CALL ME CYRIL

CALL ME CYRIL

❧ CYRIL MAGNIN
and CYNTHIA ROBINS ❧

Mc Graw-Hill Book Company

New York   St. Louis   San Francisco   Hamburg

Mexico   Toronto   London   Sydney

1 2 3 4 5 6 7 8 9 D O D O 8 7 6 5 4 3 2 1

LIBRARY OF CONGRESS CATALOGING IN PUBLICATION DATA

Magnin, Cyril.
Call me Cyril.
1. Magnin, Cyril. 2. Magnin family. 3. Business-
men—United States—Biography. 4. Art patrons—
United States—Biography. I. Robins, Cynthia.
II. Title.
HC102.5.M18A35   381'.45'000924 [B]   81-8316
ISBN 0-07-039492-X   AACR2

Book design by Andrew Roberts.

To my family and to San Francisco,
the city of my birth and the city that I love.

CYRIL MAGNIN

To my parents, Jack and Rhoda Shore

CYNTHIA ROBINS

"I am of the opinion that my life belongs to the whole community, and as long as I live it is my privilege to do for it whatever I can.

"I want to be thoroughly used up when I die, for the harder I work, the more I live. I rejoice in life for its own sake. Life is no 'brief candle' to me. It is a sort of bright torch which I have got hold of for the moment, and I want to make it burn as brightly as possible before handing it on to future generations."

GEORGE BERNARD SHAW

CONTENTS

FOREWORD

WHEN I WAS FIRST ASKED to write a "little something" for the front of this book, my first question was "Who will write the 'little something' for the other twenty-three volumes?" It will surely take two dozen books to tell the whole story. Not that Cyril has lived a long life. Men like Cyril never live long enough. It's just that he has lived so well—and so fully.

In our family we frequently refer to people as either "being born in give-y weather" or "not being born in give-y weather." Cyril was definitively "born in give-y weather."

He twinkles, he's a song-and-dance man, a sentimentalist, a tough businessman, a sucker for a hard luck story—and one of the great philanthropists. He's a prince of pleasure, a king of kindness, a formidable friend, and I am madly in love with him.

Beverly Sills

April 29, 1981

INTRODUCTION

HIS STEP IS A BIT SLOWER NOW, but Cyril Magnin moves, constantly. At the doorway to an official reception or at a performance of the opera, he'll stand poised, surveying the room with his frosty blue eyes. He is usually turned out in natty designer clothes, mostly by Ralph Lauren, chosen by his son, Jerry Magnin, whose Rodeo Drive store is a Beverly Hills landmark. With his burnished silver hair carefully blown dry and combed, Magnin looks as if he should be a famous old Shakespearean actor or a media star instead of the prototypical Jewish mercantile prince, the scion of a family whose name has meant quality since his grandmother, Mary Ann Magnin, began the family's first retail store in San Francisco in 1877.

As he wends his way across the floor, he is stopped by a constant progression of people—an amalgam of well-wishers and those who would bask in the glow of a life lived in the spotlight. For Cyril Magnin *is* one of the last of his kind—a benevolent prince, a latter-day Doge, whose personal history parallels that of his native city, San Francisco. Dubbed "Mr. San Francisco" by columnist Herb Caen, the *San Francisco Chronicle*'s ace three-dot pundit, Magnin has spent an entire life dedicated to his city, singing her praises, supporting her arts, defending her and trying to make her into the Queen of American cities. Perhaps no two men—Magnin or Caen—have done more to elevate Baghdad by the Bay to mystical status.

But it is Cyril Magnin who carries the message of San Francisco past the borders of California. As the city's protocol chief and official greeter—an unpaid position which had, until the advent of the San Francisco Host Committee, cost him thousands of out-of-pocket dollars a year—Cyril Magnin has rubbed elbows with kings, queens, princes and pretenders; presidents, prime ministers, ambassadors; dancers, divas and the darlings of society. Egyptians, Israelis, Chinese, Iranians, Japanese, Soviets, British, Irish—the entire spectrum of the United Nations—have found themselves under the benevolent and watchful care of Magnin and his good offices.

But who is this man, this high-profile do-gooder whose name decorates few edifices but whose money and influence have been spent to promote the arts, the cause of brotherhood, political campaigns, trade schools, pet charities and mercantile practices?

Twenty-five years ago when Magnin was building his empire of thirty-two stores, he was a fiery-tempered wheeler-dealer whose special talent was in eliciting innovative excellence from his family and associates. It was his own personal magnetism and vision that built Joseph Magnin from a pale copy of the I. Magnin specialty store into a fashion leader among the stylish and youthful women of the West Coast—an entire generation of women who marched to the cadences Magnin and his organization struck. As a political mover and shaker, Magnin wasn't afraid to put his money and his reputation on the line; he had the ear of presidents from FDR to LBJ. And he had an eye for beauty. Women loved him then; women are fascinated with him now. Fabulous women. Opera stars, heiresses, designers, secretaries, starlets, shopgirls. He explains it with a self-effacing shrug: "I'm magnetic . . ."

For Magnin is a doer, not a talker. He has perhaps lived enough for three lives, and at eighty-plus, he will maintain a schedule busy enough to exhaust men half his age. He is up every morning at 6:30, has his breakfast and then when his driver comes, Magnin will send his cairn terrier, Tippycanoe, to work in the car and *he* will walk the four miles down San Francisco's famous hills to his office adjacent to the south tower of the Oakland Bay Bridge. His days stretch into long evenings of dinners, receptions, opera performances, the theater, the ballet or perhaps an hour or two in the piano bar at the Mark Hopkins Hotel where Magnin has his apartment in a penthouse suite. He will sing along with the pianist for hours, often old favorites, but mostly zippy parodies of tunes—"I can't give you anything but cash, baby . . ."

Cyril Magnin is a public person with a wide private streak, a part of himself which he never shares. His thought processes usually are never voiced—he has probably never spoken a complex sentence in his life and he'll tell someone with a showier vocabulary, "You've forgotten more big words than I'll ever know." But his outward, gregarious demeanor, one developed through years of trial and error and one that has refined life down to its simplest pleasures—good company, good conversation, good health—is one of energetic calm.

And Magnin doesn't miss a thing. As he sits at his desk shuffling papers and signing checks and letters, his eye averted, his ears are open. "What did you mean by that?" he'll say, fixing his associate with a steady gaze a full fifteen minutes after a comment or an opinion has flown by. He is the consummate negotiator, not a wily schemer who will pick a situation clean, but one who will enter the ring with an open mind and a flexible goal. Cyril Magnin doesn't want to appear the Bad Guy. He will bend rather than break, yet he will not lie down as someone's private doormat. He is tough rather than ruthless and although the years and his considerable fortune have mellowed him, he is still capable of moving fiscal mountains and cutting knots of red tape with just a phone call.

I first met Cyril Magnin in 1977 when I was working as a feature writer for the *San Francisco Examiner*. I was writing a story about the lieutenants of famous people, those doers who make sure that the wheels turn smoothly and the loose ends don't strangle the powerful and busy people for whom they work. Meg Godfrey Starr was the subject of my piece. A large-boned, frank woman with an open, sweet Irish face, Meg Starr had worked for Magnin first as his part-time bookkeeper and then as his administrative assistant for nearly seven years. I first met her boss through Meg's eyes. He seemed to be impetuous, a man who couldn't say no, not even to the most frivolous request for an autograph or a hunk of philanthropy. Meg's telephone was besieged by a daily barrage of calls from people who wanted pieces of her boss—money, time, support, endorsements, company, romance.

I had expected to meet this gruff captain of industry. The reverse was true. Cyril was kittenish, flirtatious, truthful, frank to the extreme and interesting. He didn't waste time; he cut to the heart of my visit immediately, told me what I wanted to know about Meg Starr and as I found myself on the street, I wondered what had hit me. The Magnin charm.

Two years later, I received a call from Mr. Magnin's representative—would I be interested in writing Mr. Magnin's autobiography with him? The next several hundred pages are the results of our labor together—hours of conversations carefully taped and edited; hours spent perusing Magnin's extensive collection of scrapbooks. He is a pack rat's dream; he never throws out a thing. Of afternoons sharing conversation with fifty different people—relatives, business associates, political friends, lovers, an ex-wife . . . and a few who are not such friends. Magnin is not the kind of person about whom one can be wishy-washy.

In the course of writing a book, there are many people to thank, those without whose help a project like this could never have gotten into the typewriter and onto the printed page. It begins with Mr. Magnin's staff—Meg Godfrey Starr, Ellen O'Donnell, Sonja Pascoe, Michael Cowie, Peter Hamp and Sam Loflin, who I thank for their invaluable assistance. I owe a huge debt to Ellen Magnin Newman, Donald Magnin, Jerry Magnin, Elaine Hochfield Magnin and Walter Newman—Cyril's family, who were the best sources a reporter could ever find. I would like to acknowledge the cooperation of Reg Murphy, former editor and publisher of the *San Francisco Examiner* and Pamela Brunger Scott, the editor of the Scene/Arts section of the *Examiner,* whose patience, faith and cooperation led to the undertaking of this book. Thank you also to Lou Ashworth of McGraw-Hill, my editor. And to Reed Trencher, my husband, whose steady and gentle prodding helped me when the chips were down. But mostly, thanks to Cyril Magnin whose life is chronicled in these pages. God bless.

CYNTHIA ROBINS

Mill Valley, California
February 1981

CHAPTER ONE ❧

The Magnin Family History

IT WAS THE LURE OF GOLD and untold riches that brought the Magnin family to California from Europe—about thirty years too late. My grandfather, Isaac Magnin, was born in Assen, Holland, just six years before that fateful day in January, 1848, that James W. Marshall, a Mormon, picked a gold nugget out of the south fork of the American River at John Sutter's mill and started the great California gold rush. It wasn't until 1875 when the mines were already played out, that Isaac, his wife Mary Ann and their seven children weathered an arduous passage around Cape Horn to arrive, flush with expectations and little else, in the Golden State. Their third oldest child was my father, Joseph, who was born in London. I am the first and only child of Joseph Magnin—born an American, a Californian and a rare animal indeed, a native San Franciscan.

The city of San Francisco as it exists today began first as an army outpost or presidio, established for the Spanish by the

Anza Expedition of 1776. Hard on the heels of the military came the Franciscan padres who founded the Mission San Francisco de Assis, named for their patron saint, Francis of Assisi. In 1776 a Franciscan priest named Junipero Serra founded a sixth mission in Alta, California and named it the Lagoon of Our Lady of the Sorrows, which when shortened became Mission Dolores. In 1847 San Francisco was a sleepy little pueblo of 500 souls whose life revolved around the mission. By 1850, after news of the gold strike had filtered back to the East Coast, there were 50,000 people of every race, creed and color in San Francisco. It was now a burgeoning city swollen beyond its tiny borders with tents and temporary wooden lodgings to accommodate those intrepid people who had come in search of El Dorado. Shelter was scarce but there were those who were willing to pay as much as $300 per month for a single room. The city was a scalper's paradise; food prices were exorbitant. An apple cost $5; eggs were $1 apiece and a loaf of bread was 75¢. Still the people came; sailors jumped ship, school boys ran away from home, all sorts of men arrived with hope in their hearts and the gleam of gold shining in their eyes. They didn't realize that the gold fields were 100 miles away from the city and they didn't realize that the gold literally had to be coaxed out of the earth, that it wasn't lying around waiting to be plucked off the ground like so many heads of lettuce.

The discovery of gold attracted people from all walks of life, religions, including the Jews, most of whom had emigrated from Germany in search of religious and social freedom. Some Jews came directly from Europe; others remained in the East long enough to learn the language and to adjust to the new country. There were thousands of Jewish names on the manifests of ships that were sailing around Cape Horn or to the Isthmus of Panama. Many families came along with gold-seeking men, and often the trips could take five months around Cape Horn due to month-long calms in the doldrums and ferocious storms near the Cape. Very few Jews were known to have taken the overland route; many of them preferred to fork over the $380 it cost for first-class passage and others bought $200 tickets and sailed like animals in steerage.

There are records of Jewish settlers who emigrated to Northern California between 1840 and 1850, but most of those documents were destroyed in the earthquake and fire in 1906. Names like Cordoza, Rosenthal and Shannon crop up in the Jewish archives as the first Jewish "argonauts," named for Jason's hardy band of adventurers who sought their own golden fleece. The first mayor or "alcalde" of the pueblo was a U.S. Naval lieutenant named Washington Bartlett whose mother was a Jewish woman from Charleston, South Carolina. While many of the earliest Jews in California actually did pan for gold, most of them practically monopolized the clothing and dry goods business. They were like support troops providing necessary goods for the mining camps. One Jewish merchant was said to have sent his brother to see how profitable it would be to sell his wares in the camps. He received a telegram back that reported joyfully, "Come. It was richness." Another story filtering out of the period came from a showman who said that he could usually tell the prosperity of a mining town by the number of Jewish shopkeepers it held.

By 1860 possibly 980 Jewish males had come to San Francisco. The town was their first port of call, although Oakland was where most of the ships docked. Many Jews chose to remain in San Francisco rather than travel inland to the gold fields. Since the Jews were in San Francisco from the very beginning of the gold rush and helped to build the city, there was very little of the anti-Semitism they had encountered in their home countries or even on the Eastern shores of their adopted country. The Jewish migration to San Francisco, unlike migration to other areas, was concurrent with the founding of San Francisco as an American city.

When the first flush of gold fever ended, the land

surrounding San Francisco was mined for even greater riches—grain, cattle, fruits and vegetables, water and later oil. The fertile San Joaquin Valley produced a cornucopia of products from the earth. Enterprising young Jewish men capitalized on the splendor, becoming hay and grain brokers, cattle ranchers, vineyard owners and engineers. There were the Friedlanders, Anspachers, Eppingers, Blums, Frankenheimers and Newmans, hay and grain; Herbert and Mortimer Fleishhacker, hydroelectric developments; the Jostres and Koshlands, cattle; the Jacobis and Lachmans, vineyards; and Julius and Adolph Mach and Leon Guggenheim, oil. And then there were the great merchants who followed, providing clothing and hardware and those things necessary for daily living. Men like Levi Strauss who arrived in America when he was fourteen and came to California in 1850 at the age of twenty. He came West not to pan for gold but to sell dry goods and supplies to the miners. He first settled in Sacramento near the gold fields but soon moved to San Francisco to open up a dry goods and clothing establishment on California Street. He eventually developed a functional, tough overall for the workingman made from blue canvas called denim. The work clothes he made had heavily stitched pockets reinforced with distinctive copper rivets—the forerunner of today's American institution, Levi's blue jeans. There were the Verdier brothers, Felix and Émile, who arrived in 1850 on a chartered ship called *La Ville de Paris*, who named their store after it—the City of Paris. There was Raphael Weill who founded the White House and there were the Davises, the Dernborns, the Pragers and the Rooses. And later on, in 1875, came the Magnins.

You won't find the name Magnin in a lot of places in the United States, but were you to pick up a telephone book in Lyons, France, you'd probably find a whole page of them. There are also a lot of Magnins in Switzerland and in Holland. But in feudal times people didn't even have last names because they were usually serfs of the royal houses or land barons. When people left the protection of the castles and farms and came into the cities to work, men would adopt the last name of the profession in which they worked. In France, for instance, the name Magnin was taken from *magineire,* which denoted a silk factory near Lyons in the seventeenth century. Because there are a lot of Magnins there, it's possible that my grandfather Isaac's family may have gone to Holland from neighboring France. There is really not too much information about the Magnins, or Moeijons, as the name was spelled in Dutch.

Isaac was born in 1842 in Holland. His father was a professor of Semitic languages at the University of Leiden. Young Isaac was apprenticed in the gilding profession at a very early age; he learned to apply delicate gold leaf to picture frames and mirrors. It was a decorative art which was dying in Europe as fewer and fewer fine and princely homes were being built that required gold leaf emblazoned on carved moldings and worked into ceiling frescoes. When Isaac was in his late teens, he left Holland for America and somehow, the story goes, found himself conscripted into the Confederate Army during the American Civil War. He was wounded, shot in the leg, and mustered out early, broke and homeless. To make enough money to go back to Holland to find his father, Isaac wound up in New Orleans, selling buttons, needles, thread and other notions off a pushcart. By the time he had made enough money to return to Holland, his father was nowhere to be found. Neighbors advised him to look for his family in London; a family by the name of Cohen had emigrated there a few years before and they could possibly help him in his search. Isaac took their advice and left for England where he introduced himself to Rabbi Cohen and his family. I don't know if he ever found his father, but he did meet Mary Ann Cohen, my grandmother.

A winsome young woman when she met my grandfather, Mary Ann was probably no more than fifteen. She was a slender wisp of a girl in full skirts. She had a piquant face; it was almost wrenlike. She carried herself with a dignity and grace that was far beyond her tender years. No wonder my simple, uncomplicated grandfather was smitten. Mary Ann's mother was a fine seamstress and she passed her art on to her daughter. Perhaps the Cohen women made baby clothes for the British royalty—it's a story that has been passed down in my family and I have little doubt that it is true. Mary Ann married Isaac when she was sixteen and had her first child, my Uncle Samuel, when she was seventeen. She was to have six other children in Europe—Henrietta, Joseph, Emanuel John, Victor, Lucille and Flora—before she would allow my grandfather to talk her into going to California in search of work. Isaac figured that with the discovery of gold, there would be much for him to do as a gilder in the new state of California.

Isaac, Mary Ann and their large brood endured passage around Cape Horn to reach the West Coast. There isn't too much known about their journey, not even the name of their ship, but Grandmother Magnin used to tell me that they came in steerage—not a very royal way to travel in those days. The trips could be as short as $1\frac{1}{2}$ months if the winds were good and the storms around Cape Horn did not mutilate the ships. Countless souls were lost as winds and high seas buffeted poorly constructed vessels. Many ships ran into month-long calms or 12-knot winds which could blow them off course. Emigrants could be stranded on ships that took as long as $5\frac{1}{2}$ months to go the 4,000 miles from New York around the Cape and up to San Francisco Bay. For the first-class passenger, life aboard ship was fairly pleasant—the food was good as long as the ships could put into ports like Rio de Janeiro for fresh fruit and vegetables, water and meats. But the diet was usually boiled potatoes, one codfish for thirty or forty people, watery gruel and weak tea. Often the weather was so severe that no one was allowed on deck for fear of being blown overboard. Yet, the Magnins made it—all nine of them.

When Isaac and his family arrived in Oakland in 1875, Isaac did not stay, but sailed immediately for Honolulu where one of his brothers, Aisle, had settled some years before. Aisle had the reputation as the family black sheep and had wound up in the Sandwich Islands (Hawaii) married to an island princess. Isaac must have realized soon that there was nothing for him or his family in that palm-lined paradise—certainly no palaces to gild—and quickly returned to San Francisco where he tried to find work. The gold deposits had been mined years ago and many of the wealthier San Franciscans had already built their grand and garish homes, monuments of the *nouveaux riches.* With a huge family to feed, Isaac found work with Solomon Gump, a merchant who had come to San Francisco a few years before and was building a reputation as a dealer in European and American art, imported antiques and home furnishings. Gump hired Isaac as a frame gilder.

Isaac had been working for Gump for a few months when the company received a contract to decorate the ceiling of St. Mary's Cathedral. Offering Isaac a $2 a week raise (which in those days was quite substantial), Gump wanted him to take on the work. When Isaac came home all excited about more money and told Mary Ann (who at twenty-four had grown into a fierce, independent little woman with a mind all her own), she said to him with her customary frankness, "You've never worked on a scaffold. You're going to fall down and break your neck. You're *not* going to take that job." She left little room for argument, but Isaac replied that he had nine people to feed, including her, and inquired just how was he going to do it. Mary Ann was supposed to have replied, "I'll show you how we'll eat," and began to make baby clothes to sell to the gentry. I'm not really sure that the story I've just told is completely correct, but I do know that Mary Ann became the driving force in the Magnin family shortly after they arrived in the United States.

One of my cousins tells a story about what Isaac did in those first few months that his wife was stitching up baby clothes. He tried the pushcart business again, this time in Oakland where he peddled expensive, fancy buttons. Apparently they were too fancy because the business failed. Shortly after, Isaac and Mary Ann opened up a small store in Oakland at 15th Street and San Pablo Avenue, but in 1876, a year after they'd arrived in America, they moved their operation to San Francisco. It was a tiny little shop called the Yankee Notions Store located on 5th Street south of Market Street. The shelves were stocked with pins, needles, thread, buttons and tobacco, but most importantly, with Mary Ann's hand-sewn layettes and diapers. The layettes, decorated with lace trim and constructed with fine, tiny stitches, cost $5 for a nightgown or christening dress, cap and blanket; diapers were a dollar a dozen. Soon Mary Ann's reputation spread and the demand for her wares was so great that she had to take on a helper. She would arise at dawn to go to the wholesale house to buy always the finest cloth and laces available. She sold her goods during the day and after the shop closed at 6 P.M., she supervised the cutting and making of the tiny garments to be sewn and then sold the next day. It wasn't what you'd call mass production.

As her baby clothing business increased, so did requests for other handmade garments like shirtwaists, camisoles, petticoats, pantaloons and other delicate lingerie. Not only was Mary Ann making infantswear, she was also becoming well-known for her bridal trousseaux. The liveried carriages of San Francisco's rich and famous stood outside the door of the little shop. Mary Ann knew the intimate secrets of the city because of her trade—who was getting married and who was expecting—often before the families did. Her tiny emporium was a hotbed, however genteel, of gossip, which the circumspect, regal young woman never let go beyond the four walls.

In 1877 Mary Ann established I. Magnin. While the

business was really hers—Isaac dabbled in the financial end for a while, but never took a very active part in the company—Mary Ann named it for her husband because, in those days, it wasn't proper for a woman of quality to have a firm named after herself. By 1878 I. Magnin had moved to a location on Third Street between Mission and Howard and catered not only to the gentry, but to the dance-hall girls and prostitutes of the Barbary Coast district—a six-block area near the waterfront that was inhabited by seafaring men, gamblers, madames and whores. I always thought it was ironic that a woman of such high-minded ideals and such an inflexible moral code as my grandmother would seek business from questionable females, but Mary Ann was first and foremost an astute businesswoman and she knew that those "ladies," would buy her most intricate and expensive wares. In my own business, shortly after the start of the Second World War, I also tapped a market of young "ladies." They had disposable income and could afford to pay top dollar for clothes.

Mary Ann started her children in the business as soon as she could. It was a family tradition to work your way up in the store hierarchy and often there would be Magnin children marking merchandise, sweeping up and making deliveries. One of my father's earliest jobs was as a delivery boy. One day he was sent on a C.O.D. with a box of very expensive lingerie. When he got to the door of the house to make the delivery, a woman answered in a very transparent negligee and asked my father inside. I think he may have been sixteen years old at the time and very impressionable. The next thing he knew, he was in bed between two women. When they were finished with their amorous adventure, my father stood up, put on his clothes and said, "I have to collect now," and they said something to the effect, "You dirty little Jewish bastard, you get out of here. You got your money's worth." My father was afraid to go back to work because he knew his mother would probably punish him for his transgression—he

9

already had a reputation for being, if not exactly the black sheep of the family, certainly its resident playboy. My father always loved the ladies, even when he was a very old man. Rita Wohlman, our head buyer in New York, often tells the story about driving in a car with old Joe. She almost slammed into a tree when she found his hand halfway up her knee. Anyway, Joseph solved the problem at hand back then by borrowing enough money to pay for the lingerie from a tailor next door to I. Magnin. It took him about two years of working to pay off the understanding tradesman—it was *very* expensive lingerie—but I think that it was indicative of a spirit of adventure that may have been Joe's legacy to me. When he was a young man, Joe was never afraid of following his own intuition—especially if it had anything to do with women.

During the 1880s, Mary Ann's business grew. Her watchword was quality—always quality. Her clothing was made-to-order from the finest material available. By 1886 I. Magnin was located on Market Street in the heart of the business district. Along with the new location came the ninth and last baby (although Mary Ann had miscarried once since she and Isaac had come to California). Grover was born in December, 1886. Three of Mary Ann's older boys were already in the business. Victor had gone East to seek his fortune as an entertainer and wasn't spoken of much. Of the three, Emanuel John, or John as he liked to be called, showed the most talent for merchandising. He was considered a merchant of the old school—customer-oriented and in love with business. Isaac, meanwhile, spent most of his time studying, discoursing on philosophy and socialism with his cronies and staying out of Mary Ann's way. He was always a kind of dreamer with not much of a head for business and while his contributions to I. Magnin were his name and the fact that he was responsible for bringing Mary Ann and their brood to the United States in the first place, he added very little to the day-to-day running of the business.

In the early 1880s my father married a young woman named Lily Hess. The marriage lasted less than two years and until I had spent many years as an adult, I never knew about it. My father was very secretive when he felt it was necessary and in those days, a divorce was an embarrassing thing. The proceeding cost Mrs. Lily Magnin $25 plus $5 in court costs. I don't think my father had to pay any alimony. At the time, Joseph was overseeing the workrooms and the manufacturing end of the business.

By 1892 Mary Ann had been in business long enough to note which of her sons would be capable enough to carry on in her tradition of excellence and quality. She tapped John, who was then twenty-two years old, to manage the Market Street store, bypassing her older sons, Samuel and Joseph. At a dinner meeting one night in 1893, the future of the company was carefully plotted out and again, Samuel and Joseph were relegated to subsidiary positions. John could be as stubborn, bossy and single-minded as his mother, and he and my father would have jurisdictional battles all the time when John invaded the factory and tried to change the way my father was doing things. There was always tension be-tween the two of them. Sam didn't have the heart to fight and in his own gracious and elegant way remained loyal to the business but was not a driving force in it. The power struggle was really between Mary Ann and her protégé, John, on one side, and my father on the other.

In 1898 my father made a decision which perhaps dashed any hopes he may have had to take a controlling part of the business. He fell in love . . . which, in itself, wasn't terrible. The woman in question was Charlotte Davis, a milliner, who was sweet, self-effacing, attractive and diplomatic. Mary Ann adored her. But Charlotte, or Lottie as she was called, was the head milliner at I. Magnin and one of Mary Ann's dictums, inscribed in concrete perhaps, was that no one in the family was allowed to fraternize with the help. She felt that it was bad for morale, bad for business. Joseph, however, fell head-over-heels in love with Lottie and in 1898 married her. I came along the next year, two days after the Fourth of July.

My mother's father David Davis had been born in Posen, which was Germany then—it was one of those places that changed hands every time there was a border dispute in Eastern Europe. For a time, Posen was Polish, but David Davis was a German Jew. There really isn't too much known about his background, but I do know that when Grandfather Davis came to the United States, he got work as a "shamus," or sexton, of the Geary Street Temple. He had gone into the crockery business, selling china, but quite unsuccessfully. Although it was of excellent quality, no one would buy it. Rachael Davis, my grandmother, was born Rachael Silverstein in New York. She was a lovely, simple soul—very kind and loving. The typical old-fashioned housewife that existed in the 1800s. She was very much a homebody, dedicated to making life enjoyable for her husband and four children— Charlotte, Manuel, Jenny and Sadie. They were all born in San Francisco. Rachael, while she was a very unassuming woman, managed to produce a very strong daughter—my mother.

Charlotte charmed my father with her quiet manner. In later years, she became very obedient to him, but when they were at I. Magnin and later on in their own store, they worked as equal partners in an exciting, often grueling enterprise. Lottie wasn't gorgeous by any means, but she had a way about her, a style, which set her apart. She dressed very smartly. When she started to grow a little portly as she grew older, she used to take a smaller sized dress than she needed, have the seams ripped and have gussets put in. The styles were usually younger in the smaller sizes and she wanted to keep project- ing that smart image.

Joseph remained at I. Magnin as did Lottie after their marriage. They were madly in love but holding tenuously onto their positions. I think there must have been an uneasy truce between Joe and Mary Ann. In 1905 Mary Ann sent

John to New York to open up an Eastern buying office. She also started importing merchandise—gowns, lingerie and fine leather goods—from France, and soon John was in charge of both the New York office and the European operation. By 1906 the store had grown so large that a new location on Grant at Post was chosen and a six-story building was under construction to house *the* quality store of San Francisco.

On the morning of April 18, 1906, all of that changed. The great San Francisco earthquake and fire leveled the new store and I. Magnin, stripped of its stock and its fine new location, almost went under. Almost, but not quite. The morning after the quake, Mary Ann sent Joseph and Sam to the customs house in Alameda where they discovered crates of undamaged lingerie from France waiting for them. Mary Ann also instructed her sons to wire John in New York for more merchandise—as much as he could send—and then she ran an ad in the morning paper advising all I. Magnin employees to report for work as usual, but not downtown which was a total loss, but to the Magnin family home on the northeast corner of Page and Masonic, where it was business as usual. Mary Ann figured, and rightly so, that San Franciscans had probably lost everything they owned in the disaster and that they would be needing new things right away.

The house on Page Street was filled with the homeless, penniless refugees who had been shaken and burned out of their homes, but soon it became an instant I. Magnin. The butler's pantry was turned into a packing room; three bedrooms upstairs became fitting rooms and the dining room was transformed into the blouse department. With no trolley cars running in the city to bring customers, Mary Ann hired horse-driven hacks to cart her clientele to her door.

San Francisco began to rebuild right away. Again it was like the days of the gold rush when merchandise was scarce and in demand and cost what the traffic would bear. The prices were outlandish. Handmade French shirtwaists went for $150 and real lace dresses could cost as much as $350.

Business thrived in the house on Page Street. But Mary Ann knew the family had to rebuild immediately at another location; having customers in the house wasn't conducive to family life and couldn't last forever. Mary Ann was able to recoup most of the family's losses from the insurance companies (only a German company refused to pay off). And on the strength of their signatures alone, she and my Uncle John were able to secure a $50,000 loan from I. W. Hellman, Jr., president of the Wells Fargo Bank, to build a temporary store on the corner of Van Ness and Bush.

Meanwhile, a new permanent location was secured at Geary and Grant and construction began on a four-story building with three selling floors and an alterations room and a factory workroom on the top floor. Once again I. Magnin claimed its fashion leadership as the finest women's specialty store in San Francisco.

In the thirty-odd years Mary Ann had been in business, styles had changed considerably, as had prices. When she first opened her little store south of Market Street, she was making lingerie out of cottons and laces—pantalettes, corset covers, petticoats, some with pink ribbons run through the lace and some hand-embroidered with tiny flowers. In the 1890s her shirtwaists were still hand-finished—lovely creations of cream net and lace with high close-fitting collars to be worn with a fabulous black velvet suit with jet beads and appliquéd satin roses. Mary Ann always had a fashion sense and a knowledge of style and what would sell—but it was always the best. She would lecture her children by the hour about buying only the best, but she herself was very frugal. She was, in short, a penny-pinching, stubborn woman who never bought unwisely. There is a story the family tells about Mary Ann's pennywise ways. One day before the Magnins moved their business to their shop on Market Street, a district watchman came up to Mary Ann and offered his services to guard her store for $2 per month. She told him no, thinking

14

that it was an unnecessary expense. One evening when she and Isaac were returning from the opera, they found the same man standing in front of their house. The window had been broken and he said their house had been broken into. He had come along, he said, just in the nick of time and scared the prowlers away. Mary Ann didn't quite believe him but she agreed to pay him his "protection" money because she felt it was easier to do it than to have to deal with a broken window every time she and Isaac left the house.

As Mary Ann grew older, she became more and more conscious of her status as one of San Francisco's grande dames. She demanded complete loyalty from her family and her employees and she dispensed favors and gifts with the panache of visiting royalty. After Isaac's death, she moved into the baronial splendor of the St. Francis Hotel. Often, when she was getting into her seventies, she would fret and worry about her impending death (although very few of the Magnin women ever died before they were eighty—Mary Ann was no different, she lived to be a very ripe old ninety-four) and spent hours checking on her mausoleum. That task completed, she would decide that she wasn't going to die immediately and would order that her apartment in the St. Francis be redecorated, posthaste.

In 1908 Grover was twenty-two years old. Of all of her sons, he was Mary Ann's favorite. She spoiled him, babied him, kept him near to her always. Her apartment was on the fourth floor of the St. Francis and Grover's was right next door. There were adjoining suites and she demanded that Grover's door never be locked to her. I think it was because Grover was so overwhelmed by his mother's affection and sheer power that he never married until he was forty-five. Even then he and his wife, a stunning model from Louisiana named Jeanne Callahan, maintained an apartment in the St. Francis, again right near Mary Ann's, but this time, Jeanne was wise enough to have locks put on the doors between the

15

two apartments. John had married a New York woman named Rose Fleishhauer who refused to move to California, so John was made permanent head of the East Coast office. Grover was put in charge of the Pacific Coast stores and once again, my father was passed over, this time by his baby brother. It may have been that which made him realize that he could no longer advance in his family's company.

Finally, in 1913, it became too difficult to stay in the family business and Joseph cashed in his share of I. Magnin and with the money, bought into a store at O'Farrell and Stockton named Newman-Levinson, changing the name to Newman-Magnin (ironically, the same hyphenated initials as Neiman-Marcus, Dallas's great specialty store). My father was to buy out his partners in 1918, changing the name of the store once again—this time to Joseph Magnin. Mary Ann was so incensed that the rift between her and her middle son became a gulf and then an ocean. There was no contact between my family and the rest of the Magnins for quite a few years.

CHAPTER TWO

Cyril's Boyhood

I WAS BORN ON JULY 6, 1899, in a house on Bush Street in San Francisco in an area just below Pacific Heights. I imagine that it was a typical San Francisco summer day—foggy, chilly and bleak. My parents had been married about a year when I came along and I was to be their only child. Home birth was very common in those days, and while I think I was a good-sized baby, my mother had no complications and didn't have to go into the hospital. The house where I was born survived the 1906 earthquake and fire and still stands today—a three-flat, frame structure with Grecian columns in the front located directly across the street from the San Francisco Tennis Club.

Both my mother and father were working at I. Magnin when I was born. My mother was the millinery buyer. She was not a very large woman but would wear fabulous hats as befitted her profession—creations with feathered doves nesting on satin bows or straw boaters with ribboned streamers and silk flowers. She looked stately and finely bred. She had dark hair, a creamy complexion and sensitive eyes. While she was not classically beautiful, she carried herself with a poise that bespoke of warmth, authority and patience. She usually wound up getting her own way in a dispute by just waiting out the warring factions; she was a great peacemaker because she was open-minded and fair.

My father was in charge of the manufacturing end at I. Magnin. Although there were sewing machines in the factory, a lot of the work on the fine lingerie and shirtwaists was still done by hand. Merchandising was never Joe's forte; his first love was finance, something he went back to in later years with his factoring business, Donner Factors. He was a small man, about five-foot-six, if that, and was very slender. He was as careless about his manner as my mother was neat; it was to become a standing joke. Store employees at Joseph Magnin always knew what Mr. Joe had had for lunch. His shirtfront and vest wore a Blue Plate special sprinkled with cigar ashes, and his cravats, more often than not, had tiny holes burned in them by falling sparks. He was nearsighted and wore wire-rimmed spectacles. Joseph wasn't a shy man, but he was taciturn. His sense of humor was wicked—dry, subtle and almost fey. As a father he was often quite inflexible, often very stern, but he treated me as fairly as he knew how.

My mother went back to work as soon as possible after my birth and I was brought up by my Grandmother Davis, my mother's mother, and my two maiden aunts, Jenny and Sadie. My grandmother, Rachael, was a very plain woman, very motherly. She had been born in New York and it was thought that her father was a rabbi. When she was still in high school, she had won a scholarship medal but her real talent lay in being a typical Jewish mother. She was a candid woman who loved aphorisms and literally taught a lesson every time she opened her mouth with sayings like, "the world doesn't really love old people" or "the world doesn't really respect people who are totally honest." She devoted her time to taking care of her family, but she was never bitter about her lot in life; in fact, she derived great pleaure from cooking and keeping house. She had no desire to be anything but what she was. I remember how she would make her own egg noodles and then hang them out the window of her home on California Street to dry.

Of the three Davis women, I remember my Aunt Jenny the best. She was also like a typical Jewish mother although she never married. She acted like a mother to me. I loved her cooking, especially her gefilte fish; it was always my favorite. Passover seders with Aunt Jenny and the Davises were a treat. We used to make raisin wine where we would take the raisins and put them in a paper bag and then run them under the water tap; the juice would seep into a dish below. It was not allowed to ferment and I could drink it. Although my grandfather, David Davis, was the sexton at the Geary Street Temple, and my grandmother Mary Ann Magnin's own father was a rabbi in London, my own family wasn't very religious. I was brought up as a nonpracticing Jew.

I was also brought up thinking myself to be very unique and special. While there were girl cousins about my same age, I never had very much to do with them. One of my only male cousins was my Uncle Samuel's son by his first marriage, Edgar, who was ten years older than I. Sam had four other children with his second wife, a Catholic woman, but they moved to Alameda and then later to New York for a while, and we were never close. Edgar was brought up as a Fogel, with his mother's family. While he was still in his teens, he moved to Los Angeles with his mother, Lily. He and I had the same middle name, Isaac, after our grandfather Magnin, but in later years, Edgar changed it to Fogel to honor his mother's family. Today Rabbi Edgar F. Magnin is the spiritual leader of the largest and probably the wealthiest Reformed Jewish congregation in the United States, the Wilshire Boulevard

Temple in Beverly Hills. He recently celebrated his ninetieth birthday and is still very active. He has been nicknamed "the marrying rabbi", and he gave the invocation at Richard Nixon's inauguration in 1968. A very famous and wonderful man, my cousin Edgar.

As the only male Magnin child of my general age in San Francisco, I was, in a word or two, spoiled rotten—the center of attention for my two grandmothers, my two maiden aunts and my mother. I was probably not very nice to my cousins because my Uncle Sam's daughter, Mary, named for Mary Ann Magnin, thought I was a "terrible" child—self-centered and standoffish. In truth, I was really very shy, almost backward. I was overly protected and fussed over by Rachael, Jenny and Sadie. I was never very comfortable in the company of men until I was almost out of my teens. When I was a young boy, probably about eleven, my father had occasion to take me to the office of the mayor, a man named Schmidt. I was trembling, cold and sweaty, scared to death. I was so ashamed to admit it to my father that I kept my mouth shut.

Although my relatives were overly solicitous, I can understand it because I was the only boy child around for them to spoil. While I was the center of attention for the Davis family, I was also Mary Ann's favorite and continued to be even after my father left I. Magnin to start his own business when I was about fourteen. Until then I was almost like another of Mary Ann's sons. Perhaps she saw something in me the others didn't; but she lavished the kinds of attention and care on me that she would have given her own.

Mary Ann was an exquisitely patrician woman. She was the Queen, the Empress, a true matriarch with an imperious manner and ramrod-straight posture. She had the demeanor of a woman to the manor born; one would have thought she'd had ancestors on the *Mayflower* instead of coming herself perhaps packed in steerage on an anonymous ship around the

Horn. Because she stood so straight with her long neck swathed in high silk or lace collars like chokers, she appeared to be a very tall woman. I think she hardly topped five-feet-four. She was not what we would call beautiful by today's standards, but she was attractive with a narrow oval face, deep-set eyes, a prominent nose (although it's said that the so-called Magnin nose I bear really came from the Davis side of my family, my cousin Edgar and myself share craggy beaks that I think must have come from Mary Ann) and feathery eyebrows set in flight at 45-degree angles above her eyes which gave her face a permanently quizzical expression.

Mary Ann always dressed as if every day were an occasion and would wear white kid gloves when she went to oversee activities at I. Magnin. She would run her long-gloved hands over the display cases and heaven help the salespeople if the spotless white leather of her gloves should come up with a speck of dirt on them. Night or day, she wore her jewelry—a rope of pearls or a black onyx and diamond pin which she placed at the base of her neck. Her diamonds—rings and enormous earbobs—were also worn constantly whether she was at I. Magnin, playing cards with her cronies or stepping out for a night at the opera. When Mary Ann died, her jewelry was divided among her children. My father got five pieces of it and always kept them in a cigar box in a safe at Joseph Magnin. When a special customer would come into the store and the conversation would turn to Mary Ann's jewelry, Joseph would either send someone or go himself to the safe, haul out the cigar box and show off Grandma's jewelry.

As impressive as Mary Ann was or as intimidating as she might have seemed to the casual observer, she adored me, catered to me. She would pick me up in her carriage and later on in her chauffeured motorcar and take me with her to I. Magnin telling me along the way things that have stayed with me ever since—the importance of quality, the imperative of

21

being first. She would tell me never to be discouraged if I didn't get something right the first time; she told me never to be afraid of making a mistake. She taught me all the tenets I would need if I wanted to be a successful merchant. She saw in me, perhaps, qualities that my father lacked. She once told me that if I had $100, it was best to buy one very good suit rather than two mediocre suits for the same money. Throughout her long life she never stopped passing on her experience and her watchword, quality. When her youngest child, Grover, was very small, she would fasten his hands behind his back and would run different bits of lace through his fingers and ask him to identify them by touch. She never stopped instructing her own sons if she felt they showed promise for merchandising.

Mary Ann was a stern taskmaster and usually got what she wanted from people. She didn't exactly bully them into going her way, she just expected that they would. But Mary Ann could be hardheaded and inflexible. She was *the* matriarch and her word was law. Those people who had the temerity to incur her displeasure—like my father when he left I. Magnin to start his own rival retailing store—were usually subjected to an immediate cessation of affection and loyalty. In Mary Ann's mind, the unity of the family came first and those who committed the ultimate sin, those who disobeyed her, doubted her word or questioned her infallibility, were drummed out of the family, left for dead. My father's brother, Victor, for instance, was never discussed. He was the youngest of Mary Ann's London-born children, but at an early age, probably in his late teens, he struck out on his own to become an actor, something Mary Ann could never forgive. He died in New York in his mid-twenties, a victim of low life, venereal disease and probably familial neglect. Mary Ann and the family never spoke of him; it was as if he had never existed.

While Mary Ann's sons John and Grover were very much like her, dedicated to merchandising and the growth of

I. Magnin, Joseph and his older brother, Sam, were much more like their father, Isaac, who was an idealist, a scholar and a dreamer. Isaac was the complete antithesis to Mary Ann. A compact man with a barrel chest, a ruddy, freckled complexion and rusty hair, Isaac looked a little like a peasant but bore an old-world courtliness and had a gentle, bemused, almost absentminded nature. Unlike Mary Ann, he was not a snob and hated putting on airs. A self-taught philosopher and scholar, Isaac was a Marxist and would spend his afternoons pedaling around Golden Gate Park on a bicycle with his jacket pockets stuffed with socialist pamphlets. He would also stand in Union Square, down the street from I. Magnin, an immensely capitalist firm which bore his name, lecturing anyone who would stop and listen about Karl Marx and socialism. I think he was probably a great embarrassment to my grandmother. They were quite a couple. He was called, naturally, Karl Marx, and behind her back, the family called her Queen Victoria.

Both shared a passion for the opera. When they were struggling with the business in those early years before the turn of the century, they would buy standing-room tickets and watch the visiting opera companies from the highest balcony of the auditorium. Later on Mary Ann would go to the opera in her enormous black Packard touring car, decked out in her jewels, and would sit in a box. Isaac, true to his philosophical roots, remained in the gallery with his beloved common folk.

Isaac was never party to Mary Ann's intrafamily feuds. He loved all of his children equally and even when Mary Ann was not speaking to one of them, Isaac always did. When Uncle Sam divorced Lily Fogel and married his Irish-Catholic Sally, Isaac remained a gentle and loving father-in-law, often sitting in Sally's kitchen drinking tea. He was a charmer and would say to her, "Sally, never did I have such an enjoyable cup of tea," and then he would pull out a five-dollar bill and lay it by his teacup. When Isaac visited any of his children for dinner, he was most at home in the kitchen talking to the cook or the maid.

Mary Ann was not above meddling in her children's lives. She arranged marriages for her two oldest children, Sam and Henrietta (Hattie) with a brother and a sister, Lily and Jacob Fogel. The Fogels were very rich and Mary Ann was not averse to money. But when Sam's marriage failed—although Lily was a lovely woman, I don't think Sam ever loved her— Mary Ann put pressure on Hattie to divorce Jake Fogel, which she did. Hattie latter married Louis Gassner, a furrier. I don't think that Mary Ann liked to be reminded of her mistakes or of the times when she didn't get her own way. There were many long, uncomfortable years when she refused to speak to my father. By leaving I. Magnin, he had committed the ultimate sin in breaking with the family. In those years my father spoke mostly to his brothers Sam and Grover and his sister Lucy Rau. I would see my grandmother and occasionally she would ask me, "How is your father, how's your mother?", and I would say, "Grandma, you ought to have lunch with us or dinner with us." Eventually she said, "Well, bring your father down." Relations were always strained with my Uncle John. I think he died without having ever made up with my father, but he remembered all the nephews and nieces equally in his will, myself included. But my parents and Mary Ann reconciled enough for me to be married in her apartment at the St. Francis Hotel.

When I was born, my parents and I lived a fairly simple life which revolved around the business and the family. We moved to Golden Gate Avenue when I was still a baby. The street was filled with middle-class Jewish families, including the family of that famous cartoonist-humorist-inventor, Rube Goldberg. Gentleman Jim Corbett, the prizefighter, also lived in the neighborhood. We moved again, this time to a flat at 1235 Masonic Avenue between Haight and Waller Streets in the San Francisco Panhandle adjacent to Golden Gate Park.

The city was thriving then with such successful retail stores downtown as Roos Brothers, Raphael Weill's White House, Ransohoff's and The City of Paris. The silver kings and railroad barons had built ornate, princely Victorian homes atop Nob Hill, many of which had stained-glass windows, imported Italian marble floors, carved moldings and paneled walls. Compared with them, we lived very simply on the second floor of our building which was in a quiet neighborhood right near the park.

I was seven years old on the morning of April 18, 1906. It was about five o'clock and I awoke to find everything rocking and shaking. I was so frightened by things falling off the shelves that I got under the bed. It was probably the right thing to do, but must have given my parents cause for apoplexy. They were sleeping in the room next door and when the earthquake hit, they came to see if I was all right. They looked around and didn't see me for a moment, but I called out to them that I was under the bed. There was a little porch outside my bedroom window and my father told me not to go out there. He said I was very smart for getting under the bed . . . but I wasn't *that* smart. I was scared silly.

My father saw to it that my mother and I were all right and then he left to go downtown to see what had happened to the store. I. Magnin was in the process of building a new six-floor store on Grant and Geary. The building was a total loss. By mid-afternoon after the quake, the entire central city was in flames from broken gas mains. Refugees from the burning and collapsed buildings were camped out in Golden Gate Park in a temporary tent city and some of the grandest homes from Nob Hill clear to Van Ness Avenue were endangered by the explosions and the flames. With the gas and water mains bursting, we were told not to light a cook stove or open a water tap for fear of setting off another explosion or drinking contaminated water. We did our cooking right on the street in front of the house.

There was water available in Golden Gate Park, and each

morning my father and I would take a huge washtub, put it on the back of my little toy wooden wagon and fetch fresh water. About the third trip, we were coming back from the park with our laundry pan full of water when we passed Goldberg-Bowen, a grocery store which also sold liquor and some hardware. There were sawhorses blocking the entrance and a National Guard soldier standing in front carrying a rifle to keep looters from getting to the liquor inside. The soldier spotted us with our wagon and called my father over to him. He said, "I haven't had my lunch; you stay here and guard the store for me. I'll be back in about an hour." He handed my father the gun and told him, "You guard it and if anybody even wants to go near the store—shoot 'em." My father was terrified; he'd never held a gun, not even for five minutes. As soon as the soldier was out of sight, he asked me to look around to see if there was any trace of him. When I told him no, Joseph dropped the gun against a sawhorse, bolted for the front door of our house and ran upstairs. He wouldn't come out for two days.

Meanwhile, for Grandmother Mary Ann, it was business as usual—but she had to do everything by herself. Isaac was not in San Francisco. He had been visiting in London and when he heard about the catastrophe, he returned to the United States as soon as he could book passage—in steerage. He wanted to save as much money as possible figuring the family could use it.

Actually, I. Magnin as a company was never in too much danger of being destroyed just because the physical store had been. As I mentioned, Mary Ann was able to use the insurance money to rebuild at a temporary location on Bush and Van Ness while waiting for the large Geary Street location to be completed. The store on Van Ness was a frame building with offices upstairs that had noisy adding machines. Mary Ann would let me play with them when she took me to see the "new" store.

The neighborhood at Van Ness and Bush looked as if someone had dropped a bomb on it—probably because someone had. The fires had been raging out of control and were threatening to engulf the entire northwestern part of the city. Before the fires could be contained, they destroyed more than 500 city blocks from the waterfront to Nob Hill. In an attempt to stop the voracious flames, dynamiting on a small scale had been tried—houses next to a burning house would be destroyed, but the fire, driven by contrary winds, would jump the small space left by the devastated house and continue burning. Finally Mayor Schmidt ordered that a firebreak consisting of twenty-five blocks of some of the city's poshest residences on Nob and Russian Hills be destroyed by the Army Corps of Engineers. The westernmost border was to be Van Ness Avenue, which was then a promenade of tall, stately and expensive Victorian homes. The firebreak, however, ended one street farther west of Van Ness at Franklin Street—in effect, wiping out most of the showplace homes of the silver, railroad and lumber barons. A change of wind blowing eastward from the ocean and fresh water in fire hydrants north of Clay Street coupled with the planned destruction finally ended the holocaust.

It was shortly after the quake that my father began taking me to the opera. At the time, San Francisco didn't have a permanent opera company; the War Memorial Opera House would not be built until 1932, but we saw the best of the traveling companies. My father would tell me about seeing the famous coloratura soprano, Tetrazzini, a woman of such ample girth that it was a source of amusement for him that such a high and delicate little voice should have come from such a body. I never had a chance to see the famous tenor, Enrico Caruso, because he was afraid to come back to San Francisco after the quake. The first opera I saw was Verdi's *The Masked Ball.* I think I shall never forget it. The music was so lyrical and singable, you could almost dance to it. Verdi has remained a favorite of mine—*La Traviata, Rigoletto, Il Trova-tore, Aïda.* I could see them over and over again. I also developed a taste for Bizet and Gounod, but the French composers had none of the fire and excitement of the Italians like Verdi and Puccini. I could never stomach Wagner—it was like German food. Too heavy.

To the day he died, my father remained a devotee of the opera. He had an enormous Seeberg record player, the kind where you could store one hundred records, and in it was a collection of just about every opera recording he could get his hands on. There wasn't a day that he didn't wake up to opera blaring out of that record machine. He listened to opera the way young people of today listen to rock and roll—at full volume. While his tastes remained fairly pure—I may have inherited my adoration of the Italian composers from him— he liked music in just about any form. When he was already in his early seventies, he and my Uncle Sam, who was newly-retired from I. Magnin, would have either of their drivers drop them off at a movie theater on Market Street at eleven o'clock on a Saturday morning. There they would watch a Nelson Eddy-Jeanette MacDonald movie over and over again until the driver picked them up at five o'clock. They would sit in the theater, these two grand old men, humming the tunes and actually conducting the musical numbers. They must have seen movies like *Tales from the Vienna Woods* or *Naughty Marietta* a hundred times or more and each time, they would emerge from the theater, their eyes blinking in the unaccustomed light, and either Sam would turn to Joe or Joe to Sam and say, "That Jeanette MacDonald is really something, isn't she?" The two of them were quite a pair—Sam, tall and perfectly turned out in his beautifully cut suit, spats and carnation in his lapel, and my father, sort of sawed-off, his shoulders hunched over with his lunch all over his clothes, breathing fire and ashes from his cigars. How those two adored their Saturdays together.

I'm not sure whether it was because of Sam or not, but my father had a chauffeured car, a Cadillac, from about the mid-thirties until he died in 1953. He always appreciated a car that rode well, even if he was driving it himself. The first car I can remember was a White Steamer. When we would go for outings in the country, we would have to carry water buckets. Joe would chase me off the car to fill them up just in case we ran out of water. The car had no gears to shift. When my father bought a new Stanley Steamer, he sold the White to a man in Vallejo for $500. We drove the car to its new owner and had to take the ferry back across the bay. The man paid my father in twenty-dollar gold pieces so we returned home with our pockets stuffed with gold, fearing for our lives. My Grandfather Davis had a Ford with a gearshift on the floor, an open car that you had to crank. I loved watching him start it. Mary Ann, of course, had her big black cars; one was a Packard touring car. Her driver sat in the open and had a little canvas awning to pull above his head in case of rain. Later on, when she was wheelchair-bound, a special door was built into her Cadillac to accommodate her, chair and all. Her chauffeur was on duty every single day, morning or night, to take her wherever she wanted to go—even if it was three blocks down Geary from the St. Francis to I. Magnin.

My first car was a Haynes, quite a big car in those days. I was sixteen when I started to drive; it was an art I never quite mastered. When my family and I were living in Hillsborough in the late forties, I had to put used tires around the inside of the garage. I usually just aimed the car when I drove and was quite capable of tearing the side off the garage when I came home at night from the city. There were times when I drove my car like a man possessed, having little or no regard for pedestrians, other cars or traffic laws. I liked big, comfortable cars like Buicks or Cadillacs and drove them like lethal weapons—unguided missiles. A few years ago, after I had had my own driver for several years, I returned my driver's license to the Bureau of Motor Vehicles, telling them I no longer had any use for it. The streets were finally safe from my four-wheeled tyranny.

As much as my family shielded me, I still walked to school. We usually lived quite near the neighborhood schools—first, Dudley Stone where I went to elementary school and then, when we moved from Masonic to the Keystone Apartments at Hyde and Washington Streets, a building which my father helped finance, I went to Spring Valley School, which was right across the street. I was not a very good student, not even at Lowell High School, which has always been one of San Francisco's best public schools. I struggled through everything, especially foreign languages. I hated Latin, I was a lousy speller and had difficulty with English. My English teacher's name was Mr. Rogers. I think he liked me because I always called him "professor." I was a real con artist and found I could charm him very easily with just a title. Rogers was an Englishman and he filled us up with Shakespeare, Kipling and Dickens. He stuffed it down our throats day in, day out, to the extent that I was sick of all of it. I told him, "Look, Professor, is anything you're teaching me in this class gonna help me in my future life? Why do you give me all this stuff to read?" He used to call me by my last name and as he leaned way over his desk and looked me straight in the eye, he shook his finger in my face and said, "Magnin, some day, something the old professor taught you *is* gonna help you." And I never forgot.

Professor Rogers was extremely generous with his grades. If it hadn't been for him, I probably wouldn't have gotten out of high school. But it was in his class that I started to read the poetry and plays that have stuck with me to this day. When I think about the retailing business, it strikes me how much on top of things and how far ahead of others you must be to stay at the peak of your field. I remember Kipling's poem, "The Mary Glouster," and how dear old Professor Rogers almost had to beat it into me:

I knew—I knew what was coming, when we bid on the
  Byfleets's keel—
They piddled and piffled with iron. I'd given my orders for
  steel!
Steel and the first expansions. It paid, I tell you, it paid,
When we came with our nine-knot freighters and collared
  the long-run trade!
And they asked me how I did it, and I gave 'em the
  Scripture text,
"You keep your light so shining a little in front o' the
  next!"
They copied all they could follow, but they couldn't copy
  my mind,
And I left 'em sweating and stealing a year and a half
  behind.

I guess I would have to amend that for the fashion business.
You're lucky to stay even three months ahead, but those words
in "The Mary Glouster" have become almost the watchwords
of how I have lived my life and conducted my business. All
my life when I've wanted to make a point with my family or
my employees, I've quoted from my favorite poem or from
Shakespeare. The tendency to reach for someone else's words
when my own fail me perhaps is hereditary. My father was
born in England and never lost his British accent. He was a
student of Shakespeare and there was probably never a time
when he wanted to understand something that he didn't pull
out the appropriate quote from the Bard.

Eventually, school became a necessary evil—a pain in the
neck. Because of my first name, the kids would tease me and
call me "Cereal," instead of Cy or Cyril. I didn't have too
many boys who were friends (I still don't have too many close
men friends to this day) and I didn't like to play sports. That
didn't mean that I was a sissy or lacked a sense of adventure. I
have always been fascinated with charging into uncharted
territory, whether it be flying coast to coast on one of the first

flights out of San Francisco or playing the Pope in a movie; I like the excitement of discovering something new. When I was about fifteen or sixteen, I "discovered" the company of my Uncle Manuel or Manny Davis, my mother's brother. Manny wasn't at all like the Magnin side of the family. He was somewhat of a rogue, a swashbuckling type whose reputation wasn't the best. Still, he was funny and kind and I would spend my weekends helping him out in his business. My parents worked six days a week and when I went off Saturday mornings, I doubt whether they ever questioned what I had planned for the day. If they had known, I don't think I would have survived my father's wrath.

Uncle Manny was in the carnival business—that is, he ran a wheel of fortune at Neptune Beach in Alameda. He hired me to be his relief barker—a spieler. We'd sell tickets and the people would take a chance to win a big baby doll. I would holler out, "One thin dime, ten cents, one-tenth of a dollar . . . step up and take your chance right now." To get to Neptune Beach, I had to leave early in the morning and take a trolley down to the ferry which would take me to Alameda and either a big red Southern Pacific train or a Key Line train to Neptune Beach. I made a dollar a day plus car fare.

When I was spieling for Uncle Manny's wheel, one of the fellows in a neighboring booth asked me if I wanted to replace his barker. He was kind of a fortune teller, a phony magician-mind reader named Rajah who spoke in a deep, guttural accent. He had cooch dancers inside his tent; it cost a dime to get in to see them. Rajah was an expert in working a crowd. He would put on a blindfold and I would throw him questions which had been worked out carefully in advance with code words and cues. I'd say, "What's this lady doing, Rajah?" and he would put his hand up to his head as if he was visualizing the thing in his mind and he'd say, "Why, she's chewing gum," only he'd pronounce it "goom." Then

32

he would say, "Rajah knows all, tells all." Actually there was always somebody in the crowd chewing gum. He never missed. If there wasn't anybody with gum in his mouth, we didn't do it. He would also tell me if a woman was wearing a red dress or if she had on a hat. I phrased the questions so he'd know what the answer was. We gave 'em a pretty good show, but the real show was the cooch dancers inside the tent. Eventually I got a chance to do my spiel for them—which was almost exactly the same spiel I'd done for Uncle Manny— "one thin dime, one-tenth of a dollar, ten cents. One ticket, one admission takes you throughout the entire show. Hi, hi, look through the doorway . . . Don't crowd, folks . . . there's plenty of room on the inside." Everything those days, it seems, was "one thin dime."

Somehow those weekends that I worked with my Uncle Manny made my last two years at Lowell bearable. My father had left I. Magnin when I was fourteen, and from time to time, I would work in the new store, starting literally with a broom in my hands, sweeping up. Although I was never what you would call a "brain," or even a mediocre student, I entered law school at the University of California/Berkeley extension in San Francisco. I surprised myself by getting fairly good grades, but I felt pressure from my father about following him into the business.

My father had a friend named Leon Samuels, a lawyer and a political power in San Francisco. In particular, he had great influence with judges. Those who really liked him would lean over backwards to find cases in his favor. Leon was a short fellow who wore glasses. I guess he was kind of nondescript-looking, not very dapper. You wouldn't have picked him out of a crowd. But what he lacked in looks, his personality and brilliance overcame. Leon always wanted me to go into law. He knew the law better than the average lawyer. He weighed every word he said, as lawyers are wont to do.

Leon was a very crafty lawyer. His inventiveness knew no

bounds. One of his clients was a dentist who billed himself as "Painless" Parker. Painless's office was actually a truck equipped with a dental chair. He advertised that he could do painless tooth extractions, hence the nickname. Parker would shoot his clients so full of novocaine that his patients wouldn't feel anything. A professional association frowned on his entrepreneurial spirit and took him to court over the use of the name Painless. Before the court date Leon had the dentist change his first name legally to Painless and the case was thrown out of court.

When I met him, he wanted to take me under his wing, so for a while I was going to law school in the daytime and working in Leon Samuels's office in the evening. His office was in the Phelan Building at O'Farrell and Market Streets. It was my job to do research for briefs and to deliver summonses. I would get $5 for every paper I served for his office.

Leon had a varied client list. Frank Daroux was a very powerful machine politician and gambler. He was married to the madame of a very expensive bordello. In the course of his divorce proceedings, Daroux couldn't get the papers delivered. He told me that he would give me $50—which by that period's standards would be worth about $1,000 today—if I would serve his wife with the summons. I figured it wouldn't be a bad way to make some money so off I headed for her house. The "house" was known to be very expensive. It wasn't unusual for a man to pay up to $75 for a night with one of the girls. When I walked into the place, there was no one on the first floor. I took an elevator to the second floor and still didn't see anyone, not even one of the "ladies." Even if I had, I didn't have any money to spend on them—so I figured, why get all hot and bothered.

I was finally greeted by a woman, fully dressed, and she commented that she thought I was rather young to be there. I told her I was her boss's nephew. I was always good at keeping my mind on business when I had business to do.

Well, the madame came out and I handed her the paper. I didn't want to wait around to hear her reaction, so when I saw some stairs I bolted for them, ran all the way down, out of the house and hightailed it the six blocks back to Leon's office. I was shaking from excitement and fear and my face was blood red. I said to Frank Daroux, "I served your paper . . . now where's my fifty?" A hot fifty bucks. I could hardly contain myself. I took my girlfriend out on the town and spent half the money that first night, although some places wouldn't let us in because we were too young.

I remember Leon Samuels as a kind of mentor. He took an interest in me and gave me some of the confidence I lacked. I was still fairly bashful when I had to deal with people on a one-to-one basis. In Alameda I could hide behind my spiel and not have to talk to people personally, but on an everyday basis, I felt tongue-tied and intimidated. Leon helped to change all of that. I was fascinated by what went on in his office. I helped him write some bankruptcy cases during the Depression and was in his office when the banks fore-closed on United Cigar, putting them out of business. Those lessons proved to be invaluable when I was expanding Joseph Magnin into a thirty-two-store chain.

With the First World War, my schooling came to an abrupt halt. I was too young for service and was turned down. My father decided that he wanted me to go into the business and in the first years, I was more or less management. I did have to learn the business from the floor up, so to speak, from sweeping up when I was a child to marking merchandise. My parents dealt with the trade on the floor and I stayed up in the office, although every now and then I liked to come down-stairs and sell. Handbags and hosiery were my specialty. I had a gift for salesmanship but it was nothing that I ever learned in school. It was nothing I acquired on my own; it was just born with me.

As part of my training, my parents were very anxious for

me to learn all the ropes of merchandising, including buying for the store. At the time, Joseph Magnin was in direct competition with I. Magnin for the same customers and from our suppliers for the same merchandise. Unfortunately, with no antitrust laws in effect in those days, I. Magnin had all their fine suppliers tied up in exclusive contracts; in other words, a manufacturer sold only to I. Magnin. What was left for us was the dregs. Two sleeves and a zipper. Still, we did find some resources who would sell to us and I would find myself making six or seven trips a year to New York. At nineteen, I was traveling coast to coast in swaying trains that were boiling hot in the summer and freezing cold in the winter. With no air-conditioning, we had to create our own by hanging wet towels at the windows and allowing the breezes created by the speeding trains to pass through them. The trips were grueling affairs. On the old Overland Ltd., it took two nights and three days to get to Chicago and then an overnight to get to New York.

I received quite an education from some of the other salesmen and buyers on those trips. Traveling over the center of the country provided no surprises, but lots of hours which we filled swapping stories and playing gin rummy or pinochle. I was completely inexperienced and usually had nothing to contribute, but by listening, I was able to learn from the more experienced.

One regular on those trips was a salesman I'll call Mr. Brown. He had a terrible personality; he was always griping about something. You'd ask him how he was and he'd snarl at you, "Lousy!" as if you'd committed a crime just by speaking to him. But Brown was hard of hearing and often was an unintentional source for humor. One morning I found myself sitting at his table in the dining car when the steward came over and asked him how he wanted his eggs fixed. "Rotten," spat Brown, who thought the waiter was asking him how he felt.

I would always stay at the Commodore Hotel when I got to New York. There was a billboard advertising the hotel above the tracks right outside of New York that you could see if you took the New York Central Railway in from Chicago. You couldn't miss it: THE COMMODORE—A ROOM AND A BATH FOR TWO AND A HALF. I was never one to pass up a bargain and usually stayed there.

While some of the men who traveled those rigorous routes from California, St. Louis, Chicago and Cleveland to New York hated it, I always loved the experience—first on the trains, then on the ships to Europe and then, finally, the planes. Air travel out of San Francisco started in the mid-twenties, but it wasn't until 1927 that coast-to-coast flight was inaugurated. I was married by then and nearly a father, but that didn't stop me from one of the great adventures of my life—the first flight from San Francisco to New York. There was a whole entourage that followed me to the airport to wave goodbye to me; they brought me all sorts of gag gifts like diapers—they were sure I was going to wet my pants from fright. The plane was a Boeing 40, flown by Boeing Air Transport which later became part of United Airlines. The fare to Chicago was $200 and the plane made fifteen stops, in Oakland, Sacramento, Reno, Elko (Nevada), Salt Lake City, Rock Springs (Wyoming), Cheyenne, North Platte (Nebraska), Grand Island, Omaha, Lincoln, Iowa City, Des Moines, Moline (Illinois) and finally, Chicago. From Chicago to New York, we changed planes to a National Air Transport (also later on to become part of United Airlines) Ford Tri-Motor and flew to Toledo, Cleveland and Newark. The entire trip cost $400 and was not for the faint of heart—it was twenty-six hours of constant up and down, hurry and wait. I have loved flying ever since and never miss an opportunity to hop a plane to somewhere.

CHAPTER THREE

Anna Smithline Magnin

❧ I HAVE ALWAYS LOVED WOMEN and they've always loved me. My son Jerry once said that to be a Magnin woman was in and of itself an occasion. I am inclined to agree with him, but not because I was such a catch. I wasn't particularly rich or famous or dashing or handsome. But I was born with the ability to magnetize people, especially women. To attract them to me. From my earliest memories women loved and wanted to do things for me—my grandmothers, my mother, my aunts and then, my girlfriends. I have never been able to explain what my attraction for women has been and even now, I am hard pressed to understand why so many marvelous females think I'm marvelous, too. I can only go back through the years and remember them to see that it was so. In reflection, I liked a certain kind of a woman. She didn't have to be a cover girl—not that I minded a stunning face and attractive figure. But she had to have a certain style—a flair and a zest for life and a terrific sense of humor. I never really liked women who were going to play mother to me. I loved intelligent, independent women probably because most of the women I had grown up around were brilliant and highly individualistic. I guess it spoiled me.

My parents always expected that I would find a nice girl, get married and settle down. But, in the early twenties, I was in no hurry. I was enjoying sowing my wild oats; there were always pretty girls who loved going out with me although our side of the Magnin family was not the socially prominent one. When I was twenty-four, I made the mistake of sparking on a girl who worked at Joseph Magnin. Like Mary Ann before him, my father had a rule that you didn't date the help, but I allowed my heart and my glands to overrule my head and fell for a married woman who worked in the hosiery department. To get me away from her, my parents did the only thing they could. They sent me to Europe on business. It was to be my first trip—something to soften the blow of their disapproval.

In 1913 when my father left I. Magnin to start what was to become Joseph Magnin, he had a difficult time getting the same manufacturers that made goods for I. Magnin to do anything for him. There was no Federal Trade Commission around then to protect the smaller store from market domination. One of those manufacturers was Ben Gershel, a high-style design house that made classically tailored coats and suits. Time after time my father's buyers tried to get Gershel to sell us and time after time the answer would come back—a resounding "no." To circumvent this small inconvenience, Joseph Magnin made what is known in the trade as "knock-offs." We would sketch a new suit at I. Magnin and then find our own manufacturer who would make up basically the same suit out of identical material. Our Ben Gershels were line-for-line copies . . . except for the buttons.

When I fell in love with Mrs. Lee, the woman in the hosiery department, my parents dreamed up a buying trip for me. First, I was to go to New York where I was to call on Ben

Gershel to beg, borrow or steal the buttons we couldn't find to go on our "Gershel" suits. Also, I was to purchase a yard of fabric to fix the sleeve of a suit for one of our regular customers. Coincidentally, the material could only be gotten from Gershel. It was with some trepidation (and anger, because I was still smarting from my parents' reprimand— sending me away from my lady love) that I walked into Gershel's in search of buttons and cloth.

I was greeted by a pleasant young woman and I introduced myself as coming from Joseph Magnin. I explained that we were not affiliated with I. Magnin, that Gershel did not sell us, but that I would appreciate a favor. Would she sell me a yard of goods (I didn't even get around to mentioning the buttons at this point), and she said, "Sure, why not?" I thanked her and told her that it was a load off my mind, that I was going to Europe the next day and that it was the last chance I had to get the material for our customer. She mentioned that she was also sailing for Europe in the morning and asked what ship I was taking. I told her the *Leviathan* (which was nicknamed the "Levi-Nathan" after all the Jewish buyers who sailed on her regularly) and she laughed at the coincidence and said she was going on the same ship, taking her little sister, Adele, on her first trip to the Continent.

By this time, my interest was piqued. This girl was very attractive—about two years younger than I and just the right height. I was not very tall myself, about five-feet-eight, and she came up to my chin. She had lively brown eyes. Her hair was wavy and dark brown and done up in the current style, parted in the middle, marcelled down the sides in soft waves and caught up at the nape of her neck in a bun. She reminded me a little of my grandmother Mary Ann because she was petite and stylish and had a piquant, tentative kind of beauty. The more she talked, the more attractive she became because she was warm and outgoing and had an engaging sense of humor. Her name was Anna Smithline and she was Gershel's

41

head designer. She was married to a man named Herman
Bernie, brother of the entertainer, Ben Bernie, but the
marriage was over and she was in the process of waiting for
her final divorce decree. We talked business, made some small
talk about ourselves and I left the showroom. I sort of forgot
about her until I saw her the next day on the deck of the
Leviathan. She was with a tiny little girl of about seventeen
and neither of them looked very happy.

I was sitting in a deck chair, having checked into my
stateroom and come topside for the sailing. They were
walking together on deck and I waved at them and said,
"Remember me?" Anna replied, "Well, maybe . . . you're
the man I sold the goods to." I asked her if she was enjoying
the trip so far, sort of an odd opening line because we hadn't
even left the dock yet, but I couldn't think of anything else to
say. She said that she was disappointed with her stateroom,
that it was on the inside and on the wrong deck. I told her that
I would be very happy to exchange rooms with her, but that
mine had only one bunk which wouldn't be enough for both
her and her sister. I offered to go down and talk to the purser
to see if he could find something better for them. There was a
huge line of passengers waiting to talk to the purser, but he
looked up and noticed that he and I had the same Shrine
button in our lapels—something I seldom wear and then only
when I'm traveling. He glanced up and addressed me in the
familiar Shriners' greeting, "Noble," and asked me what he
could do for me. It turned out that we were both 32nd
Degree Masons and both belonged to the same Shrine body,
the Islam Temple in San Francisco. He had joined when he
was with the old Pacific Mail Steamship Company. We
chatted for a while and then I asked if he could do me a favor.
I told him that I had some lady friends and that they had a
terrible room, could he change it. I told him that the girls
would probably pay a little more if he could improve on their
accommodations, but that this young lady had done me quite

a favor the day before and I wanted to return it. He said, "Noble, we have only one thing left—the bridal suite. It has its own deck and everything." And I said that it probably would be too much money for them to pay. He told me to forget it, that he would let them have it at the regular price and he moved the Smithline sisters into a fabulous suite.

Needless to say, Anna, Adele and I became very good friends on our way across the Atlantic. The girls were going first to London and then to Paris. I was heading for Paris myself. In those days we stayed at the old Claridge Hotel (not to be confused with Claridge's in London) in Paris and I asked the girls if they wanted to meet me in Paris when they were finished in London. Anna said she wasn't sure that she had reservations and I offered to firm them up for her. When I got to Paris to check, sure enough, there were no reservations in her name, but a five-dollar bill in the correct hands fixed everything. While Anna did her buying, her little sister Adele and I went sightseeing. We had a marvelous time traipsing through Versailles where I couldn't get over the luxury and magnificence of the palace. I remember turning to Adele in amazement and cracking her up with my naiveté, saying, "That *mench* Louis XIV really knew how to live!"

Together, the three of us really saw Paris. When I got back to the States, I had decided that I wanted to see more of Ann, but she thought that I would be more suited for her little sister, Adele. But my mind was made up and I began to court Ann via long-distance line. My phone bills in the following months looked like the financial statement for Standard Oil. When Ann and I started to talk of marriage, she was young and pretty and terrifically talented. She was making $10,000 a year which, in those days, was phenomenal pay, especially for a twenty-three-year-old girl. She was a fairly well-off young lady with a marvelous career—already she was Gershel's head designer and she was training Adele to follow in her footsteps. To marry me, she would be giving up a sure thing to move to the West Coast and, perhaps, an uncertain future. For almost a year after we met, we talked on the telephone. I saw her when I could on my buying trips East, and I finally convinced her that she belonged in California with me. We set our wedding date.

Anna Smithline came from a family of five girls—Henrietta, Rose, Nina, Adele and herself. Adele was the youngest and Anna was the middle child. The girls' father was Lithuanian and had been a tailor in the Czar's army. His name, Smithline, meant "Little Smith" in German, but had been Anglicized when he processed through immigration at Ellis Island. I used to tease Anna all the time about her Lithuanian ancestors and would sing, "Ai, ai, ai, ai, I'm an old American Litvack." She was very good-natured about it and teased me right back. Ann learned her pattern-making skills from her father. She went to work first as a sketcher at the coat and suit house and then as a designer. Three of the daughters were married, including Ann, and it was she who was the main breadwinner for the family.

Ann had great taste and skill as a designer. She was a craftsman of the European school who was always in love with the feel of fine material and the principles of good design. She was a true creator who could style a suit along classic lines. At the end of the season at Ben Gershel, the company would sell off its odd pieces of material and Ann would always buy the beautiful roll ends, bring them home and make clothes for her family. She started teaching Adele everything she knew. When the two of them went to Europe that first time, Adele had gotten so adept that it was she who made both sisters' traveling ensembles. Ann's boss was very impressed with Adele's needlework and offered her a job at Gershel. Because she was still in school, Adele had to work Saturdays, apprenticing in the trimming department where she would pack buttons and put them in bags and hang them on the suits.

When Adele was about seventeen, she had been working

at Gershel for about a year and realized she didn't know enough technically about running a workroom or telling people how to do things; but she made enough money which Ann had helped her to save and she quit her job to go to school to learn professional design. Adele studied with a French seamstress at night and went to high school during the day. She used to say, "I was fascinated. To me, dressmaking was like sculpting, to take a piece of flat material and drape it and to put it together with an idea and make something beautiful was wonderful." Obviously she loved it and became quite a skilled designer in her own right. In those days women's suits were made from heavy twill material—usually a separate jacket and long skirt with a decorative trim of soutache embroidery on the bottom of the skirt and around the collar and jacket cuffs. After her schooling Adele went back to Gershel and revolutionized the entire business by cutting her clothes out of easier, softer fabric. She actually started the dress department at Gershel. But when Ann left to marry me, Adele wasn't happy and left Gershel herself to work for a man named Bass who paid her an enormous $30,000 a year, most of which she put into a bank that failed in the crash of '29. But Adele was a survivor who learned her lessons well. Today she is one of America's best and most prestigious designers . . . Adele Simpson.

A while after our trip to Europe, Ann woke Adele in the middle of the night to tell her that she was going to San Francisco to marry me. The girls had never been farther west than Philadelphia and had no idea where San Francisco was. Anna always referred to Adele as "the baby," so when I announced to my parents that I was going to marry Ann and that she was coming to California with "the baby," they automatically assumed that I had gotten away from one married woman but was marrying another one, this time, one with a child. They were relieved and quite pleased to note that "the baby" was none other than Ann's "baby" sister—all

45

of eighteen and quite pretty. To prepare for the wedding, Anna had outfitted herself with a complete trousseau and on the four-day train trip cross country, had littered her room-mette with suits and dresses, trying them on for Adele. She had exhausted both of them with her indecision trying to pick out that just-right outfit to make an impression on me and my family. They were a little confused when the train stopped in Oakland and they had to take a ferry across the Bay to get to San Francisco. Adele kept saying, "Where in the world *is* this place?" They actually thought the West was still filled with outlaws and wild Indians.

We were married in Mary Ann's apartment in the St. Francis Hotel. My grandmother had insisted that the wedding be in San Francisco because she figured that I was the last one of her grandchildren that she'd get to see married. She was seventy-five at the time and as strong as a horse. It was difficult saying no to her. She gave the wedding to Anna and me as a gift, along with $5,000. I must have been very special to her because when her other grandchildren, about twelve of them in all, married, her gift to them was a grand piano. The wedding dinner was in one of the hotel's grand public rooms. Mary Ann had decorated the place with typical panache. She was very famous for her entertainments. Her tables and settings were quite astounding. Sometimes she would decorate the tabletops with mirrors or with imported blown crystal swan vases with live gardenias floating inside. At a family gathering to celebrate a birthday or an anniversary, often she would put a $100 check under *each* person's plate in honor of the occasion. Our wedding dinner was no less spectacular. Mary Ann had her florist cut holes in the tabletops in which a bouquet of flowers was set. They appeared to be growing right out of the table. The silver flatware was gold-plated and the crystal and china were the finest the hotel could provide. It was so grand that it was almost overwhelming; I've never forgotten it. But Mary Ann never did anything unless she could do it her way—with the best that money could buy.

Even when she died in 1943, she didn't do things halfway. At the time, there was an Art Deco cocktail bar in the St. Francis in which there were flowers hanging from the ceiling—miniature purple orchids imported from Hawaii and set in tiny tubes of water. When Mary Ann died, an entire blanket of those orchids was draped over her coffin. She was the ultimate Grande Dame even up to the end.

Ann and I were married on November 19, 1925. I had just turned twenty-six the previous July, and she was twenty-four. We honeymooned at the Del Monte Hotel on the Monterey Peninsula. During World War II, the hotel and adjoining lodge were a recovery area for the navy wounded. But for us it was a place to get to know each other. Ann and I really had our courtship via telephone and had spent very little time together before our marriage. We motored down to the Peninsula and spent a very quiet time sightseeing in Carmel and enjoying each other's company. I apparently hadn't planned our finances very well and ran out of money. I had to call home to Joe for some more. We couldn't stay away any longer than a week or ten days—I couldn't afford that much time away from business and besides, Anna was anxious to start working. For her, retailing was the other side of the same coin. She knew the fashion business upside down and backwards because of designing experience. It was natural that she start in with better dresses, coats and suits. She didn't have much to learn. At first she worked with my mother. I think it was probably an even exchange. Lottie taught her retailing and merchandising and Ann shared her immaculate fashion sense. The two of them got along famously.

When we returned to San Francisco, we lived in the Alexander Hamilton Hotel for about three weeks. Ann was never a cook, so when we moved into our first apartment at 3337 Clay Street, we got a maid to handle the household chores and to do what little cooking we required. Sometimes after work—and we worked six days a week—we would go out to dinner, often stopping to visit with my parents in a more relaxed setting. We developed our own little crowd for soirees to the theater or intimate evenings in each other's homes playing gin rummy and pinochle. We were friendly with an insurance broker named Sam Markowitz and his wife Nettie. Sam was a very funny fellow—always cracking jokes. Anna was an inveterate card player. She loved to gamble and could sit for hours at the card table. I never really liked it and played "at" pinochle. Eventually, I gave it up, but Ann was so enamored of chance that she could bet on just about anything. And win.

We hadn't been married too long when we found out that our first child was on the way. Donald was born almost a year to the day of our wedding, November 17, 1926. He had a very delicate face and features. He looked like a pretty little elf with tapered fingers and a pouting pink bow-shaped mouth. He was a good combination of both of us, but as he grew older, he seemed to take after Anna. He was very thoughtful and quiet; the kind of child who liked completion—a beginning, a middle and an end, a top and a bottom. When he was born, Anna's mother came out to visit and to take care of Ann and the baby for a few weeks. I don't think she was very happy with what she saw. She asked Anna if she had any pocket money and the answer was no. Anytime we needed anything, from clothing to groceries, we just put it on account and paid at the end of the month. My mother-in-law must have thought we were terribly broke or something worse because we hardly ever used cash. We just charged. Mrs. Smithline wasn't used to doing business like that. Anna went back to work as soon as she could. After two or three months at home, she was chomping at the bit to get back to work. It wasn't that she loved retailing so much, she adored fashion. Our lives as a little family were really simple. We engaged a nurse to care for the baby, we put in our time at Joseph Magnin, spending our Sundays off on picnics in the country or at home. In April, 1928, our second child, Ellen, was born. Again Anna returned to work as soon as she was strong enough.

My wife and I made quite a team. Ann had a tremendous sense of style and of what was right. She was a born merchandiser. She was probably as skilled at buying and selling ladies' apparel as she was designing it. She had a terrific personality and the knack of getting along with everyone. She was a great mediator and conciliator. Everyone who knew her loved her, including members of the Magnin family, some of whom hadn't spoken to each other for years. One of Ann's greatest friends and allies was Sidney Sloan, Hattie Magnin Sloan's husband. Hattie was one of my Uncle Samuel's daughters by his second marriage. Sidney was the only one of the family from my generation to be at I. Magnin; he was slated to replace Grover, Mary Ann's son, when the time came. Ann had known Sidney from the time he was buying suits at Gershel. When Ann became the Joseph Magnin coat and suit buyer, the two of them were inseparable. They often covered the Eastern markets together, enjoying the long train trips back to New York. My daughter Ellen thinks that Anna "made" Sidney Sloan—that he would never have been what he was at I. Magnin had it not been for Ann's generosity and good taste. She would tell him, "Sidney, there's something hot at So-and-So's place and I'm not going to buy it; it's right for you." With Ann, there was never any jealousy or backbiting. She was always magnanimous and fair.

Ann was as generous with her time for our employees as she was for family and business associates. Working for my mother in the millinery department was a young Viennese woman named Hilda Gilgannon. My parents had hired her in the early twenties, when she was barely off the boat. She often called herself a "greenhorn" and loved my folks like second family. The feeling was mutual. My father always made a point of greeting Hilda every day and she idolized him. She

49

was also quite attached to Ann. Together they would go to market. Ann would hold an informal court in her sleeper compartment at night on those train trips, playing cards and telling stories. They would curl up on her bunk like sorority sisters and giggle all night. Often when they got to New York, Ann would make sure that Hilda and the other buyers had something to do that first night—usually the Sunday before market began. If the girls were free, Anna would take them out to her sister Adele's country place in Connecticut for dinner and an evening of cards. She took care of them just as if they were family.

Born with a graciousness that I have not seen in too many people, Ann was a devoted and loyal person to me and to her friends. She had a way of speaking to people so they thought they were the most important people in the world. There was a time when my grandmother Rachael and Aunt Jennie were living with us. We were also very close to Mary Ann and to my own mother. Unanimously, they thought Ann was marvelous. She was able to attract and please those women and at the same time keep them at bay, holding her own as the most important woman in my little family. So easily those strong women could have overrun Ann with their opinions and ways of doing things. But Ann had a no-nonsense integrity that was couched in diplomacy. When she passed away, probably 150 people came up to us at the funeral and said, "Anna Magnin was my best friend."

CHAPTER FOUR

Joseph Magnin I—
The Early Years

❧ AT HEART, I don't think that my father was a true retailer. His real calling was finance. That may have been why Mary Ann passed over him twice for leadership at I. Magnin. I think, however, that Joe's ego must have suffered when his two younger brothers were given top positions in the best store in San Francisco. For Joe's oldest brother, Sam, it was never too much of a problem. While he was assigned to the New York office before John took it over permanently, Sam was very content to return to San Francisco and be the family's "greeter" at the downtown store, reporting to work every morning in his immaculately cut suit, his spit-shined shoes with their elegant gray spats and a fresh flower in his lapel. For Joe, however, the thought of being anything less than boss was untenable and although he never told me exactly why he quit, he broke off and went on his own in 1913.

When Joe bought into Newman-Levinson, the store sold

all sorts of stuff—piece goods, buttons, notions. Some of the stock was particularly strange. For instance, the basement was filled with cartons and cartons of beads. We never knew why they were there or who would buy them. With a lot of unusable merchandise, my father had to take out a loan to buy fresh goods, and the things he couldn't use he sold to a place that specialized in odd lots and fire-sale items. For five years the business was called Newman-Magnin, and then, finally, in 1918, my father bought the Newmans out and renamed the store after himself. He sold all the dry goods, kept only the fashion end of the business and cut the area of the store down to two floors. About 1920 he also bought a tiny little store on Grant Avenue called Henkel's, which he ran under that name until Donald and Ellen came along. He renamed the shop Donnell's, after my two children, and made it into a popular-priced store. The shop, located where Podesta Baldocchi, one of San Francisco's elite florist shops is located today, never did well, and when the lease ran out, Joe gave it up.

If Joe ever thought he was going to have it easy running Joseph Magnin, he learned quickly that he had a long, hard road in front of him. And if he felt he could enter the marketplace and compete head to head with I. Magnin, he was sadly mistaken. But that was the direction he chose . . . and I. Magnin was the only game in town. In those early years I think the store made it purely on the strength of my mother's millinery business which had followed her from I. Magnin to JM. It probably comprised half our yearly sales for a long time.

My mother had a great following. People liked her. She was marvelous with the public and was attuned to what would sell. She was also the most serene person I've ever met. I never saw her angry. No matter what happened, she never got excited, but then, I think she had been trained by her experience working for Mary Ann to hide her emotions at the most crucial times. When everyone else was excited—and I found myself in noisy opposition to my father quite often—she would be a sea of calm. She would let everyone have their say, sometimes at the tops of their voices, and when all the fussing and fuming was finished, she usually found a compromise solution. She could master any situation just by smoothing things over. I think that I probably learned a lot of my negotiating skills from my mother. Lottie was a better merchant than my father. Sometimes I thought she was cowed by him because he tended to be opinionated, dominating and stubborn, but in retrospect, it was just her quiet way of letting him *think* that he had everything under control.

Ann and Lottie were very compatible. Lottie trained Ann in the beginning and found her to be an apt pupil. In some ways, I think Ann was much like my mother. I could get heated at policy-making meetings and Ann would just sit there, composed, letting me pound the table with my demands. Afterwards, sometime during the day, she would send for any of the people I may have trampled on in my fit of temper and say, "I think Cyril was right at the meeting today and I *think* it *may* work out better if you would just do so-and-so." Then she would lay out a plan which would keep us all happy.

Lottie and Ann were responsible for setting the merchandising pace of the store, given what we had available. They certainly elevated the taste. Because we were cut off from so many resources, my wife used her craft as a designer to create a lot of the clothes we sold. She'd say to one of our manufacturers, "Well, make me a tweed suit with a fur collar" or whatever. She would wind up doing her own designs out of necessity. That prejudice against Joseph Magnin in the fashion markets lasted a long time, even after Ann had passed away and my daughter Ellen was shopping for our store. Ellen would have to wait until I. Magnin had looked over the new clothes first before she could place our orders. She says that she didn't like what she saw anyhow and rather than buy second best, she, like Ann before her, became very inventive. Our things, even from those earliest days, were just a little bit different.

The Joseph Magnin store on the corner of Stockton and O'Farrell was in a multistory building, but in the first crucial years, we rented only the first two floors and the mezzanine. The rest of the building—which, by the way, is where Joseph Magnin has always been located in downtown San Francisco—was leased to light manufacturers and for office space. In the store there was a main floor with a balcony all around from which you could watch the sales action; the floor itself was highly polished linoleum. When customers walked into the store, they would be greeted either by my father or my mother. I mostly stayed upstairs in the credit office. Before I was married, I was a jack-of-all trades. I unpacked clothes, tagged dresses, swept up. I would work four to six days a week and on Saturdays would be allowed to sell—usually handbags, which I liked because you didn't have to worry about sizes. I had worked my way up to being a buyer by the time I met Ann. My mother had trained me by taking me with her on trips to New York and to Europe. When I married, I was buying hosiery, cosmetics and accessories, I handled customer relations—something which, even today, I still do for JM. I would also check the departments to see how our merchandise was selling.

Our staff was necessarily small. We all doubled as sales people and buyers at market time—something which could have been a problem for Hilda Gilgannon, who eventually became Lottie's assistant. She was hired when Donald was a baby. She was embarrassed because she thought her English was bad, but she was an extremely talented milliner. She could take a plain piece of felt and turn it into a stylish cloche in no time. A woman named Mrs. Gardner supervised the workroom and Hilda, a slender, peppy young woman with a boyish, sculptured face and strong hands, was hired to train and work under her. The millinery workroom was located off the balcony above the first floor. The girls in the shop usually brought their lunches and would eat in a little side room near their sewing machines. One day Joe walked in while Hilda was having her lunch and said, "The floor is so busy, I want you to come down and wait on someone." Hilda was panic-stricken. In her thick Viennese accent she tried to tell him that it was her lunch hour and that she couldn't come down— anything to keep from having to talk to anyone. Joe was insistent and said she could eat later. Right off the bat, Hilda sold two hats to one of our best customers. (Remember, my mother's reputation was as the best milliner in San Francisco.)

Hilda's English wasn't so terrific, but she had a real knack for hats and her knowledge transcended any language barrier. She would apologize to Joe and Lottie, but my parents would reassure her that if her English was good enough for them, it was certainly good enough for the customers. Eventually Lottie trained Hilda as her assistant and Hilda learned her lessons well. She could be absolutely tenacious when she went to markets as a buyer. When I. Magnin still had things all their own way, Hilda made an appointment to see one manufacturer who had turned her down nine different times. I had always told her to go directly to the man in charge—the shortest distance between two points is a line straight to the top—and she did. She walked into the office of the president of the company and was told by his secretary to wait. She figured that she could be waiting all day so she strolled into his office. He said to her that if anyone was that determined, he couldn't say no and she got the line for us. My father had always told me, "When you want to go to heaven, talk to God, not the angels." He was right.

Our entire family life revolved around Joseph Magnin— something that never changed through the years, even when my own children were old enough to start in the business.

Ann and I hired a series of nurse-housekeepers to watch the children when they were very small, but as soon as we could, we brought the kids with us to work. Many times Donald would fall asleep in one of the bins in the lingerie department or in a storeroom under a rack of coats. We had to work so late at times that we would have meals brought in from a restaurant across the street from the store called Helwig's. My father ate and slept the business and in those few hours that he occasionally took for himself, he was never very far away from Joseph Magnin. He would, on occasion, have lunch at John's Grill on Ellis Street, about a block and a half away from the store. John's was and still is the prototypical San Francisco male hangout, complete with continuous pinochle and bridge games up on the second floor. It was made famous by Dashiell Hammett, who put it into *The Maltese Falcon*. The second-floor room where my father liked to spend his lunch hours is called "The Maltese Falcon Room" today. Joe's regular gang included men like Charlie Helwig and Jean Blum. At John's they would sit there playing cards; Joe would have his mouth stuffed with that ubiquitous cigar, spewing ashes and food all over his vest and talking business and finance with his cronies.

Times were tough and Joe pinched pennies, often in the extreme. He was fond of picking up little pieces of string from the floor and stuffing them in his pockets. We tied the customers' packages with twine and the salesgirls didn't always cut off the exact amount. Joe made a point of going behind the counters to see how many wasted lengths of string were littering the floor. He would take Hilda by the hand and say, "See, Hilda, there go our profits." He was a notorious saver—almost a Mr. Scrooge or a skinflint. But it was a question of "waste not, want not." And nothing was wasted. In hosiery boxes, for instance, there were three pairs of stockings each separated by a piece of stiff, white paper. Those throwaways became our scratch pads. In fact, a piece of paper was never thrown away until it had been used on both sides—*all* pieces of paper, including receipts and invoices from our resources. Even Joe's cigar boxes weren't tossed out. We found that they were perfect for storing the accounts receivable ledger cards. Things were so tight that we had to make use of every dollar we had and couldn't be extravagant, even with necessary supplies. That's not to say we were one step away from the doors of debtors' prison, but when we saved money in one area, we could spend it in others to promote and develop the company.

Often Joe's money-saving ploys bordered on the ridiculous. I have to emphasize, though, that in those hard-scrabble days of the Depression when a lot of folks stood in bread lines or sold apples for a dime apiece on street corners, even the pennies counted. When Donald and Ellen were young, they were taught to read the names of the towns surrounding San Francisco. All local letters cost 2¢ to mail; out-of-town mail was 3¢. Donald sorted the out-of-town bills because he could read and Ellen, then a tiny tot, would pile up the mail that read "City," which was how letters were addressed for San Francisco. They would tie the separate piles with rubber bands and Joe would take them to post. At the time he was living in Los Altos, a small country town down the Peninsula below San Mateo, Hillsborough, Burlingame, and Palo Alto. In order to save that extra penny per bill, Joe would stop at the mail drop in each little town on his way home and deposit that day's bills so they'd have a local postmark. He would put all of our New York mail into one big envelope addressed to our East Coast office and instruct the staff to mail the contents locally, again saving that penny on out-of-town letters. Joe would make our vendors call for their payment checks. I thought it was a terrible idea, that it did not build goodwill, and I asked him why he would inconvenience people so. All he'd reply, in that fey little way of his, was, "They come into the store . . . they may buy something."

We tiptoed around financial disaster during the Depression years. Our attorney was Edgar Levy and he would worry because some of his fees were being paid in stock. He didn't think the stock was worth anything—and maybe, back then, it wasn't. As a hedge, perhaps, Joe opened another business, this time using his financial acumen. He called it Donner Factors, named first Donnell's, after Donald and Ellen. But it was too confusing when we still had a store by that name, so he changed it to Donner. Often there were small manufacturers which did not have the cash flow to keep up with their incoming orders. Most companies paid their bills in sixty days and usually the banks would not advance development capital to such small concerns. Joe would first check out the credit ratings of a prospective client, and then for a fee he would take over their accounts receivable and accept the credit risk. In effect, Donner would advance these companies money against their accounts receivable. For a long time Donner Factors was making more money than Joseph Magnin and probably kept us from going under.

Deep down, Joe was even more conservative than his oft-humorous supersavings methods indicated. There was a real ideological difference between the two of us. Because of his insistence on competing directly with I. Magnin, we were relegated to buying inferior merchandise. We were known in the trade as "the *other* Magnin," "the second-rate Magnin." The I. Magnin side of the family was very social; they were members of the city's elite—the early mercantile princes. But the Joseph Magnins were considered upstarts, parvenues, and just weren't accepted. It got so bad for a while that my father was barred from the Concordia Club, a prestigious private Jewish organization established in the late 1800s by some of the Jewish argonauts, because he wasn't the "right" Magnin. Ordinary rag merchants just weren't taken into that august body until World War II when there was a desperate need for members. The Joseph Magnin family wasn't part of any elite

58

group, Jewish or gentile. We didn't have the time to worry about it either. Every waking hour was spent working, literally living and breathing the business.

I hated being called the second-rate Magnin. Not because I had any social aspirations, but because it just didn't have to be that way. I never thought it wise trying to beat I. Magnin at their own game. They had been established more than fifty years and had a huge head start. We would always come out on the losing end if we tried to copy them and go after the same customers. The only things that were keeping us afloat as it was were Donner Factors and my mother's millinery following. Still, my father persisted. What we could buy directly from the markets, we did and what we couldn't buy, we copied and had made up by small manufacturers which my father would factor with his company. So we had nearly the same merchandise as I. Magnin—through our own ingenuity—but it wasn't the McCoy and the public knew it. I. Magnin had a long and prosperous history with the gentry of San Francisco; we got what was left when they were finished, including customers.

Toward the end of the 1930s, however, I began to notice a change in the population of the city. The country was starting to mobilize for war and had just instituted the draft. Troops were being ordered to the Hawaiian Islands and other areas in the Pacific, and San Francisco was the embarkation point. Along with these young servicemen—sailors, marines and flyers—came their sweethearts, wives, mothers and sisters and even the usual group of camp followers. The city probably had more brothels then than during the notorious Barbary Coast days at the turn of the century. All these women had no preconceived ideas of where to buy. Not only were they young and unbiased, they had money to spend. I suggested to Joseph that this was the market we should tap. Instead of beating our brains out trying to compete with I. Magnin, we should mine new territory. I was growling all the time, complaining bitterly that we were losing ground and wasting time. Joe and I had terrible arguments. Still, he refused to listen to me, to let go. It got so bad that I would sit in Union Square, a block away from the store, with my head in my hands, threatening to quit. Ann would sit there with me and talk me out of doing something foolish. In retrospect, I may have felt exactly as my father did when he was bucking his brothers and mother at I. Magnin, but I never thought Joe could see the parallel. His message to me each time I would broach the subject of changing direction was, "You'll never be successful with your crazy ideas; you're shooting for the moon." It did not inspire confidence in me to know that my father didn't believe in my ability to take his precious baby— Joseph Magnin—and turn it into something special. I kept harping on the fact that we were making a terrible mistake by not going for that new market—all those free-spending young people coming up. He told me that I was goofy in the head. I said, "Well, maybe I am, but I don't want to stick around here for the rest of my life as a second- or third-rate Magnin."

Finally my frustration got the best of me and while I didn't actually threaten Joe in the sense that I said, "Hell, I'm gonna walk out of here if I don't get what I want"—I never used those tactics to his face—I did tell him, "I don't want to sit here forever going nowhere." I was almost forty years old and had spent my entire adult life in the business. I had two children and I expected that we would have more. I didn't want to break up the family and I didn't want to tear the business apart, but I could see no future for any of us if I continued on the course my father had plotted. Finally, in 1937, it all came to a head.

One day Joe came to me and said, "I'm going to turn the business over to you. But if you go broke with your crazy ideas, don't come to me for more money. I'll be willing to bet that within a year—no, make that six months—we'll be back doing what we're doing now." He really believed I was wrong. I admitted to him that maybe I could be wrong, but that I wanted to try it. I figured, nothing ventured, nothing gained. It was an unofficial transition. There were no formal goodbyes because, while Joseph may have stepped back, he didn't step down. He remained president of the business and retained an office in the Joseph Magnin building for Donner Factors, so he never really left. I told him that if he wanted to be president, fine . . . then I'd be vice-president. *Executive* vice-president. He could stay on as president for as long as he lived. But my title didn't mean anything to me. I wanted to test my thinking to see if it was right or wrong. I had a stubborn determination to do this youth-oriented switch in direction. I think that when I look at what Joseph Magnin was to become, I was right.

With Joe's half-hearted blessing and dire warnings of imminent failure, I had my work cut out for me. If I was going to turn Joseph Magnin into a first-rate, young store, a lot of things had to be done. First I got rid of every piece of merchandise that had a matronly connotation. I marked down all the large sizes to clear them out and decided to limit the stock to clothes in sizes five to fourteen—no sixteens, twenty-two and a halfs or size forties would do. While we specialized in youthful clothes, they were not necessarily cheap ones; we bought good quality. Ann would have nothing to do with shoddy merchandise. I had learned the lesson of quality from Mary Ann and never forgot it. We had the best buys for the money, and very often it was the best that money could buy. If we couldn't find what we wanted in the marketplace, we would develop manufacturers who would work with us because what we were doing was so new, there weren't enough design houses around in those prewar days making the kinds of clothes we needed. We were far ahead of everyone, going after the so-called junior market literally before anyone thought to make junior-sized clothes. We put people like Gene Shelley and Malta of Los Angeles in business making clothes for us—financed, for the most part, through Donner Factors. Their clothes had a decidedly young look. We made history. I was selling $200 suits when we couldn't sell many dresses that cost over $60 retail. And $200, forty years ago, was a lot of bucks. After the war, when material was plentiful, we stocked fashionable suits made from gabardine and sharkskin produced by these suit houses. They were so popular we couldn't get enough of them.

I was very fortunate to have those traditionally strong Magnin women behind me in the beginning of my great adventure. I had received excellent training from Mary Ann and Charlotte, but it was Ann who helped me realize my own vision. What I had inherited from my father was a shell and while I conceptualized what I wanted to do with Joseph Magnin, Ann could take just the germ of an idea and run with it. Ann had an impeccable sense of quality and excellent taste. She had become a merchandiser in the Mary Ann mold, but she was much more creative. I was basically a gambler. I could get talked into buying 350 low-priced numbers that didn't have much of a fashion flair and Ann would say, "I think we should buy more quality." Quite often she would confide to Adele when she went East for market that I was off on a tear buying from some house in Los Angeles because they were cheaper or because we could get a better deal. It was Adele's opinion that I bought more "dogs" than anyone. I became known as "Carload" Magnin and I would say, "If it's good for one, it's good for one hundred." I was never afraid of quantity when I knew the quality and the fashion were right. I had a very wild, unpredictable side to me and it was to Ann's credit that she did not just throw up her hands and run back to New York to get away. While I had a sense of things to come, where I could spot trends, Ann could mobilize the resources to actualize them. She had a great clothes sense; she provided the class for the store. She had a marvelous integrity about dressing women, a great honesty. She was, however, not inflexible and quite often she went along with some of the crazier things I wanted to do. If she didn't like it, she bore up well and never said, "Cyril, I think you're nuts" the way my father had. Actually Ann was a mediator between old Joe and me. She performed a balancing act better than the one at Ringling Brothers—she could hold me in tow and keep my father out of my hair at the same time. She was a remarkable woman. In the end she was absolutely invaluable. Because she was already well-known in New York as having been Gershel's head designer, she could waltz into market and get the high-priced lines we couldn't have gotten before and get credit terms that were almost unheard of in those days. That proved to be most important because the store was under-capitalized. Suppliers would deal with us because of their love for Anna Magnin, rather than any affection or loyalty to Joseph Magnin.

We were a growing concern consolidating our direction in those years up to and including the Second World War. Often Joseph Magnin would be the busiest store in San Francisco and people had to be given numbered tickets to be served—just as in a delicatessen. Shipyard workers would come to shop in their filthy, dirty work clothes fresh from their jobs and buy very expensive things. Still, our finances were, at times, very rocky. Sometimes, to make payroll, we had to stage an instant sale. We used any kind of excuse—birthday sales, spring, summer, fall or winter sales, end-of-the-month sales, you name it. It was a matter of generating enough cash to pay the help. We didn't have time to put an ad in the paper, so we would stay up all night dressing the windows with sale signs and merchandise.

In a way our new customers dictated what they wanted us to sell. Prior to the war years women didn't wear trousers very much—it wasn't thought to be proper. But when women went to work in the factories and had to wear uniforms and coveralls, they realized that pants were comfortable and quite

63

acceptable for social wear. Shortly after the war marvelous material became available to us—flannels and gabardines, stuff that was used for the military and was now on the open market. We had acres of trousers made—sportswear was taking off. We opened what amounted to a boutique, capitalizing on the fervor of patriotism that was sweeping the country. We called our small shop within a shop, the All American Sport Shop. It was located off the first floor, about four steps down and to the back. The floor was covered in blue vinyl tile with red and white walls. Now, this was in an era when fashionable San Francisco stores were decorated in placid grays and beiges and where saleswomen would bring merchandise to their clients. And here we were putting together the first sportswear shop in the city and decorating it in vivid color. It was innovative and quite remarkable and on Saturday afternoons, you couldn't get into it, it was so jammed.

We developed American manufacturers for the All American Sport Shop—companies like Evan-Picone and Rudi Gernreich. We were Rudi's first customer. I could see that he had what we wanted. And while my father was still very skeptical about the direction the store was taking, even he contributed to the All American Shop. We found a shoe manufacturer named Ted Sevall—possibly my father was factoring him. Sevall had a "name" that was to the shoe business what Adrian, at the time, was to women's clothes. His were high-fashion goods. He made a thin suede wedge with an open toe—the first sport shoes. Up until that time the pump was very popular (and probably, very uncomfortable). My father made arrangements for a man named Harry Parlow to lease our very first concession, the shoe department, from us and stock it with one of Sevall's wedges. We opened that first shoe shop with a single shoe style, and decorated an entire wall with it. We had two blue leather couches on which our customers could sit and be fitted. We must have sold hundreds of pairs of that one shoe. Both the shop and the shoe were quite avant-garde for the time.

I was totally involved in the store, putting in twelve-hour days. I sold during the day and was the credit manager at night. I used to get on the telephone with a fictitious name and talk to the customers about their past-due bills. While it wouldn't be proper for Mr. Magnin to complain that their accounts were in arrears, my alter-ego Mr. Jones, had no problem at all. All those years I was cooped up in the credit department under Joe's piercing and critical eye weren't for nothing. We had such a rush of new customers, I would open accounts for them right on the floor, literally promising them everything. It's a practice I continue today. When I travel, for instance, and see an attractive flight attendant or woman seated next to me, I'll ask if she has an account at Joesph Magnin. If she says no, I'll take her name and address and make arrangements to send her a credit application when I get back to San Francisco. In those days, though, some of the accounts turned out to be bad ones. If a no-pay would show up, I'd yell at the regular credit manager. They in turn would look up to see who had opened the account. Pretty soon the girls in the credit department were wise to me and would start tagging all the accounts I had opened. I'm a salesman at heart and while I may have been careless in the matter of extending credit without a proper check, there is another side to the story. Some of our best accounts were those we hadn't verified. I let one woman walk out of the store with a couple of hundred dollars' worth of merchandise because she was new in the community and didn't have a credit record. She turned out to be one of our best customers. My desire to create sales volume could override my judgment, but mostly it paid off. At Joseph Magnin, customers were always royalty—they were always right. And I believed that you made more friends by satisfying your customers. Word-of-mouth from a happy customer was worth infinitely more than a page of advertising in the newspaper.

By the end of the war my family was completed. Our son Jerry had been born on July 30, 1938, and was in grade school in 1945. All of my family took an active part in the business. I enjoyed having them there. It was thrilling to see my ideas start to take off. What we were doing with Joseph Magnin was very forward thinking. It was a gambling move back in the late thirties to change from misses sizes to junior sizes. What may have started out as a defensive move ended up starting a trend that took the rest of the women's specialty stores at least fifteen years to catch up to. People in the business said, "That Magnin is crazy . . . he's nuts," but I proved that I was neither. I found that I had an exquisite sense of timing as to what the public wanted. I'm not saying that I was a sooth-sayer, but I could feel way down in the bottom of my gut whether things would work or not. I had a sense of adventure—perhaps something I may have learned instinc-tively way back when I was sneaking off for Saturdays with my Uncle Manny—and I was willing to put that sense of adven-ture and the future to work for me. But I also wanted to prove a point—to myself, to my father and to the rest of the retailing community—and nothing else mattered to me at the time. I was going to develop Joseph Magnin into one of the great retailing companies in the country. Secretly I wanted to surpass I. Magnin, or certainly, to be looked upon as being as great as I. Magnin. I think we accomplished both of those— but it was always seat-of-the-pants flying, as an experiment. Over the years it was a source of constant amazement to me that we accomplished what we did, starting in the late thirties as "the other Magnin."

For the next twenty-five years, nothing, but nothing, was to transcend Joseph Magnin in importance in my life.

Isaac Magnin

Mary Ann Magnin

Joseph Magnin, age five

Charlotte Davis Magnin

Cyril Magnin, age eleven

Cyril Magnin, age sixteen

Cyril, the future merchant prince, age twenty

Anna Magnin (ROMAINE PHOTOGRAPHY)

Three generations of Magnins in 1929—Joseph, Donald and Cyril

*Donald, Cyril and Joseph celebrate at Donald's
wedding in* 1952

The Sacramento, California, store opens in 1946 with Donald, Cyril and Anna on hand to do the family honors (STONE/STECCATI)

Cyril and Jerry about to fly to Hawaii in 1948

Donald, Ellen and Cyril whoop it up in 1950

Glamorous Ellen Magnin, age twenty

*Cyril turns radio commentator for Radio Free Europe
in Munich, Germany, in 1956*

CHAPTER FIVE ❧

And Jerry
Makes Three

IN THE RETAILING BUSINESS merchandise changes with the season. In the Cyril Magnin family our residences changed just about as often. The apartment on Clay Street became too small with two lively, growing children, so we moved to another place on Clay Street, and then moved into a house out in Sea Cliff, a neighborhood of lovely Spanish-style homes with green lawns and trees. The only drawback to Sea Cliff was that it was in the fog a good deal of the year. We rented our first Sea Cliff house because we had no money to buy. We hadn't been there too long before the owner advised me that he wanted to move back into his house. We were lucky to find a spectacular ten-room apartment with three bedrooms, three baths and maid's quarters, in a deluxe building at 2100 Pacific. If the times had been different, I'm sure we couldn't have afforded the place, but during the Depression, apartments like it were going empty. We paid an unbelievable $125 per month and secured a five-year lease.

Things were so inexpensive in those days that we could completely redecorate the apartment, a decision hastened by the fact that the landlord couldn't afford to do it for us. The apartment was recarpeted and Ann had brocaded silk draperies made—all very formal and elegant.

The 2100 Pacific building was an ultra-snooty residence in which children were tolerated . . . barely. Ellen and Donald either didn't know or were too young to care about decorum and blithely acted their ages, sometimes rollerskating in the lobby. The floor was made of huge Spanish tiles and as they skated, their metal skate wheels made a terrific racket. They played hopscotch and rode their bikes up and down the sidewalk in front of the building. Still, we had an ironclad lease and we paid our rent on time and while the children were considered nuisances by some of the more staid residents of the building, we weren't asked to leave. At least, not until Donald's run-in with Mrs. Hearst of the great news-paper family. Donald was a big Stanford football fan. His idol was a great player named Bobby Grayson, and for a birthday, we gave Donald a Bobby Grayson uniform in the Stanford colors, cardinal and white—a jersey, pants, pads and a helmet which was too big for him. Our apartment was on the second floor and Mrs. Hearst lived in a penthouse that took up the entire top floor. One afternoon, when Mrs. Hearst was heading up the front stairs and our "Bobby Grayson" was shooting down the stairs with his too-big football helmet on, the inevitable happened. A head-on collision. There were no bones broken and perhaps all that was bruised was Donald's pride. While Mrs. Hearst didn't herself ask us to leave the building, the landlord did.

I was on friendly terms with him, and obviously it was difficult for him to tell us to leave. He said, "Cyril, you know, this is very embarrassing. We could be sued. I tried to talk Mrs. Hearst out of starting any trouble with the understanding that you would move." I told the landlord that I had put down carpets and hung silk drapes—that I had spent a lot of money fixing up the apartment because the building's owners couldn't. We had about $15,000 in that apartment—a lot of money in those days—and I told him that I didn't want to move unless I was compensated for my expenses. He saw that we'd been in the apartment for two years and that he was forcing us to break a lease, so he agreed to prorate some of our money back to us. Meanwhile, we had stayed on social terms with our former landlord out in Sea Cliff, and one rainy Sunday we'd paid a call on him and noticed that there was a house across the street going up for auction for unpaid taxes, not an uncommon sight during the Depression. I went over to bid on the house which now, because of the money I was able to get from the landlord at 2100 Pacific to pay us back for what we'd spent on improvements, we could afford to own. The house in Sea Cliff at 28th Avenue was small and pleasant, but it proved to be too tight a fit. Eventually we bought a larger house at 5 Sea View Terrace and lived there probably longer than I've lived anywhere before or since. Ellen and Donald were raised in that house, spending their elementary and high school years there.

While our houses were always extensions of Ann's marvelous taste, we didn't lead the kind of life where personal possessions were important. We were comfortable, but not ostentatious. I think that I was more apt to reupholster a couch at the store than redo a chair at home that had springs sticking through the seat. I thought that was all right because, in those days, the business came first. Ann's designer's eye made our homes very livable and avant-garde. When everyone was decorating in beiges and off-whites, Ann painted our walls powder blue, which was very daring. She would come home from buying trips with all sorts of things that made our home just a little bit different. While everyone at the time was using the traditional Wedgwood, Spode or Minton china patterns with sterling silver tableware, Ann had fun with her table settings, pulling in marvelous colors and interesting decorating ideas such as using fresh strawberries for a party centerpiece which, back then, was unheard of. There was a real fashion flair to our surroundings.

I have mentioned that Ann was not a cook. She was a gracious hostess just the same. We had a Japanese couple working for us. The man waited on the table and his wife was our cook. He'd come in with his white jacket on and address us so formally, asking, "You want the coffee? You want the coffee?" in funny broken English. We also had a series of Filipino cooks. Now, while we were not practicing Jews and therefore did not observe the rules of a Kosher home—no mixing meat with meat products, no pork or shellfish—Ann's parents were Orthodox Jews and strictly Kosher. When Grandpa Smithline would come to California, we would have to appear observant. Unfortunately our Filipino cook didn't know anything about Jewish dietary laws and the prohibition of pork. During one visit the cook served up a pork dish for dinner and we had to tell Grandpa Smithline that he was eating veal. Visits to New York were difficult for the children because they'd gotten used to eating bread and butter with roast beef. They solved the problem by sneaking their butter onto the undersides of their bread so Grandpa wouldn't see them and get angry.

Ann's Jewish identification was much stronger than mine because of her family's religious background. She did go to temple, Shereth Israel, for the High Holidays, Rosh Hashanah and Yom Kippur, and she palled around with a group of Jewish women with whom she played mahjong. I had never even gone to Sunday School, but Ellen had gone to temple with Ann, found she liked it, and attended Sunday School, taking a streetcar from Sea Cliff each Sunday morning. Where other Jewish families were celebrating Passover and Chanukah, we observed other holidays like Thanksgiving and, of course, Christmas. The Christmas holiday season is the busiest time for all retailers, which applied to us as well. Our celebrations included working late into the night on Christmas Eve. Often we were so involved with the store that we'd have to have the display department come to the house to set up our decorations, tree and all, because Ann was working up until the last moment.

Our customers came first before our own family during Christmas and there were many times that members of my family, even after they had married and left my house, spent their Christmas Eves—and sometimes, Christmas Days—delivering packages. Our business was all important to us and if we had to devote our holiday to serving customers, we did it. *That* was very close to religion at Joseph Magnin.

As a family we traveled very little if it had nothing to do with work. I would take Ann and the children for a weekend in Yosemite or Tahoe, short trips, so we didn't have to be away from the business for great lengths of time. I brought Donald East with me on a business trip in 1939 and took him to the World's Fair, and the next year, since the Fair was still running, I took Ellen on the same trip. But we stayed fairly close to home because there was a war on. Shortly after I had married, my father bought an estate in Los Altos and that was where we spent most of our weekends.

Because Joe had his other business, Donner Factors (which, by the way, was not related to the store), it enabled him to afford the luxury of a country home. Los Altos was his *one* luxury. Now, Joe was not a particularly dapper man. I think he may have had one or two suits. He didn't gamble and he had no real indulgences except for his box at the opera and Los Altos. The "country place," as we called it, was a masterpiece. I think that in his secret soul, Joe was an English gardener. He had never quite lost his English accent or his love of order. Los Altos reflected all of that.

The estate sat on seven acres outside of a tiny town just inland and south of Palo Alto. Half of those acres were formal

71

gardens. Leading up to the house, there was a half-mile long drive lined with hedges which were constantly being trimmed by a Japanese gardener. Behind the hedges were leafy maple trees festooned with garlands of fragrant climbing roses that were trained to grow around and through the trees. Close to the house, which was a simple, brown-shingle farmhouse, were flower beds, fish ponds and fountains interspersed with Italianate silver balls on stands. The beds were well-kept and loaded with begonias, pansies and peonies. Behind the house was a wonderful lawn surrounded by walnut and citrus trees. The children loved to take a stick and knock the nuts to the ground. We played a polite game of croquet on the lawn, but anything else was verboten. Joe was unusually proud of his gardens and was very strict about anything which could tear them up—like children and animals. The children he tolerated, because they were his grandchildren, but there were no dogs, cats or ponies allowed. Our friend, Jean Blum, had a house in Los Altos adjacent to Joe's. Jean had five children, most of whom were older than mine, except for Bob, who was Donald's age. But the Blums had a swimming pool and tennis courts. Often the children would walk the two or three miles between the two homes to play with what Ellen called the "real people." The children simply weren't given the run of Joe's country place. Instead they were usually skewered with looks that could kill if they so much as ruffled the gravel on the driveway or knocked off the head of a peony with a mis-thrown tennis ball. Joe even had hard and fast rules about picking the flowers, to Ann's constant distress. It was a treat for her to drive down to sunny Los Altos, which was quite a contrast to the fog and damp of Sea Cliff. She'd seen all of Joe's colorful flowers and asked him if she could pick some to take home. His answer was always, "Nope."

Sundays were company days at Los Altos where we would be visited by friends and family. Joe had set up a barbecue area way down the lawn (and away from his precious gardens) in back of the house where I would do the honors as the weekly barbecue chef. It was just hamburgers and hot dogs, nothing fancy, but I got quite adept at turning out charcoal-broiled treats. Anyone who dropped in on Sunday stayed. The men played pinochle and the women sat around and talked. It was all very informal. Most of the Magnin family had reconciled with Joseph, and Sam would bring his family down to visit, and occasionally, Mary Ann would drive down from the city in her chauffeured limousine. Nearly everyone pitched in and helped. When it came to entertaining, Joe didn't know the meaning of the word formality. The children found enterprising things to do. They would stage fairs and theatrical events (all of this at ages five and six). They would do their entertainments and then pass around a can for pennies in exchange for a trinket or a balloon. When Joe entertained his nonfamily friends, they fell into two categories—generally Irish politicos or Jewish merchants.

Joe and Charlotte worked during the week—Lottie at JM and Joe with Donner. They had a Filipino cook-housekeeper named Emilio Evangelista working for them for many years. Since they spent long hours at their individual jobs in the city, the house in Los Altos got very little use during the week. Joe and Lottie never entertained at night because they got home so late. Emilio cooked their dinner and cleaned the house. But on the weekends he had Saturdays off, and when my father would have thirty or forty people over for Sunday dinner, Lottie and I would be pressed into service to help Emilio. My mother worked like a Trojan during those at-homes. Along with the usual barbecue, she'd serve several different kinds of salad, cold cuts, drinks and dessert. The main house was situated on the top of a big hill which dropped off slowly in every direction. On the westerly side at the base of the hill, probably 150 yards from the main house, was the barbecue area, a small bungalow called the eating house which had a big, long table down the middle and built-in benches lining the walls. It was completely screened in with a window at one end through which food could be passed. Lottie was the chief tray lugger. The trip down the hill wasn't too bad, but the trek back up must have been hard on her. She would carry down trays of corn-on-the-cob, a huge pot of baked beans, hamburger meat and buns, condiments and silverware. She never complained. But she worked six days a week and on the seventh . . . she carried trays.

Joe had a Japanese gardener to take care of the place. Of course, after Pearl Harbor, he left. It turned out that he was an officer in the Japanese navy. On his days off he would go out into the countryside just like a tourist with his cameras strapped around his neck. The Japanese who didn't return to Japan to fight were interned in this country for the balance of the war—a very shoddy time in our country's history. Joe soon found himself with no one to help him care for his three or four acres of formal gardens. In the interim my mother had fallen ill with throat cancer, a long and painful death, and when she finally succumbed in 1942, it was the straw that broke the camel's back. Without telling anybody, Joe sold off his Los Altos place for about $20,000.

When Donald was born, Mary Ann gave him a complete layette from I. Magnin and a magnificent crib. He was the first Magnin great-grandchild and she was justly proud. Ellen was born seventeen months later in April, 1928. The two of them were as close as a brother and sister could be, but they were completely different from one another. I think that Don was very much Ann's child. He had a sweet disposition and a placid nature. Donald was also a worrier, even at the tender age of five. One evening, in the midst of the Depression, I came home very discouraged. We always discussed the day's business at the dinner table and caught up with each other. That night I told Ann that I didn't know how I was going to meet Friday's payroll. In those days the employees got paid every week. Donald looked up at me and volunteered the contents of his piggybank. Donald was the kind of boy who loved "dobostorte" and Bobby Grayson, but he also loved intellectual pursuits. He is probably the most booksmart of my children. If he wanted to sit down and study, he could pick up in fifteen minutes what it would take me five hours to learn. In financial matters he was very much like Joseph. Ellen says that Don, to this day, could probably tell you the price of a case of Tab or a can of tunafish at Safeway.

Like Joseph, Donald could be very stubborn and very conservative about money. Once he had his mind made up about something, it was very hard to change it. When my father left the leadership of Joseph Magnin in my hands, he set up half of his estate in trusts for each of my children and made me executor of those trusts. One day, not many years ago, Donald came to me and said he wanted to buy tax-free bonds with some of his trust funds. I told him I didn't think it was such a good idea. He got his trust loaded with tax-free bonds at a ridiculously low interest rate. He could have been earning triple. I tried to talk him out of it, but I couldn't. I said to him, "It's your money . . . I don't *have* to approve it because I'm trustee, but I'm gonna do it because if I don't and those bonds turn out to be good, you'll never forgive me."

Because our entire family life revolved around Joseph Magnin, Ann and I got the children involved very early not only sorting bills for Joe's trips to the mail boxes down the Peninsula, but also on ground level—which was where both Joe and I started. Donald was about twelve when he started working in the store regularly. His job was to iron tissue paper. In those days all garments coming in from the East came by rail freight packed in corrugated boxes. (Today garments are shipped on hangers in huge trucks.) All pieces were tissued to minimize wrinkling. Tissue was a very important commodity because when you delivered a package to your customer by United Parcel, you re-tissued the garment and put it back into the corrugated box for shipping. In order to be profitable, we had to be economical, so Donald stood in the basement of Joseph Magnin on Saturdays and ironed the week's receipts of tissue so it would be smooth and we could re-use it.

Ellen seemed to be born with Ann's good fashion sense and my knack for organization. She also started in the business very young. Where Don would iron tissue paper, Ellen would help him build boxes and re-tissue them. The two of them did almost everything menial there was to do around JM—they marked jewelry, they tagged clothes, they posted bills. Ellen remembers even running the switchboard when she was eight or nine. The most fun job was messenger. My father trusted only one person with cash, so he didn't have cashiers all over the store. When a person made a sale, he or she would signal for a messenger and Donald or Ellen would run to get the sales checks and take the money to the central cashier, get the change and bring it back. The two of them did literally everything, including the sweeping up—which Donald did—exactly the way I started. But to them, they were big shots.

Work, my daughter Ellen has said, was fun. While my children may not have had what was considered a normal upbringing with swimming lessons, afterschool tennis games and hanging out with their friends down at the corner drugstore, their sport and hobby was working. Joseph Magnin wasn't a job. It was a way of life. At times the family's single-minded dedication got to Donald, especially when he thought that I was making him miss some of his high school activities. I did insist that, when he was given a choice of physical education or officer's training in his last year of high school, he take R.O.T.C. It was not the kind of extracurricular Donald would have preferred, I'm sure, but I thought it would be excellent training for him. He was very small in stature and the last thing he needed was to be playing football and be hit by a high school Bobby Grayson. Because he was small, he lined up in front of the rest of the boys and was given the duty to carry the company colors. The uniforms were typical military olive drab. The one thing Donald hated was coming downtown after school to work on Wednesday because it was the day he had to wear his uniform to school. It was war time and his uniform was exactly like the regular army's except for the bright blue lapels. Donald felt self-conscious. It was a real "thing" to him. He dreaded riding public transportation downtown in that uniform—he had no room at school to store his "civvies" and couldn't change. Ann would keep his street clothes down at the store, and the minute Don would arrive, he'd rush to a fitting room and get out of that hated uniform.

Another thing both Donald and Ellen would have preferred was to have gone to high school football games. Because we all worked in the store, both Ellen and Don missed a lot of their high school activities, football included. Donald worked two nights a week, Monday and Thursday. The games were on Saturdays and I'm sure the children felt I'd disapprove if they went to them. I worked on Saturday and I expected them to work. It was many, many years before Ellen and Donald even went to a Saturday game and it was only when they were in college that they went to the Stanford-Cal "Big Game," probably the only one they'd ever see in a single season. But they figured that they'd finally earned their stripes and they could take off one Saturday a year to go.

When Don was a teenager, I asked him to work full-time after school. At the time I had a general handyman named Irving Konigsberg. The store was still only two floors. There were, perhaps, thirty employees from basement to roof. Irving had been with us for twenty years. He locked up at night, took packages and mail to the Post Office and generally kept everything shipshape when the store was closed and everyone had gone home. Before he could mail the bills,

Irving had to "stuff" the ledgers in the Credit Department. Every customer had a ledger sheet and every month you had to put a bill in front of that page in the ledger because the bookkeeper would come along and type the current month's activity on the bill. Because of the carbon insert, he would also be typing a permanent credit history onto the ledger page. Afterwards, that bill was mailed to the customer. The bills were addressed on an Addressograph, with tiny plates made for each customer. The machine made a terrible *konk, konk* sound as you'd stamp your foot on a treadle to change the plate. The bills would come flying out of the Addressograph. So here were a whole stack of customers' statements, addressed and ready to stuff into the ledgers to be finished by the bookkeeper. Irving's job was to do that. At the start of the war, the only person we could get to operate the bookkeeping machine was a crippled gentleman who was 4-F because of his injury. He was the full-time bookkeeper at the Palace Hotel and moonlighted at Joseph Magnin's at night from six until nine. Don worked from three until nine. From three until six he helped Irving stuff the ledgers, then he'd do the bill-mailing procedure on the Addressograph. At six o'clock he'd go down and lock the front door and from six until nine he'd help the bookkeeper. The ledgers were looseleaf, bound in huge metal books about five inches thick. They were heavy but not so heavy that you couldn't lift them. They were stored on a truck which contained maybe thirty ledger books. The truck was wheeled into a walk-in safe every night for fire protection. Our part-time bookkeeper had a bad congenital leg condition and he couldn't handle the truck, so Don had to stay there every night just to put the truck away. Then he got on the Muni and rode all the way out to Sea Cliff and home.

Irving always carried all the keys to the store on a huge key ring—keys to the front door, keys to the bathroom, keys to the supply cupboard—keys to everything. One day he walked into my office, dropped the heavy ring of keys on my desk with a metallic clattering sound and said, "Mr. Magnin, I quit." He was going to open his own little store in Napa. At the time the phone numbers of the schools were not published in the telephone book, but I knew a lot of people around town and got hold of someone at the Board of Education and got the number of Lowell High School where Donald was in class. I called the principal's office, the only phone in the school, and they went to get Donald for me. I told him that I wanted to see him after school. He came downtown and walked into my office. I picked up the keys from the desk and said, "Irving quit . . . you're it." Again, I'm sure that Don wasn't terribly happy about it, but I wanted him to have as much training and responsibility as I could give him.

When I had turned forty and Ann was thirty-eight, we had our third and last child. We had been trying to have another baby for years, but Ann miscarried. When our son Jerry was born on July 30, 1938, Ellen was already ten years old. Jerry was like a second family—almost like starting over again. Our birth announcement showed a picture of a baby and the Tower of the Sun, the central building erected on Treasure Island for the 1939 San Francisco Exposition. Our slogan for Jerry's birth was, "Here in time for '39." Jerry, as the youngest, was my special baby, probably because he was ten years younger than his sister. And because he was so much younger, I could be more affectionate with him. I nicknamed him Boaky. He followed me around like a little puppy tail; I would have to say that he was a pretty spoiled kid. His brother and sister had been brought up by nurses, but usually their nurses would be strict with them and make them sit at the table until they finished their meal. If they didn't, the same food would be waiting for them at lunch, then dinner until they ate it. Jerry wasn't treated like that. He had a nurse named Vicki who used to walk him to Miss Burke's School on 32nd Avenue. One day he didn't want to go to school and he pushed her down the stairs. She broke her leg and quit.

Jerry terrorized quite a few nurses, but he adored his great-grandmother Davis, Rachael, my mother's mother, who was living with us for a while. She would take Jerry downtown on the old trolley cars with the wicker seats that used to run from the Ferry Building clear around the Embarcadero to the Marina. Jerry would look forward to those outings with great anticipation. Ann was a fairly strict mother, but her discipline was always accomplished with loving care. She taught all the children about the quality of time a parent spends with his or her child and not the quantity, because, of necessity, she was working and couldn't be home to kiss bruised knees or drive to Cub Scouts or make cookies like some of the other mothers did. We would take Jerry to work with us when we could. I shooed him out of my office when I had work to do, so Jerry would find his mother's department which was on the second floor. Like Donald before him, he would get very tired and find a place to fall asleep. He would take a couple of chairs and line them up under the women's coats, letting the coat hems cover him and keep him warm like a blanket. Jerry drew pictures for everyone's office— some of my staff kept those pictures for years. And it was Jerry, a six-year-old with the heart of a born entrepreneur, who charged admission to the store one Saturday afternoon.

Jerry was an active, enterprising child who was always getting himself into jams. The house on Sea View Terrace had a long, sloping driveway and once, when I told Jerry that we couldn't go snow skiing like some of his friends, he got angry and improvised. He poured Ivory Flakes on the driveway to make his own private ski run. I was perturbed, to say the least, and thought he should have to pay to have the mess cleaned up. So he thought up a novel, money-making scheme. He put a rope across the front door of the store on O'Farrell Street and charged our customers a penny entrance fee. The child might have had the devil in him, but darned if he didn't make money doing it.

As he grew older, Jerry became more and more like me to the extent that we walk and talk alike and he seems to adore women as much as I do—except that he always married his special girlfriends and I didn't. When I was going to New York on a regular basis, I would get a shave every morning at 1400 Broadway from an Italian barber named Leo. One day when Jerry was first coming into the business, I suggested that he might want to give himself a treat and have Leo shave him. The next time I came back to New York and settled down in Leo's chair, he said to me, "Somebody came to see me that looksa lot like you. In fact, he talksa lot like you." It's not unusual for someone to say that Jerry is the spitting image of me. He has the same kind of ability to attract people. The same Magnin magnetism.

Home life when you are a retailer is never the way you would prefer. Retailing is a demanding business—you open the doors in the morning and close at night and then you sit down and work on the books. Ann was a dedicated retailer, the driving force behind a lot of the good things that were beginning to happen to Joseph Magnin. She was also an exceptionally fine mother, able to shift gears after a long, hard day. She was very harried, trying to fit it all in—cleaning out Ellen's closet, getting to a teacher's conference or some other activity that involved the children. I never learned to do a thing—can't even boil water—but I learned to entertain my kids which I did night after night with fanciful tales sprung from imagination about sheriffs, Black Bart, policemen, firemen and some of the politicos I knew. Ellen would squeal with delight, "Tell the sheriff story, Daddy . . . tell the policemen."

Looking back, I think my children must have had a very unusual time growing up in a family where both parents and both grandparents were involved in time-consuming businesses. It even affected the kids' birthdays. I don't know if we ever had a pin-the-tail-on-the-donkey kind of party, but Ann did arrange for the children and their friends to have lunch out at a restaurant called Townsends and then go to a movie. For Ellen's eighteenth birthday, Ann cooked up a marvelous surprise. Ellen was away at Stanford, a lonely freshman, who felt that nobody loved her. Everyone else in her dorm had gotten a cake for her birthday—everyone, that is, except Ellen. Very blue, she drove up to the city to have lunch with her mother and there was every friend she'd ever had, assembled to help her celebrate.

Ellen grew into a very strong-willed, capable woman; she was equally as self-directed when she was a teenager. Ellen took pictures of the family down to Stanford with her and put them up in her room. All she could see were our noses, which, especially on Jerry and me, are quite prominent. She said it gave her quite a complex, but she decided to do something about it on her own. Ellen was working both at Joseph Magnin and part-time at Roos/Atkins at Stanford and she saved every cent she made. She took herself to a plastic surgeon at the Stanford Medical Center to see about having her nose bobbed. The doctor called Ann and me and told us, "Your daughter has checked into the hospital here to have her nose fixed and there isn't really anything we can do for her. Her nose is fat and it's going to stay fat and that's what's bothering her." And Ann was very wise. She said to the doctor, "Go ahead. Let her pay for it and let her do it. It's cheaper in the long run than a psychiatrist."

Ann was marvelous about teaching Ellen how to be a good merchandiser. If Jerry followed me around like a little tail, Ellen stuck very close to her mother. When Ellen first started school, Ann gave her money to buy school supplies, about a dollar or two, but wouldn't go shopping with the child. She told Ellen that she wanted to see what she could get for the money. Later on Ann would send Ellen into the fashion markets in the East to select items for the store, but wouldn't have her write orders. Ann would go herself the next day to approve what Ellen had selected and tell her why something was good or something wouldn't work. It was on-the-job training.

For the most part Ann was a much calmer parent than I was. I had a terrible temper. I wanted things done immediately, if not sooner, and would flare up very easily at the slightest infraction. Those close to me like Ann and some of my employees learned to defuse the situation quickly. Ann would simply turn her back and walk away, taking all the wind out of my sails. I also lost my temper at Ellen—we would have some very loud disagreements. But she'd get back at me by walking into V. C. Morris, a specialty gift shop in exclusive Maiden Lane, and charging the most expensive thing in the store, which probably amounted to $90 or $100. I think that in the past few years, I've mellowed considerably. People new to San Francisco don't know the paper tyrant I used to be.

CHAPTER SIX 〰

Single Parent,
Eligible Bachelor

ANN HAD ONE TERRIBLE HABIT. She smoked incessantly. Lucky Strikes . . . probably three packs a day. I think it killed her. I tried to talk her out of it, but as long as I or anyone else remembers, she was never without a cigarette in her hands. It was worse than Joe and his smelly cigars. At least he lived into his eighties.

I had been on the Heart Association board, and in those days they had just determined that cigarette smoking was one of the major causes of heart problems—they weren't blaming fat in the diet so much as they were insisting that cigarette smoking was the great culprit. I would come home from those meetings and tell Ann that she was killing herself and she'd just pooh-pooh the whole idea by saying, "How can you listen to those phonies talk?" I'd try to convince her that the doctors had no ax to grind, that they were dedicated people who did research in an attempt to save lives, including hers, if she'd only listen. But she wouldn't quit. She suffered terrible circulatory problems—her sister Adele always remembered Ann's fingernails having a bluish cast—she didn't sleep well at night and she was fatigued constantly. I attributed all of it to her smoking.

I kept after her to see a doctor, our family physician, Dr. Harry Pruett. He listened to her chest and took X rays and told her that if she didn't quit smoking, she wouldn't last five years. Her lungs were deteriorating and while he didn't think she would get cancer or emphysema, he expected that her heart would just give out on her. The doctor suggested a change in diet, more exercise, a change in climate, and of course, a radical change in her smoking habit. He told her point-blank to quit. None of the other things he suggested could do her much good, he added, unless she stopped. The change in climate was accomplished with a move. Those foggy, clammy San Francisco days out in Sea Cliff weren't doing her any good. We bought a beautiful Spanish-style home in Hillsborough, a sunny suburb of San Francisco, at 1006 Bromfield Road. It was a gracious, wonderful house, but Ann lived only a year after we moved and never really got to enjoy it.

Anna died on July 12, 1948. I wasn't even in San Francisco. I was one of the California delegates to the Democratic National Convention in Philadelphia the year Truman was nominated. I was sitting in the convention hall in Philadelphia listening to the nominating speeches. It was hot as blazes with no air-conditioning and I was sitting there in my shirt sleeves; I'd left my jacket at the hotel. All of a sudden a policeman came over to our delegation and asked, "Who's Mr. Magnin?" I put my right hand up and said, "What I'd do?" He said, "The captain would like to see you—some problem at home." I said to a friend of mine, Harold Berliner, who was then an officer with the Internal Revenue Service, "Listen, if I don't come back in a few minutes, you come and bail me out. I don't know what they want me for." I was told that I had an important phone call and when I got on the phone, one of our employees, a woman named Mae Nichols, was on the line. She was very calm and she told me,

"Ann's been sick; you'd better come home." When I heard that, I knew there was something terribly wrong and said, "Hey, Nichols, don't give me that. I think she's passed away." My son Jerry got on the phone crying and told me Ann had died. I turned to the police captain and asked him what was the first plane I could get home to San Francisco. He phoned the airlines.

In those days it wasn't easy to get to California, and nonstops were unheard of. The police captain helped me secure a reservation. But the only plane I could get stopped first in Dallas and then flew on to San Francisco. I had only thirty-five minutes to get to the airport to make the plane, which posed quite a time and logistics problem. Again the captain helped me out. He said, "I'll tell you what I'll do. I know what's happened to you; they told me before I called you and I want to help. You won't have time to go back to the hotel to get your things. You wanna go in your shirt sleeves?" He then told me that there wasn't a police car or a taxi immediately available but that there was a motorcycle with a sidecar and he offered to put me in it to send me to the airport. He also called the airline and told them that I might be five or ten minutes late and he asked them to hold the plane. He told me that he had the authority to do that. They held the plane twenty minutes for me and I drove up in a motorcycle sidecar, my hair all ruffled from the wind, in my shirt sleeves. Under any other circumstances, it probably would have been an exciting experience, but I was too upset to enjoy it.

When I got home, I found out exactly what had happened. When Ann and I moved into the Hillsborough house, she was having a hard time sleeping at night and her restlessness kept me up, so sometimes, she would sleep in Ellen's room where there were twin beds. On this particular night she had been to a party and had returned and was sleeping with Ellen, which she did when I was away. She awakened sometime after midnight and said she didn't feel well. We had been in Hillsborough less than a year and our family doctor lived many miles away in San Francisco. We had not thought about an emergency and had no physician in the area. When Ann awoke ill, my son Donald, who was going to Stanford summer school, living at home and commuting, called the nearest hospital, which was in San Mateo, and they sent out a young doctor, barely out of his residency. He may have been so hungry for patients that he didn't mind making a housecall in the middle of the night. Donald speculates that perhaps if they'd done things differently, the outcome might have been different, but I don't think so. Probably, by that time, the damage was past repairing. Anyhow, the doctor put a nitroglycerin pill under Ann's tongue, which is one of the basic treatments for coronary, but he told her that he thought she just had a touch of indigestion. The symptoms were the same. The doctor suggested that she have a glass of milk and go back to bed.

Mae Nichols was one of our top buyers who had been with the store a long time. She lived somewhat near us, probably five or ten minutes away, and she would pick Ann up every morning to drive her into the city to work—I was always out of the house much earlier. Ellen was up and about that morning preparing to drive in with Ann and Mae, and Donald was up although he'd decided to cut his eight o'clock class. Mae was probably having a cup of coffee in the kitchen waiting for Ann and noticed that my wife was very late. Mae went upstairs to check on Ann and I think Ann must have stood up and said, "I don't feel well" and was dead before she hit the floor. Ann was forty-six years old. Donald and Ellen were out of their teens and were at Stanford, but it wasn't for them that I was concerned. My young son Jerry was only nine years old.

Ann's death came as a great shock to everyone who knew her, especially those who had worked with her so closely. When she died, Joseph took over and provided the strength we all needed. He called Hilda Gilgannon, who had worked so closely with both Lottie and Ann, to help keep things in order. He was so saddened by Ann's passing that he remarked to Hilda, "I wish it had been me. I've lived such a long time and she had so much life ahead of her." The night before she died, Ann had worn one of her sister Adele's dresses to a professional women's meeting. We requested that she be buried in it. The store, for which Ann had given so much, was in a state of mourning. We closed in memory of Ann the day she was buried. There were memorial wreaths and bouquets of long-stemmed roses with placards all over the store noting her passing. Messages came from all over the United States from friends and business associates who had considered Ann such a joy in their life. Adele, with whom she'd been so near and dear, was absolutely devastated by her death. She was in shock and once remarked that it took her two years to get over it. Ann's thoughtfulness while living caused Adele an additional sadness, however, the Christmas after she died. Often, when Ann was on a buying trip to Chicago, she would purchase some personal things at a linen store on Michigan Avenue, one that specialized in luxurious items. On her last trip before she died, Ann had ordered a beautiful set of monogrammed table linens for Adele. During the following Christmas a package came with the linens and an enclosed card in Ann's handwriting.

At the age of forty-eight, I found myself a widower and a single father to a child who required as much love and attention as I could give him. I had to love Jerry for two. I began spending as much time with him as I could, playing baseball in the backyard and keeping him company. I've never been a terrific athlete. I love to walk and have for years walked to work from wherever I was living—except, of course, Hillsborough which would have been a marathon trek every morning. I did, however, try to teach Jerry to play ball. I could hit a baseball a country mile and was continually batting it over the fence. Jerry would cry and beg me not to hit it so hard, but the next time, bang, it would go over the fence. We often spent quiet times in the yard relaxing in the sun. Joe was living with us in Hillsborough. There wasn't a minute that opera wasn't playing in the house. Joe had an enormous Seeberg record player and each morning he'd put on another opera album. I continued the practice even after Joe passed away. Jerry grew up listening to Verdi, Puccini, Bizet and Rossini instead of Fats Domino and Bo Diddley.

As soon as it was proper, I took Jerry away on a holiday. United Airlines had instituted service to the Hawaiian Islands the year before on May 29, 1947. I had been one of the only paying passengers on board a plane full of press, airline executives and Chamber of Commerce officials. Jerry and I flew to Hawaii the summer after Ann's death to enjoy a father-son vacation. It was a bittersweet time for both of us because we missed Ann very much. There were times when Jerry would be playing out in the backyard by himself and he'd just be sitting there, tears running down his little face, not really comprehending that she wasn't coming back.

Throughout Ellen's teen years she had been very close to her mother, learning not only about the workings of the store and about fashion and buying, but also the art of being a gracious hostess. After Ann's passing, Ellen at age twenty became my official hostess. One of her first duties was to organize a party for the opening of our second Palo Alto store. It had been designed by Victor Gruen and Associates and was quite innovative, with a circular staircase right in the middle of the first floor. It was an award-winning design and it attracted a lot of attention from other retailers, including officials of Detroit's J. L. Hudson Company, who were coming for the opening to check it out. Hudson's was in the process of planning its huge Northland Shopping Center in suburban Detroit, though it was a big secret in the retailing community that the store was even on the boards. I invited the Hudson people to my home and Ellen had to prepare for it. She did, and as always, it was a bang-up job.

For the first few weeks after Ann's death, I could hardly function for my grief. At one time I was even going to sell the business to I. Magnin—just a passing thought, but one that upset Ellen very much. She sat me down and said, "Dad, you're not gonna do that to my brothers and me. I'm leaving school." And that was that. Ellen, in fact, stepped right into her mother's shoes with very little effort. She left Stanford at age twenty to take over where her mother had left off. Seventh Avenue had a great regard for Ann and perhaps, because of it, the resources accepted Ellen readily. It was an exceptional period, those few years after the war, and the women's ready-to-wear business was exploding. Ellen earned her credentials in a hurry and was soon spending millions of dollars, buying for Joseph Magnin. She operated differently than Ann, developing her own style. She also had the security of not being fired. I was somewhat tough with her, but it never discouraged her. I taught Ellen and my sons that they shouldn't be afraid to make mistakes—that they should make them big, learn from them, and then not make the same mistake again. Ellen had the energy of three or four people and when she finally did step out of active participation when she married two years later, I think that five people had to fill her slot. Ellen had dated some very nice fellows, but her first love had always been merchandising and Joseph Magnin. Then she met a soft-spoken, tall, athletic young man with an agricultural background named Walter Newman.

About twenty-six miles west of Modesto, California, is a small (population 3,000) town named Newman at the Southern Pacific railhead. Walter's grandfather Simon Newman founded it in about 1880. Simon had come to California from Germany in the 1870s as a young boy. One of his kin was a man named Saul Langeheim, who had a dry goods store in Markleeville in the mountains of the Mother Lode. When the gold and silver ran out, the two young Jewish men moved to the San Joaquin Valley to start a business and to acquire land—something the Jews had not been able to do in Europe. At a place called Hills Ferry on the banks of a river, they built a warehouse and store. They were the town grain brokers in the heart of the fertile cornucopia that was the Central Valley. They acquired huge tracts of farm land as a corporation and when the railroad came through, Simon was asked to move his business from the river at Hills Ferry to the railhead. Simon named the new location after himself and founded the town of Newman.

In those days before the turn of the century, Newman was a thriving town, a major factor in the agricultural life of California. One of old Simon's rivals was a man named Henry Miller, considered the "cattle king" of the San Joaquin. He had come to California as a butcher boy under a forged passport—his name was really Kaiser. He saw the possibilities for raising beef in the Valley. At the height of his success it was reputed that a person could ride from Canada to Mexico without leaving Miller's land. Newman and Miller were arch-rivals, competitors. When Simon established the town of Newman, Miller built his own town four miles away and named it Gustine after his daughter. The men were lifelong enemies, but when old Simon was dying of cancer, Henry Miller came to see him and shook hands, forgiving old enmities.

Simon had a son named S. Walter who was president of a very fine old homewares and hardware shop, Charles Brown and Sons. His son, Walter, was born and raised in San Francisco. Young Walter always loved his family's ranching business and would go to the Valley in the summer and work on the farms. The family corporation wanted him to get an agricultural science education, so he attended Berkeley for two years and then went to the University of California at Davis and studied for a degree in animal husbandry. Walter was an affable, active young man who was vice-president of the Davis student body, editor of the school paper and C.O. of his R.O.T.C. unit. When he graduated, it was during the war and as a young lieutenant, he fought as an infantry officer and was wounded in the invasion of Normandy. He finished his service as an instructor in the general staff school at Fort Leavenworth, Kansas, and decided then that he did not want to make the army his career.

When Walt got out of the service, he lived in San Francisco and took a job with the Harry Camp Company, which operated millinery concessions in department stores. But the family wanted him in the business and he settled in his namesake town to assist in the management of the Simon Newman Corporation, which also had the biggest department store between Stockton and Los Angeles. Walter worked for a time in that business. He was also very active in the Republican Central Committee and at one time was asked to run for Congress, which he declined to do. He was making quite a life for himself as a desirable, eligible bachelor, but the pickings were fairly lean for a young man of property in Newman and Walter would come to San Francisco for his social life. One evening he was invited to a cocktail party. A friend had told him, "I'm going to introduce you to the girl you're going to marry." That girl was my daughter, Ellen.

Walter says that for him, meeting Ellen was love at first sight. Even with their very different backgrounds, they became, in the words of the columns, "an item." Ellen was traveling back and forth to New York constantly and their courtship was filled with questions as to what the future held for this agricultural tyro and my fashion-conscious, business-woman daughter. Ellen and Walt went together for two years. He would come to San Francisco and date Ellen on the weekends. They spent hours discussing whether she could give it all up to live in Newman. That it was a somewhat different environment than she was used to is gross under-statement. I guess they decided, the hell with it, and married. Shortly after the wedding Joe and I discussed taking Walter into the business. We needed someone with management training and a real estate background; it seemed custom-tailored for Walter's abilities. Ellen was extremely supportive of any decision Walt would have made, even if he had opted for Newman, California. But they decided to live in San Francisco for a while and Walter came into the business and was put in charge of store operations—all store activities but merchandising. From the start, also, Walter handled the leases for our fast-expanding branch-store operation.

Ellen had attracted as her future husband a member of an "Our Crowd" Jewish family—pioneering California Jewish aristocracy. On their first date Walt came and picked her up with his cousin and it was the cousin who asked her out for himself for the second date. I think that Ellen must have seemed as exotic to Walter as he seemed to her. Their wedding was a sumptuous, lavish, grand, large and expensive do. It was also a lot of fun. We thought it was a glittering success in spite of the fact that four of our lady guests showed up wearing identical gowns that had been purchased, coincidentally, at Joseph Magnin. The night before the wedding a thief broke into our City Assessor Russ Wolden's car and got away with a huge gift box, wrapped in Joseph Magnin's fanciest paper. It was a regulation straitjacket covered in sequins and satin bows—a gag gift for me for a Father of the Bride party my friends were throwing me the night before the ceremony. On the evening of October 15, 1950, my little girl was married to Walter Newman. My cousin Rabbi Edgar Magnin officiated at the Fairmont Hotel. Ellen wore an original Adele Simpson creation—a lovely shirtwaist sheath design with a low-cut bodice and huge collar and a removable overskirt. She had nine attendants who also wore Simpson gowns in periwinkle blue organza. It was a magnificent sight.

For my one and only daughter, nothing but a complete wingding would do. It was a very expensive wingding, a point not missed by anyone, including a few of my enterprising employees who cooked up a "balance sheet" of my remaining assets, dated October 16, 1950.

ASSETS

CURRENT ASSETS:

Cash on hand or in bank	$ .17
Postage stamps:	
New stamps	.11
Cancelled stamps	.21
1 suit (torn and threadbare)	1.30
1 pair shoes (hole in right sole)	.44
6 pair socks (darned)	.72
Underwear, fountain pen, Dick Tracy badge, and other miscellaneous assets	4.40
1 carton empty Coke bottles—salvage value	.12
1 bundle last year's newspapers	.10
TOTAL CURRENT ASSETS	$7.57

FIXED ASSETS:

4,498 empty champagne bottles (no corks)	—0—
1 living room rug (with 137 cigarette burns resulting from the reception)	—0—
1 new Cadillac	$5,000
(less bank lien on Cadillac, $5,000)	—0—
1 bank book (Bank of America)	no balance
172 dozen cut flowers, two days old left over from wedding	—0—
1,258,123 shares Joseph Magnin common stock—no par value and no value	—0—
1 membership in the Democratic Party— dues not paid	—0—
TOTAL FIXED ASSETS	—0—

NOTE: All inventories are valued at cost or market, whichever is higher.

No direct confirmation was made of amount of blood still remaining on hand since amount is apparently negligible.

LIABILITIES

CURRENT LIABILITIES:

Due to Benjamin H. Swig for use of the Venetian Room Powder Room for wedding—regular price, $6,125.49, but by special arrangement with Mr. Swig, special price to Mr. Cyril Magnin	$ 10,195.50
Podesta and Baldocchi (florists)	4,798.62
Max Sobel Liquors (one year's supply, French champagne)	11,641.30
Wayne Peters (two dozen candid shots of wedding)	7,043.24
Freddy Martin, Ernie Heckscher, Guy Lombardo, Xavier Cugat	25,500.98
Loan—Donner Factors	10,000.00
Interest on above loan (ten easy installments)	13,543.67
Selix Clothiers (rental on cutaway), deposit refunded upon return of garment	7.50
Pacific Telephone & Telegraph—long distance division to Adele Simpson, et. al.	9,540.56

LONG TERM LIABILITIES:

1,006 assorted friends (former) not invited to wedding and/or not seated close enough to the bride's table—the amount of business lost per year	250,000.00
102 new relatives—at average Christmas gift of $10.00 per year—Newmans, Lilenthals, Pateks, etc.	1,020.00
Doctor bills for future ulcers (estimated)	55,100.00
NET CAPITAL AND SURPLUS (OR DEFICIT)	$257,580.67

P.S.: HELP!!!

When Ellen married Walter, she began to soft-pedal her activities with Joseph Magnin. She was still my official hostess, but her interests became more in keeping with her newly married status. She, like Ann before her, couldn't cook—couldn't even boil water. She had no idea what to do with a simple lamb chop, which, the first time she attempted to cook one, she boiled. Ellen became active in her local garden club; she learned flower arranging and she started the gift shop at Mt. Zion Hospital. I think she proved that she could be as domestic as any young woman who had been brought up with dolls and coloring books instead of cash registers, sales slips and inventory ledgers. But Ellen was never far away from JM. Within the tradition that Lottie had started and Ann continued, Ellen's inventiveness and taste could still be felt in the store even though she was no longer there very much. As dynamic and opinionated as Ellen could be, I must say, to her grace and credit, she never once flaunted her strengths in public. I'm sure, as with most young couples, she and Walter disagreed, but they never displayed any disharmony in public. Ellen and Walter had been married nearly two years when they presented me with my first grandchild, Walter Newman, Jr., in April of 1952.

Just as my new son-in-law had been considered quite a catch when he was still among the ranks of the unmarried, I found that at age fifty I had become an eligible bachelor. I was thrust back on the market, so to speak. I had discovered at a very early age that I had the power to attract women. During my marriage—and while there was a powerful emotional bond between Ann and me, we also had a working partnership—I wandered. My infidelities were very casual; I would never let anything come between Ann and myself. She understood me. It was as simple as that. She knew that it was an integral part of my personality to have female diversion. My interests have always been piqued by things new and different, including a variety of women. Ann discovered

97

quickly that because of my curiosity and diverse interests, jealousy was perhaps a wasted emotion. I never discussed my private life very much and in recent years made light of my fascination with women by saying that it was just part and parcel of the rag business—to change with the seasons. Ann, however, knew that no one could take her place in my life and in my affection and if people ever said unkind things about my so-called philandering to her face, she was the first person to defend me.

After Ann's death, however, my unconscious ability to attract women seemed to be working overtime. I had more than my share of pretty girls, probably more than I wanted. When I began dating again, I was seeing one woman who informed me that she was expecting and that it was my child. She told me she didn't want the baby, and while two doctors disagreed as to whether she was pregnant or not, I couldn't take the chance and gave her the money to take care of herself. To prevent it from happening again, I had a vasectomy, then a fairly innovative procedure. I figured that I had three wonderful children, I had done my job. Besides, I was always concerned about the women who were attracted to me—whether it was me or my money or the fact that I ran one of the most exciting women's fashion stores in town. By the time I was widowed, I was "comfortable." I remember a Shakespeare quote that I mangle all the time: "When paupers are born, no comets are seen; when princes are born, the sky is ablaze with fire." That's not true of everybody, but my money had become to me an aid, a comfort and an immense stumbling block. I couldn't separate myself from my money, although there were several women interested in me at the time who would have been very glad to do it for me. When another one of my lady friends informed me that she was expecting, I had my attorney send her attorney a copy of the hospital report where I had my surgery. She never bothered me again. I guess you can't argue with nature.

In spite of all the lovely women available to me, I missed the companionship of a wife. I had met a small, pert woman with a sculptured, sharp-featured face, hazel eyes and dark hair named Lillian Ryan Helwig, who was the manager of the San Mateo Store. She had worked for Joseph Magnin since 1944, first as a saleswoman, then as a buyer and then as the manager of the Palo Alto store. Lillian was a native San Franciscan who had been in parochial schools all her life. She had a college degree from Holy Name. She was a bright woman, a good merchandiser and extremely chic. While she had a tall woman's taste, she was a petite five-feet-two and wore Larry Aldrich clothes. She was never without a hat and white gloves which were all the style back in the 1950s. As a fashion person Lillian always insisted that her buyers wear good-looking clothes and hats when they were in New York for market. A great deal of our business still derived from my mother's millinery department, and Lillian, always the good merchandiser, wanted her women to set a good example.

Lillian and I started dating probably a year or so after Ann died. I suppose in the beginning we were madly in love. She had a young son, Gregory, by her first marriage, and when we were married on June 21, 1951, Lilli and Greg moved into the Hillsborough house. Our marriage was more of a working agreement than Ann's and mine had been. Lillian and I had the business in common. She and I worked very hard and I suspect that we would have had more of a chance to stay married had we spent more of our private time for ourselves. She was as dedicated to Joseph Magnin in her way as I was in mine, but we still had terrible arguments and fights. I was very demanding of all of my intimates—family, friends, lovers and employees, all. Perhaps I was more demanding of Lillian than she could stand. Sometimes I feel I've made few mistakes in my life. One of them that I will admit to was marrying Lillian. We have, however, remained on fairly good terms since our divorce. In fact, Lillian stayed with Joseph

Magnin. She had been an integral part of the business and remained with us until her death in November, 1980.

Meanwhile, Donald had met and fallen in love with a tall, dark-haired beauty from Portland named Elaine Hochfield. They actually met in a nightclub shortly after the end of World War II. It was a place called the Bal Tabarin on Columbus Avenue in North Beach and was owned by a friend of mine. There was live entertainment and one evening Donald took his steady girlfriend to see Sophie Tucker. He announced himself as Cyril Magnin's son to the owner and was ushered to a table for ten. The two of them looked like two lost peas in a great big pod. Donald's date noticed three couples at the entrance to the club and remarked that one of the girls was Elaine Hochfield, who was there with her two cousins and their dates. Donald suggested that they join their table and was introduced to the three girls from Portland who had just moved to San Francisco. The next time Don and Elaine met was at a cocktail party thrown by the three cousins to reciprocate to all those who had been so nice to them when they first moved to the city. None of the girls looked alike and Donald, who had been invited as his girlfriend's date, remarked to Elaine that it was nice of her to invite him. He called her mistakenly by her cousin Geraldine's name and Elaine corrected him. Not an auspicious beginning.

Elaine, meanwhile, had met Ellen and approached her for a job at Joseph Magnin, right before the Christmas holidays. She had gotten her job and was planning to fly to Portland to be with her family when Donald saw her standing in the store and invited her to a Christmas formal. Per usual, Donald says he waited until the last minute and it was all he could do to persuade Elaine to give up a very valuable plane reservation to date him. At first she declined, saying she had to catch a plane, but Donald wouldn't take no for an answer and struck up a deal with her. If he could get her out on another plane in time to spend Christmas at home in Portland, would she consider going to the dance with him? She agreed; however, Don could only get Elaine a train ticket—a fourteen-hour ride to Portland. Still, Elaine agreed to go to the dance with Don. They were out until three in the morning. Don dropped Elaine off and spent the rest of what was left of the night in a hotel room, having promised Elaine that he would see to it that she got to the railway station in time to catch an eight o'clock train. He left a wake-up call for 5:30 A.M., and at the appointed time he was physically awakened by someone shaking him. He thought it was a burglar. In his sleep he mumbled, "The money's on the dresser," but it was just the bellman. The hotel switchboard had caught fire and the bellboys were going around to the rooms and personally awakening guests who had early calls.

When Elaine returned to San Francisco, she went to work at Joseph Magnin and came up through the ranks to be the assistant better-dress buyer. I had hired a marvelously stately, gray-haired fashion person from Neiman-Marcus named Helen Baum to be our better-dress buyer. Unfortunately she had no feeling for the young market, one which we were going after. Her specialty was buying conservative and elegant designers like James Galanos, who certainly did not design for our target customer. I took Elaine aside and told her that Helen didn't really understand the young clothes, and I put Elaine in charge of buying from houses like Ann Fogarty and some of the other up-and-coming youthful designers. Elaine's office was on the third floor and Donald was in the executive offices on the fifth floor. They started seeing each other on a casual basis, perhaps too casual for Elaine, for Don would call her up on a Friday night, when she was dated up perhaps, and ask her out. If she had a date, he told her to break it, which she usually did. She became available, perhaps *too* available. I had a secretary named Barbara Ritter—more than my personal secretary. She was also purchasing agent, personnel director, Mother Confessor.

101

Barbara was a capable woman who could do anything. Once Ann and I were leaving town on a buying trip and we asked Barbara to organize Don's thirteenth birthday party. Barbara had just started working for me and she did it—in style—without blinking an eye. She had become very good friends with Elaine, who would cry on her shoulder about Don's cavalier attitude. Barbara sat Elaine down and told her straightaway that she was much too available to Donald and that if she expected him to marry her, he would never do it if she worked in the store. Elaine simply quit one day and it must have worked, because they became engaged and then married on June 15, 1952.

Just before Ann passed away, my father had written me a very wistful, sad, yet businesslike letter. It was dated June 22, 1948, and it read:

My Dear Son:

When one becomes fourscore then life becomes serious and it is my sincere wish that when I pass away that you do the following:
A. Do not close any store.
B. Bury me the cheapest way possible.
C. Do not have anyone officiate over my body.
D. Request that you and Ann only escort me to my home of rest.
E. No public notices until I have been buried for four days.
F. Then if you wish to announce the same, it would be up to you.

By exercising the above, you have fulfilled my sincere wish.

YOUR DAD JOE

While my father was still sharp mentally, he had been in failing health for several years. His eyesight was very bad and he was troubled by the infirmities of old age. His request that only Anna and I see him to his "home of rest" seemed sad.

Joseph was eighty-one when he wrote the note; he lived five more years, dying on April 29, 1953. The announcement in the newspaper was a scant twelve paragraphs, giving a capsule history of his life and accomplishments. We followed most of Joe's requests, burying him very simply in the place he'd already provided for himself. There was no great memorial service and little pomp and pageantry. We did, however, ignore one of his requests. It was not business as usual at Joseph Magnin. We felt that it was absolutely fitting that the stores which bore his name honor their founder by closing in his memory.

With Joe gone and my two oldest children married, it was Jerry and me, Lillian and Greg, living in Hillsborough. Before I was married, I tried to be both mother and father to Jerry, giving him everything he wanted, within reason. The only thing I couldn't give him that he wanted was more of my time because I was still responsible for Joseph Magnin. While I may have spoiled Jerry terribly, I still tried to teach him some basic values. When he was a teenager, he came to me wanting a car, which I bought him. But when he wanted another car, I told him, "Fine, but you gotta work for it"; so Jerry gave up afterschool sports when he was a high school senior (which was pretty difficult to do because he was proficient and had lettered nine times during his high school years) and worked in the San Mateo store, sweeping floors and handling incoming merchandise in the receiving room. With all three of my children I never played favorites when it came to understanding the value of things—not even with Jerry. He understood at an early age about the nature of business.

Business was always business with our family, and perhaps, as my father was with me, I was a lot harder on my own children than I was on other employees. I demanded from them and from the people I liked the best that they give their best. I never took the time to bawl anyone out if I didn't care for him (or her). With Jerry, as with Ellen and Donald, I would take him to task for a mistake, but I think they knew I really cared for them and loved them all the time I was yelling at them. They knew I didn't mean it.

Jerry and I, in spite of the flare-ups that happen between fathers and teenaged sons, got on well. One summer we traveled by car throughout the entire Western half of the country to all the great national parks—Yellowstone, Glacier, Sun Valley, Yosemite. It was before the interstate highway system made a direct route more convenient for most traffic and we had the opportunity to see the U.S.A. in all of its summer glory—Indian paintbrush, blue bonnets, sunsets, rock formations. It was magnificent. I knew that my time with Jerry was limited, that sooner or later he'd be graduated from high school and then away at college. I thought he'd be going to Stanford—I think Jerry did, too. He had grown up singing the Stanford fight song along with Don and Ellen. But Jerry went East to school instead.

At Burlingame High School Jerry was very popular. He was president of the boy students and vice-president of the student body—a born leader. He had all the right stuff. While he was a good student, there were fifteen other kids who were just a little brighter than he was who also wanted to go to Stanford and got in. Jerry did not, but he had the opportunity to talk to the recruiters from all the schools who came looking for potential students. While the schools sent their people out each year, they didn't come to Burlingame High School annually. For the first time in four years the representative from the University of Pennsylvania sent a man out to interview. One day I got a call from Harold Zellerbach, one of the chief executive officers of the Crown-Zellerbach Corporation, who graduated from Penn in 1917. He told me that he was a trustee and that one of the Penn interviewers had talked to Jerry and that they wanted a Magnin at Penn. Harold wouldn't take no for an answer. Since Jerry had been turned down at Stanford, he decided to

104

go to Penn. The experience, he says, taught him a lot of humility. The values in the Eastern United States, especially at the Wharton School of Finance, are much more conservative than they are in the West, and while we Magnins were not what you would call ostentatious or free-spending, Jerry was still considered, in his words, a "gross Westerner"—not in keeping with the image of the staid University of Pennsylvania.

Jerry had come for summer vacation in 1959 to find that we had exciting doings at our Hillsborough home. Lillian was in New York and then Europe on a buying trip for the store when the State Department called me requesting that we play host to a visiting contingent of Russians. The First Deputy Premier of the Soviet Union, Frol Koslov, and his entourage were touring the country. Their welcome had not been gracious in some places and while Lillian felt that it would not be a popular move for me to make, I consented to have a party at our home on July 4—a bang-up barbecue. It was very hot in Hillsborough that summer and Lillian was concerned that the lawn would be burnt to a cinder. Unfortunately no one thought to water it, but the State Department thinks of everything and we had Podesta Baldocchi come out and plant such exotics as orchids, daisies and mums in the yard. It was quite a sight.

We wanted to show the Russians a typical American barbecue—but I wasn't to show off my skills learned at Los Altos. Instead the Fairmont Hotel catered with charcoal-broiled steaks, California avocados stuffed with black caviar and one of Ellen's specially designed desserts. For this occasion she had flower pots stuffed with chocolate pudding for the "dirt" and live flowers growing out of the top. It was quite spectacular and was a big hit with the Soviets. When they first saw it, they thought it was real and Koslov said through his interpreter, "Is this a typical American plant?"

We had gotten word from the Soviets that they were to

105

arrive at noon for a casual luncheon and then a swim in our pool. I had bought all sizes and shapes of bathing suits to accommodate them. Then we heard that they were on their way an hour early. They walked into a mess with the catering trucks. It was a terribly hot day and all of the Soviets were dressed in suits and ties. Some even wore sweaters because they'd just come from a cruise on the Bay and it was chilly in San Francisco. Lillian whispered in my ear that maybe we'd all be more comfortable without our coats so when I doffed mine, the Soviets followed suit.

The Secret Service of both our countries were all over the place checking every conceivable thing. Our Secret Servicemen even ran surveillance machines over the food to see that nothing toxic had been put in it. We had received many hate letters prior to the Soviets' visit and couldn't be too careful. However, as the afternoon wore on, spirits rose and soon all the visitors were enjoying our swimming pool.

The Russians enjoyed a typical July 4th. We had a wonderful lunch and then from 4:30 to 6:30 P.M., we held a reception for San Francisco dignitaries. Initially we had received a lot of "sorry, we can't come" answers to our invitations, but President Eisenhower had issued a statement over radio and television that the Russians were guests in our country and that they should be accorded special courtesy because it was very rare that we have them. At the reception about 300 people came—including some of those who had said they couldn't make it. The Soviets had a marvelous time; they even decided not to go back to the city to see the fireworks display over the Bay. Around ten o'clock, however, someone who had had too much to drink made an insulting remark to one of our guests and in an instant the Russians disappeared.

Perhaps my marriage to Lillian Helwig had been doomed from the moment I met a young woman by the name of

Eleanor Ford. In 1955 Ellie was a leggy, high-spirited girl in her mid-twenties. She was of Portuguese-Catholic extraction, had a marvelous sense of humor and just as stubborn in her way as I was in mine. Joseph Magnin had built a store in Sacramento, and one afternoon I was returning to San Francisco and stopped for a bite to eat at the Nut Tree Restaurant, which was on the road between the two cities. Ellie was sitting with one of our buyers from Joseph Magnin, a woman named Jeri Naditz who was, in fact, Lillian's assistant buyer. The women had just come from a ski weekend and were on their way back to town. I've always been attracted to women who were knowledgeable about fashion and art, but what really attracted me to Eleanor was her beauty. I walked over to the table and had Jeri introduce us. Eleanor remarked that she thought I looked like Gladstone, the English Prime Minister. I think that may have struck a chord, because from then on I was determined to date her. When I got back to San Francisco, I called Jeri and asked her to give me Eleanor's phone number; I called Ellie and asked her out to dinner and she gave me a maybe. I said, "What do you mean, maybe? You can't live your life on maybe's; you have to have definition in your life." Finally she said to call her again and then we went to dinner, at a place called Monroe's on Lombard Street in San Francisco. Eleanor was going with someone else at the time and my marriage to Lillian was pretty much on the skids, although we were to remain together another six years.

I found Eleanor Ford to be one of the most exciting women I'd ever met. We grew to be great friends, although we fought like cats and dogs. She had a very hot temper and could match me, invective for invective. It was never dull with Eleanor. She was a marvelous traveling companion. The summer that the Soviets came to Hillsborough, they recipro-cated by inviting a group of San Francisco businessmen to the Soviet Union on an unofficial trade mission, one of the first

American business groups to be invited to the Soviet Union. I took Jerry along with me. I asked him to carry the gifts I'd brought along for Deputy Premier Koslov, his wife and family—a blender, some sporting goods and some tennis shoes. When we got off the plane, Jerry disappeared. After an hour he still hadn't shown up. That's when we realized that he had been arrested coming through customs for carrying contraband—the gifts for the Soviet officials. It took us a while to bail him out. Meanwhile, we had made arrangements at the end of the trip to meet Eleanor in Vienna and then to take Jerry on the grand tour. He and Eleanor got on famously. We had no reservations anywhere. Eleanor, by this time, was used to the way I liked to have fun—including bluffing my way through situations. When we arrived in Venice, we got to the Danieli Royal Excelsior and I walked up to the desk and asked for our reservations—three rooms with bathrooms. Of course, they didn't have reservations for Cyril Magnin. I flung my briefcase on the counter and started shuffling papers, throwing them in a heap on the desk saying, "I've got the letter of confirmation in here somewhere." They still refused to honor our nonexistent reservations. I threw a mock temper tantrum saying that my company spent many hundreds of thousands of dollars in their country and didn't they know who I was. Eleanor and Jerry were mortified. They slunk off down the lobby and hid behind a palm tree until it was over. Of course, we got our three rooms with bath.

CHAPTER SEVEN

Joseph Magnin II— Building an Image

IN A SENSE Joseph Magnin was a war baby. By the early forties our business started to take off. In a way we out-Magnined I. Magnin by capturing and holding a brand-new buying public—the younger woman. I. Magnin was going along in the way that had made them very successful, catering to a wealthy, mature clientele, and we were doing something fresh and new.

When my father started concentrating his efforts on Donner Factors, I changed more about the store than the merchandise. We spiffed up our image, although in those first few years we did it in a haphazard way with no conscious plan as to what direction things were going to take. I took chances, that's all, and had the guts and determination to make it all work. The key, I think, was to find the right people who understood my vision and could carry it out. After we'd become successful, someone wrote in one of those publications that service the retail business, "The more we look for evidence of free thinking, the more we realize that stores have a mortal fear of being different." The article went on to say, "Thank heavens Joseph Magnin defies the rules." I'm not sure that we were *that* defiant. We were different because we had no choice but to create a new market and it was that difference that put us on the retailing map. I also had a feeling that the industry was changing and I wanted to be the first to take advantage of it.

We were still considered upstarts by the gentry—albeit successful ones. We became trendsetters. Even so, we started out thinking that we'd be catering mostly to middle- and high-income businesswomen and the collegiate crowd. But other women got interested, even some older ones. Our customers were not all young people, but people who were young in spirit, who thought young, including a marvelous woman I'll never forget. She was eighty-five years old and married to a wholesale grocer. She would come in and say, "You know, stores like I. Magnin and Ransohoff's, that's stuff for old people. I want to be young." She'd always buy our most expensive clothes.

Still, with all of our first successes, the store had no precise merchandising policy. We had no definitive advertising style and were we to forge ahead, it was necessary to build an unmistakable fashion image both in our print ads and in the merchandise we carried. Then two young college girls in pastel-colored polo coats walked into my office—Virginia Sisk and Anabel Hagyard. It was as though the heavens had opened to answer an unspoken prayer.

Ginny and Anabel were Stanford grads who had been working in the advertising department at Roos Brothers. They couldn't have been more than twenty-one or twenty-two at the time. Now, let me explain that I have always been very accessible; anyone could walk off the street and talk to me and that's exactly what these girls did. They just walked in and plunked themselves down in my office with an interesting proposition. Virginia said, "I've got a whole concept, a new concept about an advertising format and they won't let me get to first base at Roos." She went on to say that she and Anabel could see the direction that Joseph Magnin was taking, but they suggested that what we needed was a plan, an advertising program to help us cement our market—one that dealt with building an image rather than realizing quick sales volume the minute the newspapers hit the streets. They showed me their ideas and told me that I should hire them. I took them at their word and virtually swung for the fences, hiring them on little more than that tingling feeling in my gut. My instincts were boiling again. There was something in their attitudes that told me, "Go ahead. They're on the right track."

In the next few years terrific things began to happen. We hired more and more young people, mostly women, who were talented and innovative and who agreed with what we wanted to do with the burgeoning youth market—a full fifteen years ahead of the 1960s when everyone started to think young for a profit. I really can't take the credit for all the things that happened. I just had sense enough to leave our advertising department alone to do what they wanted. I let them do their job. I never interfered as long as I thought they were going in the right direction . . . which, through the years, meant I *never* interfered. I felt then as I do now that perhaps I was lucky. We got the right people. Many years later, as a result of my growing "kiddie corps," all those bright young people who were to create the JM style, we were acknowledged by one of the greatest merchandisers of all, Stanley Marcus of the Texas specialty store, Neiman-Marcus. When he sent me a copy of his book, *Minding the Store,* he inscribed it, "To Cyril Magnin—A great merchant who led retailing to the young market . . . With great admiration, Stanley Marcus." I am very proud of that. Compliments from the cognoscenti always rate higher because you know they know and understand better than anyone what you're trying to do and whether you are really successful.

Our Joseph Magnin family was very small—I had my

family involved, Donald and Ellen and Ann up until her death in 1948, plus about five or six buyers, the salesclerks and office help. We were still leasing out the upper floors of the building to other businesses and when we took on an advertising department, we had to rent space elsewhere until those leases were up. Often our tenants would call Joseph and get him involved in lease renewals, playing him against me to get better terms. But we just let their leases lapse and little by little began taking over more space in the building. Until then I located some of our ad department in Jean Blum's office. Jean was an old friend of my father's and, subsequently, of mine. He was quiet in the extreme and it seemed that he was never in a good humor, but he was just shy and didn't like to talk to people. His office was located south of Market Street at Fourth and Mission. We had to put Ginny and her advertising department over there. One of the girls in the office was a young woman recently moved to California from the East Coast named Toni Moran. She was married to a navy man and arrived in San Francisco, as she puts it, "shortly before Hiroshima." She was to become one of the most valuable members in my growing kiddie corps.

Toni's background was as extraordinary as her talent. She was from a good, if quirky, Southern family. Her grandfather was a physician and her grandmother on her mother's side was a horsewoman from Greenville, Tennessee, who carried on a lifelong correspondence with Rudyard Kipling. Another grandfather was Christian Hammer, an art collector of some renown in Europe who had once owned Rubens's *Salome.* Toni's father was a Major Wheeler-Nicholson, a career army man who had been cashiered out of the service for criticizing the subordinate system.

Wheeler-Nicholson was a seven-goal polo player whom Toni called a bit of a playboy. He became interested in writing and began turning out adventure-fiction for pulp magazines. He lived a very gay, Bohemian life and moved his

112

family to and from France a couple of times and then to the seat of American bohemianism, Greenwich Village. At one time they lived in the famous Dolly Sisters' apartment in Paris. It was a very glamorous life complete with servants which, Toni said, the Wheeler-Nicholsons could ill afford. Whether they had money or not, Toni's family lived as if they did, but during the Depression, things started to fall apart and they moved back to the States, to Long Island, where Toni says she had some semblance of normalcy.

When she finished high school in Great Neck, L.I., she had to go to work. Funds had run out and there was no question that she would *not* be going to college. She went to work at the Macy's exhibition at the 1939 New York World's Fair. The company retained some of their special hires, Toni included. She was put to work in New York City on the comparison shopper squad. Often when she shopped stores like Gimbels, someone recognized her and her cover was blown. There would be a bell rung on the floor announcing to one and all that Macy's was in the store—look out. Toni quit Macy's to work at Lord and Taylor. Eventually, through a friend, she wound up in the promotion department at Simplicity Patterns where she was a stylist for their catalogue. She chose accessories for catalogues and then traveled extensively putting on style shows at department stores throughout the country. She met and married Forrest Moran, a submarine officer whose family lived in Marin County right outside of San Francisco. When he was transferred to the West Coast, Toni came with him.

Toni arrived in the Bay Area looking for a job in advertising. She inquired as to what the "good" stores were and was told the usual list. She didn't even consider coming to Joseph Magnin for work. She knew nothing about advertising but took around samples she'd made up. She walked into JM not as a job-seeker, but as a customer, attracted by a pair of shoes she'd seen in a window. She was chatting with Fred

Esgar, Harry Parlow's partner in the shoe concession, about
being new in San Francisco and about wanting to get a job in
advertising. When he heard her story—including the fact that
she had worked for Lord and Taylor in New York—Fred
whipped her up to my office. I was chewing somebody out—
probably yelling up a storm—when this marvelous-looking,
smart young woman walked in. She had a great smile that
made her eyes crinkle up at the corners; she was about five-
feet-five and dressed youthfully but conservatively. She had a
no-nonsense air about her coupled with a wonderful sense of
humor. She was not cowed by my display of bad temper,
which pleased me. I respect people who stand up to me. I was
seated in front of venetian blinds and she couldn't see my face
because of the glare of sunlight streaming in behind me. I
asked her a couple of questions as a disembodied voice and
told her I was looking for an advertising girl, that I had two
Stanford grads—Anabel, the artist, and Ginny, the copywriter—who needed a Girl Friday. I wound up hiring her on the
spot and told her to report for work the next day at our
rented cubbyhole in Jean Blum's office above the blood bank
at Fourth and Mission. Little did I know at the time that Toni
was to become one of the driving forces behind Joseph
Magnin's reputation and image.

When I hired Toni Moran, it wasn't a split-second decision; it was my instinct working. I didn't hire everyone I
spoke with by any means, but we were looking for young
talent—people who were compatible with the store's direction. I liked Toni's looks from the start—she was frank and I
enjoyed that. She had an honesty that brooked no nonsense
and she worked well with people. During the ten-year course
of our association, we mixed it up pretty well. Nobody
survived with me unless they learned to yell, argue and stand
their ground. And Toni was very good at carving out her own
territory. On one occasion, she even took on my father. It was
after she was head of the department and my father was

insisting that all advertising budgets be approved by him. Toni was so incensed, because she felt that he was challenging her jurisdiction, that she threatened to quit if he didn't stop.

By this time Joseph was past eighty. He was the elder statesman around JM. He had become diminutive with age, all hunched over in our typical Magnin posture. He was balding and his blue eyes, although weak, sparkled with the devil. He was never without his odoriferous cigar and people could see him coming 'round corners, preceded by a cloud of smoke. In his own way he had become as imperious as Mary Ann had been, but mostly it was his sly, puckish sense of humor that motivated him. Toni, however, wasn't having any and she took him on by telling him that he was still treating Joseph Magnin as if it were a little "mom and pop" store. I smoothed things over with Toni by having a talk with Joe about letting her do her job unmolested. But he was such an imp. He had to have the last word, which he delivered by sticking his head inside her office door, cigar clamped firmly in his teeth and eyes definitely a-twinkle, saying, "I'll just go and ruin someone else's temper."

I grew to respect Toni's integrity so much. We became very close, although there was never any hanky-panky between us. My wife had passed away and I was very lonely and decided perhaps, since Toni and I understood each other so well, we should get married. We were sitting in a restaurant named Galli's having dinner when I made that suggestion. She looked at me quite stunned and remarked, "I can't marry you—you don't even ski." The issue was settled before dessert and we resumed our business relationship as if it had never happened.

When Toni was hired on, she eventually worked her way up to being the head of the department. Our advertising at the time was good, but it was to become a pacesetter in the industry with the addition of two more key women, Betty Brader and Marget Larsen. Until Toni found and hired them, we tried some outrageous things and were successful with some of them—maybe too successful in the case of the Gossard lingerie promotion. We had run an ad showing a woman in a black girdle, black stockings and black brassiere with a filmy black negligee flung over her shoulders. Around her neck was a rope of pearls. She was quite soigné. The ad copy read, "Last night I dreamed I had nothing on but my black Gossard . . . and I remembered feeling quite smug about how smooth it looked—how well it fit." We recreated the ad in a window display on Stockton Street with a mannequin gotten up in her black girdle and bra, complete with the pearls. The morning after the ad and the display appeared, we found a huge hole in the store window. The only thing that was missing was the girdle.

Most of the young people I was hiring were women. It was not coincidental. I had always thought that women comprised a huge, untapped segment of the labor force. There was a built-in prejudice against hiring women and all that woman- and brainpower had been going to waste. Besides, women worked cheap. Toni once said that women didn't think they were worth any more than they were being paid and that they were lucky to have any kind of job. She was quite surprised when job offers came to her from other parts of the country offering her many thousands of dollars more than what we were paying her. But the women we hired were very loyal to me. They knew, as Toni did, that they could probably be making more money elsewhere, but where else would they have the freedom to create and develop their ideas without some corporate Big Brother leaning over their shoulders to monitor their every move. Also, we were training these women and when you start to promote employees in-house, they will not command the salaries of a person you've recruited from outside the company. In the process of learning there was a trade-off. They might have been making less money, but they were getting something valuable in return. Besides, there was great merit in encouraging women to express their ideas. They were also consumers and by and large they were exactly the same audience that JM catered to—the young, vibrant, original working woman with disposable income and strong taste levels.

In our hiring practices at Joseph Magnin we were never discriminatory, not against women, blacks or any other minority. We were first to hire Japanese-Americans after those terrible days of World War II when they were interned in detention camps. I really felt sorry for them and for the injustice that had been done them. A lot of them were American-born and shouldn't have been made to pay for the mistakes of the Japanese government over which they had no control. I felt a moral obligation to put them to work. My nondiscriminatory stance came from Grandfather Isaac—he was always for the underdog, the dispossessed. Today people would call him a socialist or a communist, but his concern for other people became inbred in me. We put our Japanese employees on the elevators. When the operators' salaries went up so high, the union complained that the rest of their membership was being discriminated against because all we hired for the job were the Japanese. I guess when you tried to be fair, you just couldn't win.

When Toni first started, she worked for Ginny and Anabel as a go-fer, doing all sorts of menial things like running errands and going for coffee. She was also writing advertising copy, a job for which she showed enormous talent. It was a valuable apprenticeship for her, because six months later, when Ginny was offered the post of advertising manager at Neiman-Marcus (an offer she just couldn't refuse), she recommended that I try Toni for the job. Toni was twenty-four and pregnant with her first child. Her marriage was on the rocks and she says that it was probably the most awful time in her life. But she dug in and made her mark very early. It was during the early fifties that she found two brilliant artists, Betty Brader and Marget Larsen.

Toni had discovered Betty's work in a fashion magazine

117

out of Southern California. In the course of her day, Toni browsed through volumes of fashion magazines and retailing publications to see what the competition was doing. Betty's art just stood out—like a light in a darkened room. She was one of those rare artists who can express an entire concept with a simple, stylish and graphic drawing. Toni knew that this young woman was exactly what we needed and she came tearing into my office all a-buzz, wanting to get Betty Brader at any cost. That is . . . if Betty wanted to become associated with us. Luckily, she did. She was responsible for our distinctive advertising style—one which won prizes year after year. Our ads were so dynamic and striking, they could have stood alone as poster art. Betty could do a young, flip look and then something rather sophisticated. In the ad business she was legend. Department stores all over the country copied her style—sometimes, I've been told by her fellow artists, tracing her designs right off our pages. There's probably been no one then or since who has been as influential in newspaper fashion advertising as Betty Brader.

Toni's second important hire was a statuesque young graphic artist named Marget Larsen. She was absolutely stunning—tall and stately and dark with a turned-up nose and an elegantly casual personal style that she carried over into her work. She had started working at I. Magnin when she was very young, doing lettering for the windows. The atmosphere there was conservative and she found it suffocating and suffered under the dictates of their newspaper style which, compared with what we were developing, was typical of most contemporary advertising—nondescript and gray. Unfortunately, Marget had contracted tuberculosis and had just come out of a sanitorium and was very shaky. When she came to Joseph Magnin toting a portfolio of things she had tried unsuccessfully to get I. Magnin to use, she wasn't even sure *we* were the place for her.

Marget was a second-generation native San Franciscan

118

with Scandinavian antecedents—Norwegian and Danish. Her mother had trained with Dirk van Erp, the international flatware designer, and was creating silver and metal flatware for Shreve's Jewelers. Marget's father was a contractor in business with his father. They built a number of buildings on the Stanford campus and in Burlingame. Marget's design talent seemed to be passed on in her genes. She herself was interested in jewelry-making and studied metalwork at the California School of Fine Arts. She got her marvelous color sense from her grandmother, who always wore magnificent hues. Marget was five-eleven; you couldn't miss her in a crowd. You also couldn't miss her contribution to Joseph Magnin. She was born with a natural eye and a sense of color, proportion and harmony. She had an ongoing love affair with the print medium, especially typeface. She knew how different type could create a mood—such as not putting heavy headline type on an ad for a filmy evening dress. She understood the mechanics of print reproduction and could tell by the way a print-ready ad looked if it was going to reproduce well.

With Marget's wizardry with type, Betty's hard-edged, graphic drawings and Toni's inventive copy, our advertising began to receive both local and national attention. We had a small, unique and effective operation consisting of Toni, Marget, Betty, a second copywriter and another artist. They were all under thirty. What they did was spontaneous and creative. Often the girls would have to model for each other. If Betty needed a hand or a body shape, Marget or Toni were pressed into service. Our ads made strong statements. Betty developed the prototypical JM woman—one with large, sloe eyes, a pert nose (Marget perhaps?) and luxuriant hair. She was young and beautiful—exotic but clean-cut. She was a very strong image which stated that Joseph Magnin was the place to come if you were an individual. Couple those vivid pictures with Marget's unfailing technical sense and we had a lot going for us. It was Marget who found the master engravers who, if we were advertising a tweed suit, would strip in a photo of the actual tweed onto our art work. If any engraver had a problem, it was Marget with whom they worked to arrive at a solution. All of those women were quick. Toni was sharp enough to see if something in stock was very hot. She would pull it, hand it to Betty to sketch up (sometimes Betty could draw it in a half-hour), shoot it and *voila!* instant ad. Some of the best things happened when there wasn't much time to prepare between conception and deadline.

I think our advertising department broke all standard art school rules for newspaper advertising. You'd have been hard-pressed to find a brand-name logo or even the JM signature that stuck out in an ad. We also realized that an advertisement is competing with a lot of other stuff on a page and that if we had a mushy, gray-toned ad, it could get lost. But you couldn't ignore our ads. Often we took odd spaces in the newspaper, not because they were cheap or strange, but because they were appropriate to what we wanted to present. We wanted to be innovative, but we were merchandise-oriented and that was what dictated the size and shape of the ad. We were the first advertisers to buy the gutter, the one place in the center of the newspaper between two connecting pages where there isn't any print. We had the papers dummy in their news stories on either side of our ads. At the time there were four newspapers in San Francisco, each hungry for advertising revenues. They were very pleased to sell us space that hadn't been a money-maker before. We were not the largest advertiser, but we became one of the most important because we set a high standard and a pace that everyone tried to copy. I would kid Toni and say, "We've taken advertising into the gutter." But we were always trying something new and different.

We bought entire pages—sometimes two adjoining, in what are called "double-truck" ads. We used color which was also an innovation. After the holidays and the January sales when it is traditionally a slow time in the retailing business, we would run a huge color ad to pick up everyone's flagging spirits. We would have four separate small block ads stacked up on top of each other down one side of a page, and once we bought seven of the eight available columns for an ad which featured one gigantic shoe from a firm run by protégés of Herbert and Beth Levine, Margaret Jerrold. The name came from owners Jerry Miller and his designer wife, Margaret. I was all excited about that particular shoe. It had a pointed toe and was made of pleated silk. It was absolutely gorgeous. I thought that Jerrold required a special ad to introduce them to San Francisco and I gave the assignment to Toni, Marget and Betty.

The women never really showed me a layout. I just turned them loose, knowing they'd come up with something smashing. And it was . . . all seven columns of it. In color. Unheard of. The Joseph Magnin sig was in tiny print at the bottom. Perhaps I was surprised that they would come up with such an extravagant presentation—to use nearly an entire page on one high-fashion item. All they had left was a single column so no one could give us any competition. But I wouldn't have cared if they'd taken three pages. The purpose of that ad and others like it was not to sell merchandise but to relay a message to our customers that we were the store for high-fashion young clothes and excitement in San Francisco. I also wouldn't have cared if the ad had sold only one shoe, but it did both—it delivered our message *and* sold shoes. We could hardly keep them in stock and they were a very high-ticket item for what they were.

I was a big believer in advertising and I tripled our ad budgets. It got to the point where people actually looked forward to seeing what Joseph Magnin was going to do next. It was entertainment. But the ads were only part of our effort to make a splash in San Francisco and elsewhere with our branches. The easiest way to make an exciting statement is through the use of eye-catching color. We redesigned our windows in pinks, reds, purples and oranges—outrageous colors in an era of dull beiges, grays and powder blues. Long before that wonderful Bloomingdale's bag with the rose and the woman's face, we had our own designer bag printed in red and pink harlequin diamonds. That, too, was a daring departure because most retail stores were handing out glorified grocery bags in browns and beiges. I think I. Magnin countered our harlequin diamonds with a brown and white striped bag.

And then, there was the matter of Marget's boxes.

In one of her creative flurries, Toni suggested that perhaps we should have specially-designed boxes for our Christmas merchandise. We asked Marget, who was and is a packaging whiz, to come up with something terrific. Marget met with Walter Newman and together they previewed all the seasonal merchandise to decide how many boxes and what sizes would be necessary. They also tried to make an accurate estimate of how many in each size we would need—there's nothing more useless than a leftover Christmas box on December 26. They came up with fifty-four separate sized boxes for things as small as jewelry and scarves to the odd sizes needed for umbrellas, giftware and fur coats.

Marget's first effort was a smash—a pyramid made from silver-coated stock, stuffed with flame-colored tissue and fastened with colorful seals instead of ribbon. Her subsequent designs were equally innovative. One year she designed an entire gingerbread toyland village which grew with each different sized and shaped box; another year featured a design adapted from the end papers of antiquarian books and still another featured sea shells. While they may have been more expensive to produce than conventional boxes, ours could be stacked flat underneath the counter instead of taking up valuable storage room needed for

122

merchandise. We also saved the money ribbon cost and for further convenience, the customer could take them home and assemble them—which also saved valuable time for our salespeople who, incidentally, were taught how to assemble the boxes just in case they were asked. We went with the idea that if you had a folding box with exciting graphics, the customer would want to get it. People used to come in and buy all sorts of merchandise just so they could get one of each of the boxes.

Our customers were so supportive through the years that our Christmas box became a collector's item attracting perhaps people who shopped with us only at Christmastime just to get our box. In fact, people still have them under their Christmas trees each year and a museum in Oakland displays the entire collection. We also featured them in our advertising, often building an entire campaign around them starting on Thanksgiving Day, traditionally the beginning of the holiday buying season. That first Christmas, we estimate that our business went up twenty-five percent—attributable, I think, to that something extra: Marget's boxes.

Of course, you can't make everyone happy and as much as we were complimented for our special Christmas gift to our customers, we would get letters complaining, "Where is the traditional red and green?" I would just tell our staff that I thought it was better to be talked about than forgotten about.

One year I asked Marget what our design was going to be and she replied, "Cyril, let me surprise you." I trusted her artistic judgment implicitly, as I did the ability of all my creative people. I left everything in the capable hands of the art department. If any buyer or executive didn't like the design of a face in an ad or the color or pattern on store wrapping paper, it wasn't any of their business. Those were solely the province of the art department and I backed them up one hundred percent. I was very much involved in wanting to know what was going on, but not in a nit-picking way. You can't put handcuffs on creativity. While I knew I was a good salesman and that I had excellent merchandising people around me, I left the artists to what they knew best. You hire people who are supposed to be expert and knowledgeable in their fields—then you let them do what they were hired for. However, I didn't want anyone working for me who didn't make any mistakes. That meant they weren't doing anything creative or interesting. I always said that it was fine to make a mistake—just don't make the same one twice.

When Toni hired Betty and Marget, their ads were actually more exciting than some of the merchandise we stocked. We were still getting good buys on boring clothes and it drove Toni mad. She said she used to have to write zippy captions for some of our clothes which taxed her imagination.

I had an assistant who had been with the store for a long time and was, in fact, a very good merchandiser and a hard worker. She could handle all the details I didn't have time for, but she was also a thorn in Toni's side. They mixed about as well as oil and water. When the assistant claimed she had to OK all of Toni's ads, Toni blew up and threatened again to quit if she couldn't run her own department autonomously. It was at that point that Toni started getting involved with merchandising. She told me that she couldn't have decent ads without decent merchandise. There were many exciting things happening in fashion that perhaps started with Walter Hoving and Dorothy Shaver at Lord and Taylor in New York—an emphasis on new American designers like Claire McCardell, whose draped jerseys are still being copied; Ann Fogarty, who was designing specifically for the junior-sized figure and Ceil Chapman, whose gowns were both youthful and elegant. Toni thought that Lord and Taylor was on the right track, but bringing an East Coast sensibility to San Francisco has not always been an easy thing to do. Our lifestyle has always been a lot less formal, so Toni adapted what she had seen for our customers. We were still being hampered in the market. We were still getting chicken tracks from some of the better suppliers, so we were still creating our own resources. Often, for instance, if we couldn't find the right accessory to go in an ad, Marget would create it and then we'd find someone to make it up for us. I was always very enthusiastic when one of my kiddie corps came up with a new idea. I couldn't express myself in any other way than to say over and over again, "That's the greatest."

We had a unique organization in Joseph Magnin. In those days JM was a good example of creative anarchy. We weren't formal the way businesses are today, where I think that there are too many people reporting to too many people. Creativity tends to get lost in the paperwork. But back then we had no chain of command. Anyone could walk into my office at any time. It would never have dawned on some of my people to make an appointment to see me. I think it drove my secretaries to distraction. But my door was always open and instead of using an intercom or the telephone when I wanted to see someone, I simply yelled down the hall. If I wanted to summon Walter Newman, for instance, I would simply holler, "Newman!" at the top of my voice. Often he wouldn't come until I'd barked his name twice (I was rather abrupt). He knew how impetuous I was and figured if I wanted him badly enough, I'd call again. There may have been a loosely structured organizational chart, but no one paid any attention to it. In fact, a lot of typical retailing positions weren't even filled. For a long time we had no merchandising manager, leaving that job up to the buyers and the advertising department. What we did have was a lot of chaos—a hurricane of activity where ideas were born and batted back and forth ferociously. (Some ideas came from unlikely sources. Once, when my youngest son, Jerry, was still in grade school, he made an observation that perhaps our credit department would be more convenient for our customers who wanted to pay on their accounts if it were laid out differently—this from a ten-year-old who was right on the money.) All in all, I held my staff responsible for results, not methods. Strong, capable executives came out of all of it and those who couldn't take the commotion simply dropped out.

With all the changes we did not even consider firing any of the old Joseph Magnin employees, people who'd been there for years when my father was in charge. One woman in the credit department named Frances Hutchinson was eventually mechanized out of her job when we put our accounting and stock control on computer, but we kept her on allowing her to post her records by hand. She'd been with the company a long time and was a loyal employee. I knew that if we let her go, she'd probably have passed away and I couldn't bear that. But then I never really fired anybody. Those with the ability to recognize what we were trying to do were more than happy to climb on board; those who couldn't fit into the tumultuous kind of atmosphere that surrounded our changes just quit. Many resigned because they didn't like what we were doing and thought we were crazy.

A lot of the "Joseph" people did stay, including Hilda Gilgannon in the millinery department and Ruth Yoell, our fur buyer. Hilda remained although millinery was not playing as important a role as it once had when the department was responsible for keeping the store going. The department took up half the first floor, but no one was wearing hats by then. I think probably we had maintained the space because it was once one of Charlotte's strengths, but Toni pointed out to me that I was using all that floor space for something that wasn't generating enough business. We put in a hat bar instead which was very successful. Eventually, when hats were no longer selling and wigs were all the rage, Hilda bought the hair goods. Her department was so lively in the late sixties that she would attract a crowd around her when she fitted a wig or made a hairpiece.

126

Miss Yoell was another one of our "old" Joseph Magnin people who opted to stay. She was a tiny, round little woman with a pert face; she looked very French. She always dressed in the latest fashion whether it was designed for her figure or not. She was fiery and had a quick temper; she loved to argue and would fight with me at the drop of a hat. She was a great fur buyer with a natural sales ability and a tremendous sense of quality. Customers were very loyal and would wait for her insisting that only *she* could take care of them. In proportion to our business, the fur department was very important and she had a lot of high-ticket sales. She oozed creative excitement. We got into fights all the time because she didn't agree with me. She would burst into staff meetings and shake her forefinger in my face. The finger had been broken and had a crick in it and she would stand there, invited or not, telling me what she thought. One day I got so fed up that I ducked into the men's room and yelled at her through a crack in the door, "This is one place you can't follow me."

The fashion business, by necessity, has to change with every season, but sometimes we at Joseph Magnin were able to change even faster. We could tell, for instance, if an item was going to sell within the first two weeks it was on the floor. If it was a slow mover, we were not afraid to make markdowns. I may have been called "Carload" Magnin for some of my unfortunate purchases, but I was not cowed by that red pencil which I would use with abandon, marking down things to make room for fresh, salable merchandise. We opened a sale room on the sixth floor of our building called Magnarama where we would send the markdowns. We even marked down the markdowns after a few weeks if they weren't moving in the sale room. A smart shopper could get a real bargain if she checked the sixth floor regularly.

We were always operating under extreme pressure. But we functioned best when we were up against deadlines. While it was stimulating, we worked long, hard hours. Toni, for instance, was working six days a week. She would get to work at 9 A.M. and was rarely ready to leave for home until after 7:30 P.M. She never went out for lunch, usually preferring to grab a sandwich in the store cafeteria. But she had remarried and had enlarged her family. She threatened to quit again if she couldn't have her Saturdays off to be with her husband and children. It caused a large furor, but she won the point. I knew it was a small price to pay for her talent.

Under Toni's sharp eye our merchandising policies began to change with the advertising and art departments setting the pace. That's not to say that our buyers weren't capable, but since we had no merchandising manager to scout new resources, our buyers were doing double duty, familiarizing themselves with what our tried and true manufacturers were carrying each season and staying on the lookout for new resources. After a while they found they couldn't do both well. It was then that we added a young man named Al Duarte to our growing bunch of creative kids.

Duarte was twenty years old when June Curran, the manager of the Palo Alto store, hired him to freelance for the display department. He worked at the old store on University Avenue and when the new Victor Gruen–designed store with the circular staircase was opened in 1945, he joined us full-time. Duarte was a native of San Jose and had gone to San Jose State for two years in the art department. He left to study art with Rudolph Schaeffer in San Francisco. When he came to my attention, he had been designing windows that were different and quite arresting. One set of windows he'd done in Palo Alto were in pink, red and orange. Back in the mid-forties that was a very daring color combination and June wasn't at all sure whether she should like it or not. She called me to come down to the store to check it out and when I saw it, I thought it was marvelous—exactly the kind of idea I was looking for.

About that time the charity fashion show was just starting

to catch on. Al inaugurated a series of Friday shows every other week at a restaurant where he'd use "real" models, community women from the various charitable organizations. It was a great way for them to make money and it was a marvelous way for us to get our clothes seen. We liked what he was doing, and gave him the San Mateo store for shows on alternate Fridays. He'd pull the clothes and dress and train the models. It was about this time also that Toni suggested to me that we needed some sort of fashion coordinator. She explained that buyers had a different view of the market than promotion people. She said that they usually liked to stay with what's tried and true, what sold last year, but things in the fashion business didn't stand still and it was necessary to get new things, new resources into the store. That's where Al came in. Toni thought that he would be the perfect liaison between the buyers and the advertising department. Instead of asking the buyers to take the time to scour the market for new things, we would send Al. He was a natural. He could recognize trends—he had a golden gut, just like me, but he had a fashion sense and the artistic background to know exactly how to promote it.

One of Al's great coups was to scoop the Paris collections of the summer of 1954 before the merchandise could be copied down and land in the stores. In the spring of 1954 Chanel, who had been inactive for years, reopened with a collection of simple, elegant suits that had straight skirts and the classic, Chanel box jacket. It was not a success; the press crucified her as being dated and old hat. It was simply a bomb. Al had been to New York and saw a Chanel influence—the great American suitmakers, Ben Zuckerman and Davidow, were all doing their versions of it; nobody had picked it up to copy it—they had all developed it on their own. Al's instincts told him that whether she had been successful or not, Chanel's influence was going to be with us. He went into the market and told the manufacturers what he wanted—not a true Chanel copy, but the feeling. He had a boxy jacket in gray flannel made up at Sportwhirl which he put with another gray flannel skirt to be sold as a suit. There was also a Larry Aldrich black velvet shirtwaist dress in our "new look" which retailed for $98. In our kickoff ad for the "Chanel look," Al had found a two-piece tweed dress from Junior Sophisticates, then an up-and-coming junior house for whom Anne Klein designed. It was done up in either black-and-white or brown-and-white tweed and we bought six pieces of it to cover the ad. Junior Sophisticates wasn't even cutting the dress at the time; we had to talk them into making it again. We did so well with it—we must have sold at least 500 pieces before we dropped the outfit and Sophisticates carried variations of it in their line for several more years.

What was so prophetic, however, was that Al scooped the Paris showings because in the summer of 1954, Christian Dior came out with his own version of the Chanel suit which was the success of the collections. They were held in Paris in the end of July and on August 2 we ran our own Chanel promotion with merchandise ready to sell already in our store. We had been running teaser ads for ten days before with just a silhouette and the line, "Chanel is coming . . ." Meanwhile, Evelyn Hannay, the fashion editor of the *San Francisco Chronicle,* picked up on it and ran a fashion article on the front page of the paper which indicated that we had "scooped" the Paris collections. Then the wire services got hold of it and shortly after the local TV news cameras were pushing their way down our aisles in the suit department to have their look-see.

The Chanel promotion included everything from the clothes to Chanel perfume and tons and tons of long gold chains and ropes of pearls. Al had told me that the ropes were going to be the coming thing. They had been the principal accessory in the collections. I said, "For Godsakes, get a few manufacturers to make 'em for us, ask 'em not to sell 'em to anybody else. Tell 'em that I want two months; at least, six weeks advance. I want to do something sensational." I then told Al to buy all he could get. I was a real gambler. While I'd never been one to bet the horses or play the slot machines in Las Vegas—if I played at blackjack, I'd usually quit if I was ten dollars up or down—I went all out on those ropes. We couldn't keep them in stock. Not only did we have them made, we couldn't get them on the counters fast enough. At first it was all we could do to have enough to decorate the mannequins. I lived in Hillsborough, south of the city, at that time and had to pass San Francisco Airport on my way to work. I would have our buyers in New York pick the ropes up directly from the manufacturer and put them on the first plane out. They would call me to tell me what plane the ropes were coming in on and I'd get them the next morning on my way into the city. We flung that jewelry onto counters with no price tags. We didn't even have a chance to inventory them.

Al seems to think that if I hadn't been excited about the Chanel thing, it probably wouldn't have gotten off the ground. It wasn't an easy thing to accomplish because there were no available resources. We had to create everything ourselves, from talking Junior Sophisticates into continuing with that little two-piece suit to having our own manufacturers supply us with boxes of pearl ropes. We even had to have the hats that had been shown in the Chanel collection made up locally—little boaters and those flat bows made from velvet and grosgrain ribbon that fit like headbands. I was so excited about it that I got on the phone and contacted the buyers, encouraging them to find anything they could that would fit the new style. This was nothing we had planned; it was strictly an emotional decision that paid off. Again I simply let my creative people do their jobs.

I must reemphasize that the Joseph Magnin look was a very young look. At the time, in the mid-fifties, there was not the focus on youth that there was to be in the 1960s, but a

131

more serious department store wouldn't have stepped out on a limb as we did to promote junior clothes and the new American designers. Oh, they may have had a few items, but certainly, not a whole store built around youthful styles. We were offering fashion at a price and we did it in such a way that our promotions became famous. The store was always full of young people. Their vitality was catching. There was almost nothing we wouldn't try if we thought it would bring us good press and loads of new customers.

One promotion involved a new Revlon nail color called "Kissing Pink." At the time, Hal March was the MC of a top-rated quiz show called "The $64,000 Question." Before the quiz show scandals ended his reign, March was playing to 60 million people a week. He was a native San Franciscan who had gone to George Washington High School. We got the idea that Hal should come back to San Francisco, to his home town, to help kick off the "Kissing Pink" campaign. We flew him into the city in a helicopter and landed it in front of City Hall where the mayor gave Hal the key to the city. We had a "Hal March box" made up with five dollars' worth of Revlon products in it. The box must have cost us six bucks, but we didn't care. We almost had a riot with all the women trying to reach March to have him autograph the box. We painted the front of the building "Kissing Pink" with water-based paint and prayed that it wouldn't rain.

Before March came, we had him tape a thirty-second message that if you dialed a certain telephone number, he would come on and say, "Hello, this is Hal March. I'm coming back to my home town, San Francisco, and I'll be at Joseph Magnin on [such-and-such a day] between noon and 2 P.M." We burned out the phone company's regional switchboards because not only did we publicize the number in the newspaper, he mentioned it on the air. On March's first show when he got back from San Francisco, he thanked the people of the city—mentioning me and the Joseph Magnin stores by name—for making his homecoming such a grand event. My son Donald and Walter got hold of a friend of theirs at BBDO, the big advertising agency, and found out the price of a national television spot and got an official billing receipt. They dummied up a fake bill addressed to me in care of JM for special promotions—it was some fantastic amount, perhaps $50,000. They asked our comptroller to put the bill through, which he did. The prank worked. I was, to say the least, very shocked until they told me the truth.

We built our promotions around the darnedest things—usually a color, like our "White Smoke" campaign where we decorated our long front window with a huge cigarette with smoke curling out of the end of it. We filled the window with twenty-five hats in the white smoke color and by tne end of the day we'd sold every hat in the display. There was a time when we built an entire campaign around blue denim. Al took a Dior navy silk serge suit that had been designed by Mark Bohan, who had treated it like blue jeans with tiny rhinestones on the seams for "stitching." We had a local manufacturer make it up for us in actual denim with white top-stitching. Every department in the store had some article in denim—shoes, handbags, even underwear and sleepwear. We even had denim-and-striped ticking printed on wrapping paper. It was a summer promotion designed to bring us out of the summer doldrums. One of our fall promotions was "Popcorn and Cider," which was Ellen's brainstorm. It was a very easy theme from the standpoint of the display department. They made up windows in pretty shades of camel, rust and taupe with bales of hay, autumn leaves, bowls of popcorn and apples. Our ideas could come from anywhere, even the Broadway stage. When *The King and I* was popular, we copied some of the jewelry and decorated our windows in exotic fashion.

While our promotions were entertainments for our customers, we had in-house activities to keep our department heads and salespeople apprised of what was coming from each new market. It was Al's job to organize a huge fashion showcase to which we'd invite every store manager and assistant—even from stores as far away as Reno and Sacramento. We'd take over a theater and there would be a lavish production with music and a storyline. For those local salespeople who couldn't come in from the outlying stores, we'd have traveling shows to acquaint them with what they'd be selling in a couple of months. One show was particularly memorable. It was Al at his theatrical best. For the finale, he used music from Respighi's *The Fountains of Rome*. The models were dressed in very expensive, floaty chiffon gowns from Helen Rose, the Hollywood designer. The models were to waltz through a cloud of dry ice and down the ramp. Al couldn't get theatrical dry ice, so he had one of the guys from the display department chip up regular commercial dry ice and throw it into buckets of water which had been heated over a hot plate behind the set. Next to these buckets waited the girls in their frou-frou chiffons. Not only did the dry ice steam right on schedule, it spit and popped and pretty soon the girls were screaming that they were being burned. Al hustled them onto the runway, yelling, "Go, go . . . don't stop," but it was too late. The hems of the delicate chiffons were starting to pull up. Of course, the dresses were ruined, but the fog effect was wonderful. I loved it.

Under Al's savvy direction we opened up what amounted to the first boutiques—tiny shops which handled one-of-a-kind pieces or which were set up for special occasions. We were one of the first stores in the country to concentrate on Italian imports; our shoes and leather goods were always magnificent and we were able to sell them at a good price. We opened a men-only, pre-Christmas boutique called the Wolves' Den. There, a gentleman could come into the store and receive personal attention from a pretty woman who would show him items for his lady—furs, jewelry, filmy

134

lingerie, perfume—things that were out in the regular store, but had been pulled together in one place to make shopping easier for him. A man could come in, relax, have a drink (before the Alcoholic Beverage Control got so strict), look at a beautiful model in sexy lingerie and then make his purchase, which then would be wrapped in a special way. The idea was personal service. It was a huge success—something which other stores would take five or six years to copy.

One evening, Al was having dinner with me and my second wife, Lillian, and he mentioned that it was sad that JM didn't have a department in the store for very special merchandise—the avant-garde stuff. Maybe it didn't fit into a regular department or perhaps it was too expensive or a little quirky. There was a tiny round section on the fashion floor that used to be our bridal department. We turned it over to Al and had a terrible time naming it. We had always called it The Little Room because the space was so small, so the name stuck. It was a precursor of the boutique. We filled it with marvelous things—like those high-fashion items Rudi Gernreich was making that wouldn't have sold elsewhere, or Andy Warhol's shoe sketches for I. Miller that were selling for $35 apiece or Bonnie Cashin's leather and mohair reversible poncho. I gave Al *carte blanche* to buy whatever he wanted to buy with no discussion of price.

I wasn't afraid to go out on a limb if I thought that the results would be exciting and help build an image for the store. Once I even advertised a $100,000 sable coat in *Town & Country* magazine. The ad was completely my baby—I'd even written the copy. There was a sketch of a gorgeous woman reclining in the coat on a plush seat and the ad said, "For the private railway car set, a sable coat, full length, $100,000 . . . ever so much more practical because it can go every place." Well, we had to send the coat back because nobody bit. Eventually, Princess Grace of Monaco bought it from the supplier.

Not everything ran smoothly in those glittery, gambling, build-an-image years. In a fit of efficiency I decided that I was going to investigate how many man-hours it took the creative people to come up with things that we spent our money on. I hired a precise little man who fit every stereotype of what you'd imagine a time-study man to be, down to the pad and paper he carried and the worried look that never left his face. He had to know exactly how long it took to get things done— creative things to which you can't attach a time schedule. He made the ad department artists uncomfortable with his questions. In return my people would give him vague answers because sometimes the gals in the art department would get the germ of an idea while they were setting their hair at night or when they straightened their stockings in the ladies room. He would disrupt this crew by trying to put a box around their creativity. We parted company during the Chanel promotion. The time-study man tried to organize the receiving department, saying that deliveries had to be made at certain times and that merchandise was to be tagged and out on the counters according to a specific schedule. Of course, deliveries came in when they came in, especially during the Chanel promotion when I was making them myself. We couldn't mark the pearl ropes fast enough to get them to our customers, so we never marked them at all. The salespeople knew the prices. Things not accomplished quickly had a tendency to get on my nerves and I knew that we had to get that jewelry to our customers who were clamoring for it. My expert almost had a complete collapse. I said, "The hell with it," and let him go.

The retailing business is a nervous kind of business because it's made up of people who want things created yesterday and who don't want to wait around a week for things to happen. At Joseph Magnin that maxim was doubly true. We were looked on as crazies by people in our own field. We'd sometimes get new people in the company from other organizations and our form of anarchy confused them at first. They never knew to whom to report. But for the most part we preferred to get our own young people and train them. A lot of my personal success has to do with the loyalty that I and Joseph Magnin engendered in these people. I realized that what might move one person to action would have stymied another. I tried to treat my people as individuals, catering to their individual problems. It was a lesson I learned long ago from my father. I remember we had a terrific lingerie salesgirl but she was taking little things home with her—it was employee pilferage. Joe looked at me and said, "What if I hired a girl who was scrupulously honest who couldn't sell a damned thing?" We had a good salesperson and we let her take things that didn't amount to much because she made up for it by being a terrific salesgirl.

I do know how to extract the best out of the people who work with me. Often I would use reverse psychology. I would get them mad, perhaps tell them that their ideas were all wet. Perhaps I'd tell a store manager, "You can't run that store." Well, that manager would break her back to prove I was wrong, she was so mad at me. But I knew what kind of competitive spirit she had—what motivated her. Other people needed hand-holding. My son Donald and I were 180 degrees apart in that respect. Donald would want to adhere to a set policy for everyone saying, "Cyril, we're running an organization with 2,000 people; they all punch the clock at 9 A.M. and they punch the clock at 5 P.M. to go home." Well, we had one buyer who was enormously talented. Like Toni Moran before her, one of the conditions of her employment was that she not work on Saturday in a period where every buyer worked on Saturday. She wanted to spend the time with her husband. I just told Donald that "if that's what it takes to keep her—and I need her particular talent in her particular area—then I make the exception."

I was prepared to be enthusiastic and to go along with

137

anyone's good idea as long as that person stuck by his guns regardless of what I said or did. I loved retailing, especially the game of it. Often I would make the meetings between me and the buyers into a verbal tennis match. They would come to me and want me to extend their budgets to include a really hot item. I think that without exception I said no just to see how hard they would fight for what they wanted. We had one buyer in the New York office named Rita Wohlman—a sparkly, beautiful woman who was filled with that high energy that so many New Yorkers have. She bubbled over with enthusiasm and creativity and she was an indefatigable worker. Rita started working for Joseph Magnin in 1946 when she was twenty-three and she stayed twenty-five years. She was another one of those people whom I hired on the spot—and then I didn't see her again for about two years. Rita bought better dresses and she and my daughter Ellen would work together when Ellen went East to market. Ellen must have been twenty-one; Rita, twenty-three—two smart-alecky kids who were, in Rita's words, "scared spitless" with all the big-shot buyers with whom these two upstarts had to compete. Rita and Ellen came to me with a real jazzy item—a five-piece Donegal tweed suit which was very "in" at the moment. It was to retail for $55 and included a coat, skirt, pants, vest and matching cap. I said to them, "It's too much for the money; the customers will never believe it's genuine." They simply wouldn't take no for an answer. I figured that if they had so much faith in their decision, I should back them up, so I gave in. They ordered 1,000 pieces and Joseph Magnin had to eat them . . . which was all right. There isn't anyone in the fashion business who hasn't had a bad call once in a while. The fashion business is a series of mistakes and those who make the fewest will last. There is an old saying that "the mistakes of yesterday are the wisdom of tomorrow." I don't think that either Ellen or Rita ever overbought on an "iffy" piece of bad goods again.

138

Ellen was a whiz at buying. She started following Anna to the markets when she was a teenager and showed extraordinary talent for improvisation. It was her idea to make up velveteen coats in orange, lemon and lime colors. They were fabulous and we couldn't keep them in stock. While everyone else was featuring that particular style coat in dark green, navy and maroon, Ellen went for the brights. She tied up all the fabric and if anyone wanted one of those Life Saver-flavored coats, they had to come to us.

When Rita started with Joseph Magnin back in 1946, we were still having trouble getting in to see resources. Not too much was available to us and we would walk into a showroom and literally have to bluff our way into a solid commitment from a firm which was reluctant to sell us anything lest they incur the wrath of another San Francisco store. Rita was often flying by the seat of her pants; it was up to her to follow my lead. I put her on the spot many times by asking her to tell our prospective resource how much we'd spent at one of his rivals—when we hadn't spent a dime. She'd make up a figure and I'd agree—something outlandish like $100,000—and soon we'd have our order, mostly because the supplier didn't want to be bested by his competitor. Often white lies were the order of the day . . . and I wasn't the only one who indulged in them.

One afternoon Rita and I were having lunch with Charles Revson, the creative mind behind Revlon beauty products. It was before Charlie had become king of the hill. Rita and I had a 2:30 curtain for a Broadway show and as we were sitting at the table, Charlie said to me, "Well, I might put $2 million into this project," and I countered with a mythical $3 million of my own. We bullshitted each other through the lunch hour. Rita interrupted us by informing me that we'd be late if we didn't leave, but I was enjoying myself so much with Charlie that I suggested that I would meet her after the show. Rita didn't have cab fare and I looked in my pockets for money and had none. I said to Revson, "Charlie, do you have a five?" After shooting the breeze about millions and millions of dollars, neither one of us big shots had a dime to give her.

Charles Revson was a tough guy and a brilliant merchandiser. He had a great sense of loyalty for anyone who helped him out, but if he wanted to play rough, he could be mean. As I recall, he was in the dress business at one time. He recognized the importance of women using liquid nail polish and developed the rest of his business from there. He could see change coming and was always on the bandwagon ahead of everyone else. He had a lot of courage and knew the direction in which he was going. No one laster longer (although he's dead now) because of the strong foundation he laid for his business. I respected him, but I don't think I was ever as tough as he was. I could scream and holler and carry on—often it was one big act just to test some of my employees—but I don't think I had the reputation for toughness or ruthlessness with which some people had labeled Revson.

Like Charlie, however, I was extremely loyal to people we'd worked with for years. Some of them had been kind to us when no one else would be. I'd ask Rita, for instance, how's so-and-so's line? She'd say, "Mr. C., it's awful." But I'd tell her to buy something from him. We must have had twenty of those companies running around. But I could never pass up the line whether it was good or bad because of my loyalty to them. Those people gave me credit when they shouldn't have; money can't buy help like that. But every manufacturer has his ups and downs—it's the history of the fashion business. Sometimes a company lost a designer and then the line would get out of touch with the current fashion. What we did was to buy a few things out of loyalty, but it wasn't charity. We didn't just stop there. We told them what they could do to improve their line, not just take an order because they were nice to us when we needed them. In many cases they took our advice.

I had confidence in all of my people, especially the buyers. They worked very hard, particularly around market time. We had a suite at the Essex House in New York, and then at the Hampshire House, and during market we'd work until three or four in the morning seeing salesmen and writing orders. We'd invite the salesmen to bring their lines directly to the hotel room and the buyers would see them at any time of the day or night. On Saturdays and Sundays the women in the buying office—Rita and Selma Gross and Ellen when she came East—would be writing orders in their bathrobes. On off-season our New York buyers relaxed, sometimes playing hooky if things were slow. They deserved it. But they didn't do it in season.

Rita went from being a buyer to being a scout. She didn't buy as much as look for new resources. She and Al Duarte would go in to see a new fashion house and if the line looked good, they'd send a buyer in to buy it. That would give us two opinions—one from the fashion office and one from a buyer. The buyers couldn't possibly cover every available house and when they had to go to markets in Los Angeles, Dallas and Chicago in addition to New York, it became impossible to do it well. I think it's hard enough for a conscientious buyer to see his or her regular resources and do it well. It takes an hour and a half to view the line modeled and another two hours or so to pick out the things you want—a minimum of a half-day to service just one resource. Al, Selma and Rita as our fashion scouts saved us not only man-hours, but money, too, because they found us the hot resources, and in the long term we had merchandise that moved and took fewer markdowns.

There's a momentum that goes with this business and when manufacturers and designers know you've got it, they'll want to be on the bus with you. What we were doing was to become a self-fulfilling prophecy. The more we were successful in spreading the JM message—fashion at a price for the young at heart—the more people wanted to be in our corner.

141

Excellence greets excellence. For instance, *Glamour* and *Mademoiselle* were the hot, young fashion books and we started accumulating credits. We were the only store in San Francisco carrying the kind of merchandise featured in those magazines. We were definitely making our own rules. Rodeo Drive didn't exist in those days as it does now and there was only one other store cross-country who had the kind of fashion hipness we were exhibiting—Neiman-Marcus. It was a terrific thing for a manufacturer to be in a Joseph Magnin ad because the ads were so spectacular. They got noticed. But a dress house or a shoe company would have been hard-pressed to find his logo in a prominent position. Our artists wanted not to advertise a particular company, but an idea. It took us a while to train our resources not to expect prominent display of their label.

The same went for our seasonal catalogues. We didn't sell a page in the catalogue for the sake of getting it paid for. It wouldn't have done us any good to have merchandise that wouldn't sell or wouldn't support our image. We wanted to sell goods and the catalogue was the vehicle. We picked the items first and then contacted the manufacturer about being in the catalogue. If they didn't want to give us the item *we* wanted, we told them we'd go to the competition. We never dictated; we never forced them to do it—that would have been illegal. Instead, we said, "If you *want* to do it our way, we'd be glad to consider putting you in our catalogue." We finally got to the point where each of our manufacturers knew what our policy was. We had a few more stores then and had more buying clout. It was the same policy we used in asking a company to sell to us exclusively—when the Federal Trade Commission outlawed confining goods as a restraint of trade, we found a legal way to do it. We would tell a company that we would take 100 of a certain item as long as we didn't find it in another store. But we never put it in writing. We simply said that if they wanted to sell another store, we wouldn't take the item. We wanted exclusivity, but we stayed on the right side of the law. It was also a question of how badly they wanted to be in our stores or in our catalogues. I'm sure had those companies found some store to give them a larger order, they'd have dropped us like a hot potato.

With Toni Harley, Rita Wohlman, Al Duarte, Marget Larsen, Betty Brader, Ellen, Donald and the rest of our kiddie corps, we established Joseph Magnin as the most exciting store in the nation. Growth brings change and we couldn't stay as we had been—a loosely organized, highly energetic place in which ideas had free reign. Toni married a man named John Harley whose business took him to Stockton. When she left us in 1955, it was a very sad day. We gave her a marvelous surprise party at the Fairmont Hotel. Everyone wore a hat Al designed that had something to do with advertising. Donald pinned a Stockton city limit sign on the back of his suit—the type which lists every fraternal order in town from Moose to Shrine to Rotary Club; and Ellen, who was pregnant with her first child, wore an amusing banner to remind Toni of a private joke they shared about their mutual run-ins with a member of my staff with whom they fought continuously. I had on a crown of flowers that lit up like a Christmas tree in the dark and when Toni walked into the party, all she could see was this ghostly face illuminated by twinkly little lights. Our arguments had been legend, so a parody of "Anything You Can Do, I Can Do Better" was sung for our benefit. To this day, I doubt if anyone could have done things better than Toni.

Al left us twice—once to go to New York to work for Condé Nast's publications and then again, for good, to open up his own modeling agency. I knew we couldn't keep someone like Betty Brader forever. She married and is now Betty Ashley. She lives with her husband, also an artist, in

143

Carmel and freelances. Marget quit to go into her own design business and has been responsible for designing packages for national companies.

It is to my credit that I recognized their talent and let them alone, but it was their talent, drive and ability that built Joseph Magnin into a young fashion leader and established a niche all our own. I am thrilled when I look back and realize what we accomplished, but I am reluctant to get too swellheaded, preferring to remember a Shakespearean quote from *Julius Caesar* that the old professor, Mr. Rogers, shoved down my throat:

> But 'tis a common proof,
> That lowliness is young ambition's ladder,
> Whereto the climber-upward turns his face;
> But when he once attains the upmost round,
> He then unto the ladder turns his back,
> Looks in the clouds, scorning the base degrees
> By which he did ascend.

So said Brutus to Lucius about Julius Caesar—and I never wanted the same thing that happened to Caesar—to be so out of touch with reality that it kills you—to happen to me.

CHAPTER EIGHT ❧

Joseph Magnin III— Building an Empire

❧ IN THE EARLY 1940S Joseph Magnin began seeing itself as a true fashion independent and started buying, promoting and selling what came to be recognized as that special JM flair. Suddenly we realized that the United States was becoming a nation of young people, not necessarily in years, but in thinking. We became conscious that women were beginning to color their hair; using more make-up; dieting and exercising to improve their figures. They were thinking in terms of youth. At that point, we also colored our thinking. We changed the make-up of Joseph Magnin; we lost the weight of years and we exercised our brains. We changed our entire merchandising, promotion and advertising policies.

In the years following the changeover in 1937 from trying to copy the more established San Francisco store, we did a lot of exciting things. We searched the markets for a new kind of fashion—contemporary, trend-setting and youthful. We incorporated brilliant colors, not only in our advertising and

145

window displays, but in the store itself. We often adhered to a
central theme throughout the store from first to top floors.
During the mid-sixties, for instance, at the height of the
flower-child-psychedelia craze, Joseph Magnin went theatri-
cally psychedelic with vividly painted walls, mini-skirted
salesgirls, Peter Max-style surrealistic ads and in-store
graphics with merchandise to suit the times like Rudi
Gernreich's topless bathing suit (I may have been the first
merchant in the country to buy it, feature it and sell it), paper
dresses and textured stockings. I was quoted in *Newsweek* at
the time saying, "We're dedicated to trying not just the new
but the unheard of." The effort paid off. Joseph Magnin sales
jumped from $17 million in 1957 to $47 million in 1967. As
the *Newsweek* article put it, "The idea behind the complex go-
go Magnin empire is quite simple: sell youth because that's
where the action is and put everything you've got into doing it."

We did not arrive at that exalted place overnight. It was
seat-of-the-pants flying all the way. Most of the credit for our
good press and national reputation for being an innovative,
exciting store came from our advertising department. As they
created our image on paper, we received many awards for
their excellence, including the William Randolph Hearst
Award for Newspaper Advertising and the Client of the Year
award from both the New York and San Francisco Art
Director Clubs. And we also received the prestigious Gold
Cut Award from *Retail Advertising Week,* a trade publication.
Writing in the 1970 Gold Cup edition which featured a
twenty-year retrospective of our advertising, M. Seklemian,
the chairman of the Gold Cup Committee, wrote:

> To receive *Retail Advertising Week's* Gold Cup, a store
> must do many things. The advertising must not only be
> the kind of advertising the trade admires, but it must also
> be admired by the people and be the topic of conversation

in the homes of customers. It must not only be an example of outstanding advertising craftsmanship, but it must have demonstrated this leadership over many years.

Technically, the Gold Cup winner must be doing a beautiful job. Every ad, every day, has to be excellent, a shining example of good copy and good graphics. But customer response has to be excellent, too. Store management must be able to say, "our advertising has been an important factor in our continuing growth."

Finally, the Gold Cup winner's advertising must interpret the store. It has to be an unquestionable demonstration of what the store stands for, a daily appeal to the particular audience to which the store seeks to sell.

In all respects Joseph Magnin qualifies. JM's advertising over the years has had an amazing consistency. It has never deviated from its basic precept: To be a true reflection of the kind of store it is, and to constantly reach out to the particular Joseph Magnin customer.

There may be those in retailing who do not admire or understand Joseph Magnin's advertising. Older generations, perhaps, who think JM advertising is bizarre and hard to take. If this be so, JM couldn't care less. If the "squares" of the world, the "over 30" people, don't like what they see in the newspapers, the men and women at Joseph Magnin would consider it a compliment. This store is for the now generation, the aware ones who know where they are going, and in Joseph Magnin, they've found a store in their groove.

Perhaps Seklemian capsulized exactly what the Joseph Magnin ad department had tried to do from the time that Anabel Hagyard and Ginny Sisk walked into my office and turned the image of our store around. And I must reiterate that at the time, with the exception of perhaps Neiman-Marcus in Dallas and Bloomingdale's in New York, we were the only store in the country which was lively, youth-oriented and totally in a class by itself. It always amazed me that it took so long for other retail operations to catch up with us—and as old Kipling said in the quote which became my watchword, "They copied all they could follow, but they couldn't copy my mind/And I left 'em sweating and stealing a year and a half behind."

Meanwhile, in addition to the many awards our advertising department was winning, I was snagging a few myself as president of Joseph Magnin. With Ann gone, I felt I had to work for two and was clocking ten-hour days that started at 8:30 A.M. and ended after 6:30 P.M., either in a meeting two or three times a week, or at a civic function. By this time Jerry was in college and I was spending more of my time on civic and political matters. But our merchandising programs were not escaping my retailing peers. In 1950, for instance, I was awarded a trade "oscar" from the San Francisco Manufacturers and Wholesalers Association along with other outstanding San Francisco merchants. I was also chosen Retailer of the Year in 1962 by the National Association of Women and Children's Apparel Salesmen and received the same honor in 1964 from the Southern California Fashion Industry Club of Cedars-Sinai Hospital at the First International Fashion Festival in Las Vegas. I accepted on behalf of everyone at JM who created our wild, wonderful and very *profitable* image.

As we started to get awards from trade-related organizations, we also started getting excellent press, not only in *Women's Wear Daily,* but also in publications like *Mademoiselle* and *Glamour,* two fashion magazines aimed at our target audience. For a while we were getting many picture credits for featured merchandise because, frankly, we were one of the few stores in the country that specifically handled youth-oriented clothes. Our kiddie corps of young artists and our fresh advertising style made *Look* magazine as early as June, 1948, in an issue with a striking pose of a young Lauren Bacall on the front. The article showed a picture of Toni Moran with one of our artists, Vivienne Blanquie, with the headline: HOW COEDS SEE THEMSELVES. The copy read, "The Joseph Magnin store newspaper ads feature lean-shanked, lank-haired campus queens cavorting in the clothes they want to sell. Some four years ago, astute store president Cyril Magnin entrusted his advertising to two young girls in Shetland coats and the successful format they evolved has been making dollars and sense ever since."

We were riding the crest of success with our San Francisco store. Our national reputation was assured even though we were known mainly as a West Coast organization. Although we had established two "twig" stores, one in Palo Alto and the other in Reno, Nevada, as early as 1928 and 1940, respectively, we started branching out in earnest in the late 1940s and early 1950s. But to be absolutely truthful, the first time I ever discussed the concept of the branch store with a friend I didn't think the idea was so hot.

When Ann and I moved to Sea Cliff, I would walk to work with a young attorney named Marvin Lewis, who was to become famous in San Francisco for defending, successfully, a young woman who claimed that a fall from a moving cable car turned her into a nymphomaniac. I think he got a record million-dollar judgment for her. I first met Marvin when he was working in Leon Samuels's office, and we became not only close friends, but associates in our civic work. Marvin was a tall, friendly looking man with a long, open face, a terrific smile and heavy John L. Lewis (no relation) eyebrows that turned quite imposing with age. Young Marvin was a crusader and original thinker. He was to become a city supervisor and worker for causes, some of which were not always popular. Back in the late 1920s we would start our morning jaunt to work at 29th and Lake Streets, rain or shine. It was about an hour and a half stroll that took us over to and down California Street, paralleling the cable car tracks over Russian and Nob Hills. We would pick up Leon Samuels at

149

Hyde and California, and once over Nob Hill at Stockton Street I would turn off and go to the store while Marvin and Leon would continue down the hill to their respective offices.

We discussed all sorts of things during those morning constitutionals—from city politics (and it was noted in a very early Herb Caen column in the *San Francisco Chronicle* that perhaps more city policy was originated on those walks than in the mayor's chambers), to major-league sports, to a plan for a nine-county commuter railway which eventually found itself realized by our five-county Bay Area Rapid Transit System (BART) and, of all things, to the future of the branch store. On one of our morning walks, Marvin noticed an enormous vacant lot at the corner of Presidio Avenue and California, the present site of Fireman's Fund Insurance. Marvin suggested to me that perhaps I should think about building a Joseph Magnin branch there or someplace like it, and at the time I thought his idea wouldn't work. First of all, San Francisco had a workable public transportation system and downtown wasn't all that difficult to get to. Geographically San Francisco is a huge fist of land that covers only 47 square miles, set on seven hills, like Rome. It was a city of neighborhoods with a central downtown area second to none in the entire country for art galleries, theater, restaurants and fabulous shopping. The city had a marvelous cachet—it was a very special place and was known in cities as far away as Portland, Oregon, and Los Angeles as "The City." All people needed was the slightest excuse to come to San Francisco to shop. People could make a day of it, a family outing, and come to The City for luncheon and shopping. Besides, I felt at the time that there wasn't enough demand in the outlying areas for any depth of stock in a branch store when the buying habits of the times dictated that people were used to shopping downtown. In a larger city, one in which the downtown was more inaccessible, yes, perhaps a neighborhood branch not five miles distant from the central shopping area might have worked. At the time I disagreed with Marvin, but ultimately I came to believe in the concept. As I mentioned, we did have a "twig" store in Palo Alto which had originally been called Donnell's, to match the small Grant Avenue store that eventually was closed. It wasn't until the 1940s that Joseph Magnin started to grow more than just twigs. We developed a network of fashion-conscious stores from Reno, Sacramento and Lake Tahoe in the north to Santa Barbara, Ventura, Century City, Palm Springs and Las Vegas in the south—an empire of thirty-two shops by the end of 1969.

I. Magnin had begun branching out in the mid-1920s, but they located their stores in the "Golden Ghettoes" of the very rich, catering to the carriage trade in communities like Santa Barbara and Beverly Hills. We had smaller stores that were true suburban shops in which we aimed our merchandise at the suburban customer. Right after the war the suburbs started to grow at an amazing rate. San Francisco started losing population to outlying areas where there were yards and playgrounds and rambling houses for children to grow up in. The move away from the cities was a nationwide trend. Bedroom communities sprang up in areas around San Francisco in the East Bay, on the Peninsula, in Marin and Contra Costa counties. Major highways were under construction and the suburban dweller discovered that it was difficult, at best, inconvenient, to come to San Francisco to do her shopping on a regular basis.

We geared our suburban stores to that shopper, offering her just about everything she needed or could get in the downtown store. We didn't load any of our branches with merchandise that people would generally come to the city for, like opera clothes. If a woman wanted to buy a dress for the opera or for a very special occasion, she knew she could find a larger selection in the city at stores like Saks, I. Magnin, Maison Mendessolle, etc. (She wasn't usually our customer, anyhow.) But if a woman wanted to buy a summer dress, we

151

had it. We didn't carry certain things in the inventory because the stores just weren't large enough and the risk, in the beginning, was too great. We had to use our floor space with great economy and put in merchandise we could move.

We did, however, understand that to attract the suburban customer, we were not going to have to compete with the San Francisco store. Our stores stood as entities, servicing the communities in which they were located. As my son Donald put it, "The easiest way to encourage people to come to the city is to give them skeleton stocks in the branches." In other words, I gave the Joseph Magnin suburban customers a reason for *not* coming to the city. They recognized they could find as much of the merchandise that suited their area in the branches as they could have in the downtown store. (I must say that it took a little time to educate the suburban customer as to what we had to offer in our branch stores. It was often very frustrating to Donald, for instance, when he was managing the Sacramento store. He would ask a customer, "Where did you get that dress?" and she would say, "I got it in The City," meaning in San Francisco. He would have the exact item hanging in his stockroom.)

Eventually I realized that the suburban store was an *essential* part of our present and projected pattern of living. Our outlying stores did not take business away from the downtown or parent store because of the concentration of customers in the suburban area who weren't shopping in the city anyway.

Before we opened a new store, we wrote letters to the residents of the community to find out what type of shop and merchandise they wanted. We had amazingly good response and patterned our stores accordingly. In Palo Alto, for instance, we learned that our Stanford-oriented customers wanted sportswear, not formal dresses. In Reno our JM woman wanted the extremes in casual dressing—riding habits and jeans for the hot summers and ski clothes and sweaters for the snowy Sierra winters. The same buyers purchased clothing for all of our stores, keeping merchandise standards high. Those buyers also kept in mind the specific needs of the area for which they were buying.

When my father opened Joseph Magnin at Stockton and O'Farrell in 1918, the store incorporated two 50-by-100-foot floors in a six-story location which, by the mid-fifties, had expanded to include the entire building and 55,000 square feet. We went into Palo Alto in 1928 because of the college town market. It was the first time in Northern California history that a woman's specialty shop moved into a suburban area, and it set the pattern for future moves by JM in years to come. It was in 1940 that we opened our second branch and our first out-of-state store, in Reno, Nevada. It was my father's friend, Jean Blum, who suggested that we do so. My father was very conservative and didn't like the idea of going far away from home. In fact, every time we opened another store, until the day he passed away, he *never* liked the idea and expressed his displeasure by throwing up his hands and telling me that I was crazy.

Jean Blum had been a longtime friend of my father's. He was a man of medium build with luxuriant salt-and-pepper gray hair which he combed straight back off his forehead. He had a prominent nose and his ears were large and stuck out from his head like Clark Gable's. He had heavy eyebrows which curled lazily over his warm, gentle eyes. His was a kindly face, an uncomplicated, almost nondescript face. Jean was a silent kind of gentleman. When Toni, Ginny and Anabel were quartered in his offices, Toni often said that she didn't think Jean liked any of them that much because he never spoke to them. But Jean was a very shy, nondemonstrative kind of person who was economical with his words. His opinions were never given in haste and small talk was anathema to him. Like Leon Samuels, Jean was one of the few men in my life to whom I looked for advice. I considered him very much a mentor. He was as loyal and dedicated to me as he had been to my father.

Jean had been born in Rumania and was self-educated. He and I would talk by the hour about business and politics. He had an enormous direct-mail business and mailed the bills for PG&E and the telephone company. He also did direct mailings for political campaigns. Because of this billing service, he became conscious of the high percentages of telephones in the residences in Reno and he interpreted from that that there must be a pretty affluent group of people living there if they all had phones. It wasn't so common to have a telephone in the 1930s because during the Depression not too many folks could afford it. Jean came to me and said that we should open a store in Reno. I told him we didn't have enough money and he said he'd put up half. The initial investment was $50,000, half of which Jean paid. We closed the deal with a handshake. There was never any contract in writing. We started a separate corporation called Specialty Shops, Inc., for which we used the Joseph Magnin name. I think we probably made back our original investment within the first few years because Reno was ripe for our kind of operation. When Joseph Magnin planned to go public in 1958, it was necessary that the family own all of its stores, including the half of the Reno operation that Jean owned. I went to explain the situation to him and he asked, "What do you think is a fair price?" I named a figure, he countered and modified the sum a bit and said, "That's it." Again we shook hands and closed the deal. He was a most honorable man.

The Reno store, as I've said, was a gold mine—an excuse to mint money. Reno then was the divorce capital of the United States and was filled with women who had money to spend who were waiting out their six-week residency requirement for the state. Of course, the Magnin name didn't hurt us a bit, but if it wasn't for Jean, we couldn't have capitalized on any of it. We had no competition in Reno and, at the time, it

154

was the most profitable store per square foot we had. Jean's loyalty to my father and me, coupled with his faith in our ability to be successful, put us there. Of course, he was well-rewarded for his investment.

Our Palo Alto and Reno stores were so successful that we opened a third store in San Mateo in 1942. The war halted any further expansion until 1946 when we went into Sacramento, the California state capital, where we had a built-in clientele of young women who worked in the state bureaucracy. The store cost $400,000 and was 30,000 square feet of selling space. Then we went into Oakland in 1948, moving the store in 1951 to a downtown site occupied by Lindburgh's, a fine fashion store which catered to a more conservative customer than we did. We also took over a Lindburgh store in the Claremont Hotel in Berkeley. In 1950 two other stores were built, each of them unique. The first was a summer-only resort store in Lake Tahoe on the California-Nevada line in Cal-Neva. We catered to our customer who wanted to be able to shop JM when she was on vacation. It was an unusual store—literally a tent, a gaily-striped coral-and-white one that rose up twenty-eight feet over a permanent concrete slab floor. It was fitted with removable glass windows, and in the winter the canvas and windows were put away and only the native fir supports and the concrete foundation remained to bear the cold Tahoe winters.

The other store, while more conventional in design, was our first shopping-center store in the Town and Country Shopping Center on the outskirts of Sacramento. It was here that we offered for the first time the same merchandise in the suburban store that we had in the downtown San Francisco area. Our growth rate put us in Berkeley, Modesto, Walnut Creek and San Jose. We also opened another shop called JM for Juniors in Palo Alto near Stanford. But in 1956 we consolidated our Stanford junior store and Palo Alto locations with a Victor Gruen–designed store which was striking architecturally. It had a circular staircase, live plants, pastel walls and cylindrical little shops, echoing the shape of the staircase. These shops were forerunners of little boutiques. The junior store, however, was designed specifically for juniors only—the Stanford collegiate crowd—and like so many of our new ideas, it was innovative and very successful.

In January, 1957, we broke ground for our Las Vegas store. Again it was Jean Blum who told us that it would be like mining gold in the streets to locate there—not only because of the gamblers, tourists and their wives and girlfriends, but because the people who worked the casinos had no major stores for their shopping needs. It always amazed me that no other companies came to Las Vegas with sizable stores until very recently. Still, at the time, it did seem strange to go into a town where time was upside-down and where there were slot machines in the airport and no clocks in the casinos. Most of the action in Las Vegas began after midnight.

Appropriately Las Vegas was called our "lucky thirteen" store, and just as appropriately we opened it in a burst of fireworks at 1:15 A.M., August 31, 1957. The store had cost a half-million dollars and was located adjacent to the Desert Inn. For the opening we had TV's Uncle Miltie, Milton Berle, emcee the festivities. Jane Powell, a musical-screen star and Las Vegas headliner, cut a twenty-foot, four-inch-wide satin ribbon to let in the public and our invited guests. Two days before the opening the store was a mess. We were flying our buyers and department heads down to put out the merchandise and to set up the store, but carpets weren't laid and some of the walls weren't even painted. It was symptomatic every time we opened a new store, but in this case, to hurry the process, I came in early and brought the workers some whiskey and beer to "help" them finish the job. I think that the carpet was still being put down in the fitting rooms as the celebrants were coming through the front door.

We chartered a plane from New York and for the opening

flew in some of the country's leading designers, including Oleg Cassini, Herbert and Beth Levine, Harvey Berin, Herbert Sondheim and my dear and talented sister-in-law, Adele Simpson. Four famous high-fashion models were met at the Las Vegas airport by the sheriff, his posse and a Brinks truck. The girls were to slink out of the back of the armored car at the appointed time wearing $2,500,000 worth of fabulous furs and jewels—in 100-degree heat. The stunt had been dreamed up by Al Duarte, our fashion coordinator, and he was panicked at the thought of opening up the back of the truck to find four fabulously garbed human french fries expired in a heap of expensive finery. Everything went off without a hitch and the models and Al survived. We had flown in guests from all over the country, including, of course, our own buyers and executives from San Francisco, each of whom was given a silver dollar and a bag full of quarters for gambling. We had a gala dinner at the Sands Hotel and then with champagne running like water, we had our ribbon-cutting ceremony and opened the store. The public was so enthralled and probably so well-oiled by the fountains of bubbly and the late hour, that some of them took the new shoes off the displays and drank their champagne out of them.

We were right about Las Vegas. We had very free-spending customers there. On one occasion I saved the biggest customer we had. She used to come in and spend two or three thousand a month with us—on credit. During one billing period the credit department mistakenly sent her a letter and told her she was over her limit. This gal probably could have bought our company and wouldn't have even missed the money. She wrote me a letter, threatening to close her charge account if I didn't do something. To make amends I sent her a magnificent floral arrangement and flew her and her husband up to San Francisco for dinner. By the time I got through with them, they really believed in the company.

We always did our best to please our customers. If any of

157

them were overdue on their bills, we enclosed, not official-sounding letters, but pastel-colored notes with funny cartoon characters on them and a cute verse—a soft-sell, gentle nudge to remind them that they owed us money. We also instituted a preferred customer charge card called the 24 Karat Club. It was a promotional gimmick, a charge account with no limit issued to celebrity customers in the form of a gold charge plate. We had opened stores in Southern California by that time—Canoga Park, Ventura and then finally, in 1965, Century City in Los Angeles on the old backlot of Twentieth Century Fox. We issued cards there for actresses, producers' wives, studio heads and their wives, selected press and civic leaders. We had sent a card to gossip columnist Hedda Hopper and Donald received a note from her which said, "I couldn't have been more delighted to have a membership in your 24 Karat Club. I have never had a gold credit card before; I shall carry it and use it with great pride. Can't wait for your opening in 1965 and you can wager, I'll be one of your best customers." As I remember, Hedda *was* a good customer. I must emphasize that JM was the complete innovator. Most of our original ideas such as the preferred customer, the Wolves' Den for men, our Christmas boxes, our advertising and our small boutiques within the main store were later copied by other stores nationwide . . . but to my knowledge, we were the first stores to use and promote those ideas.

During those years of expansion we also went into small, conveniently located stores in towns throughout California and Nevada. To Walter Newman fell the task of finding and obtaining good locations and excellent leases for us. Jerry and Donald both expressed to me that we were expanding into nowhere, but it was a calculated decision on my part to go where we could maximize profit and minimize expenses. I told Walter what I wanted—no minimum rent and a fixturized deal. I wanted to put the company's money into merchandise and promotion instead of dead assets. Joseph Magnin had an electricity about it that people liked. We were very much in demand and we took the approach that we didn't want to get into the typical (and usually expensive) leasing situation—ones that included only the shell of a store that we would have to outfit ourselves. We simply did not have the money to expand in the way we wanted *and* outfit a store from the floors up.

We had had a few outstanding successes like Sacramento, Reno and Stonestown in suburban San Francisco which convinced developers that Joseph Magnin was a star in terms of volume of sales, rents realized, numbers of customers attracted and quality trade—all the things that a developer wants for his shopping center. In that way we could convince a prospective landlord to write a lease for us for the percentage of the gross with either no minimum or very low minimum rent. In return he would not only build the store but would equip it with furniture, fixtures, carpets, drapes, and in a few places, merchandise and the hangers. What they got in return was an exciting anchor tenant. Their gamble was that they would get a substantial rent *without* a guaranty. But JM was a proven winner with a good reputation. Still, it required a lot of cash flow and investment capital for the developers to swallow that tough a deal. We were able to make the deals because Walter was a very tough negotiator.

Perhaps those leases, as Don and Jerry thought, were not good for the long-term health of the company. We did not go into major out-of-state markets because they were much too expensive to get into—expensive, that is, at the time we were expanding. Perhaps we could have postured ourselves better had we opened in Chicago, Houston, St. Louis, Washington, Denver or eventually New York. But, at the time, we didn't.

Long before a group of Joseph Magnin stores became a reality, I recognized the fact that a multiple operation would require policies and techniques never needed in a single, independently operated store. The time-tested methods of single-store operation became hopelessly antiquated as buyers were faced with the complex problems of merchandise distribution. I realized that additional merchandise records would have to supply the missing contact with customers' wants if the basic character of the stores was to remain unchanged. Long before automation became an accepted form of accounting and merchandise control, I was studying ways to mechanize. I realized that we had to institute an electronic data processing system—a computer—for a complete tabulation of each store function from buying merchandise to keeping track of it (unit control) to accounting and customer billing. The system was set up by the Remington Rand Corporation with the help of our comptroller, a woman named Zelva McMilan, who came to me through Toni Moran Harley.

Zelva, or Mac as we were to call her, started working part-time for Toni, posting advertising bills on Saturdays. I walked in one weekend to find her in Toni's office and I asked her what she was doing. I liked her looks and her forthright manner and I hired her full-time. The personnel director was upset. She said, "You don't know anything about this woman. She's just down here from Portland and she hasn't even filled out an application." When I learned she was a C.P.A., I hired Zelva as an internal auditor where she worked for eight months and then I named her our comptroller. The male accountants were disturbed when I promoted her. One or two of them left. But Zelva knew accounting. She was extremely loyal to me and to the store and she was creative and innovative. I like to keep people like that working close to me. They are helpful with new ideas and original thinking whether they be gifted in fashion merchandising or in accounting. Creativeness in business is one of the most important aspects of a successful enterprise.

I realize that the words "creative accounting" have come

160

to mean under-the-table dealings these days, but when I hired Zelva, her creativity was not only legal, it was to be far-reaching in the entire retailing industry. As for myself, I tried always to be scrupulously honest—something I learned from my father. Zelva was always getting after me to report to the IRS any business expenses like long-distance phone calls or entertainments for clients that I incurred at home. I consistently refused and once during an audit the poor Internal Revenue agent couldn't believe that he couldn't find anything wrong. He said I was "too honest."

Zelva McMilan was certainly qualified to be comptroller. She was extremely professional and circumspect in her approach to her job. Zelva didn't like loose ends. For the first couple of years she was with me, I'm not sure she liked me. I had shown her my very worst side when she first came with us by flying into rages and arguing at the drop of a hat. Zelva, a mild-mannered woman who was completely ladylike, was shocked. She'd never been in a work atmosphere as charged as ours in her life.

Zelva had grown up in Oregon and had worked for six years for Price Waterhouse, a national accounting firm. She received her C.P.A. by passing a proficiency test because she didn't have a college education. She had worked for the Janzen Knitting Mills right before coming to San Francisco. She quit her job and wanted to see some of the country, and was working odd jobs to support her wanderlust when I met her.

Zelva was the kind of person I like the best—a bright self-starter. In spite of her initial distrust of my methods, she stuck it out. It was trial by fire, because I didn't believe in spending money foolishly and had to be convinced every step of the way that she was dedicated to the task at hand. I think that anyone could have developed at Joseph Magnin who showed gumption and initiative. I had no use for a buyer, for instance, who would not try to overbuy. Buyers have to have confidence in themselves. I, in turn, had tremendous confidence in Zelva and began to depend on her judgment about the accounting operation in the store. Toni had noticed that buyers were spending a great deal of their valuable time toting around massive inventory control books in which they had to hand post their transactions. Zelva and I put together an inventory control system that made it easy, when the time came, to mechanize. In some ways, Joseph Magnin operated in a haphazard way—I've called it creative anarchy. For instance, many years in the past, I had an infamous left-hand drawer into which went the bills I couldn't afford to pay, including the newspaper advertising bills which Toni insisted we pay right away to take advantage of a ten percent discount for promptness. I would tell her that I'd paid the bills and then she'd discover them under my blotter or in that left-hand drawer. With Mac around, however, we became very precise in the way that we did business.

In those first two years Mac and I had terrific arguments. She did learn to fight with me—for survival, I think—and once I remember getting into the elevator with her on the first floor and fighting all the way upstairs to the executive offices, getting off at every floor, spatting, and then getting back on the elevator again. The customers got a free show, but we solved our problem by the time we got off on the sixth floor. I often wondered why she just didn't quit, but she had contracted to set up a new accounting system and she didn't want to leave the job unfinished even though I refused to hire an assistant for her. She told me that with some help she could reorganize us in two years. It took her five years all by herself, but she did it. By the time she was finished, she was well dug-in in our corporate structure as a great innovator, peacemaker and leavening agent. When she quit to marry, I sent someone out to buy her something very special and said, "Whatever it is, it has to be solid gold because that's the way we feel about her."

Zelva recognized that the Joseph Magnin stores had to face new and different problems. How much centralization was desirable? It had its obvious advantages in that centralization eliminated duplication, standardized procedures, prevented waste and kept central management informed far better than was otherwise possible. On the other hand, there were inherent problems with centralization of all record-keeping and buying functions. Would it stifle initiative in the separate stores? Would it turn store managers into puppets who were unable to act independently? These questions and more had to be answered in the process of Joseph Magnin's growth from a single store to an important group.

We never knew quite how she did it, but out of Zelva's mysterious Outer Space Department, that region of her offices in which she had installed a creative think tank to figure out all the problems inherent in a multistore operation, she, along with Remington Rand and later, Unitotes, worked out a system of record-keeping that reflected the merchant's view in all of our operations. In many stores, perhaps most in those days, the accounting office was a detached work center that paid invoices, collected bills, maintained historical records and generally had little or no interest in the fundamental problems of merchandising. In all too many businesses there was a widening chasm between the "money people" and the "product people." Office managers and comptrollers regarded themselves as the most important members of the team, shrugging off the unreasonable demands and the "arty" temperaments of the group of buyers, advertising and promotion people. Such was not the case with the system that Zelva and the computer people developed.

I believed that stores were not built primarily for the purpose of buying and selling merchandise and not merely for the purpose of paying bills and sending out statements. It was all interrelated. I considered all records and reports to be the by-products of the basic merchandising records. Certainly,

163

bills of the vendors had to be paid promptly and proper accounting methods had to be maintained. But in the JM concept these operations were corollary to the main function of recording what was purchased from whom and for how much and at what markup. Similarly the payroll department paid employees and maintained the most modern records for the internal revenue, social security and health plans. Again, however, I felt that this was secondary to the maintenance of efficiency records—telling who sold how much and how much of what they sold was returned.

The central office function then was to maintain merchant-inspired records of goods bought and sold by style number, price line, fabric, color and size. The underlying principle started with the purchase order, continued through marking, bill paying, selling, commission, and would extend in the future to the billing of customer accounts. So what we had in reality was three separate accounting systems interlocked on one Univac 120 computer. One was for merchandise and unit control. Another was for accounting and billing our customers, and it included a complete credit history of what they bought and when they paid for it. The third was payroll accounting. Our Univac kept track of the merchandise from the time it was ordered from a vendor to when it was tagged and put out on the selling floor to when it was sold (and sometimes returned) to when the vendor was paid. We developed a four-part sales tag which had punchmarks in it and included not only the garment's identity, size and style numbers, but also a record of when it was received. There were two sections on the sales tag which kept track of when the item was sold the first time, and in the case of returned merchandise when it sold again or when it was marked down. All data was fed into the computer which kept complete records of what was selling and how fast. Every week or two, depending on the department, I would get a printout of the best- and the slowest-selling numbers. It was instant inventory. We were capturing approximately 400,000 transactions monthly and transmitting some of them up to 600 miles from our farthest branch to our headquarters with less than one percent recoverable error in transmission.

To facilitate not only unit control but customer records, we put in a new type of register which was tied into the Univac 120, called the Unitote system—I think we were the first large operation to use it. The Unitote was a point-of-sale recorder, a full-keyboard register, that had been designed specifically for our needs. It captured all the necessary data from the sales tag at the point of sale and gave on-line credit authorization. It saved the customer's time and also that of the salesperson by automatically preparing the salescheck when the correct numbers were punched in. That information went straight into the computer and directly onto the customer's account. Not only were we able to have accurate and instant inventory control, we could update our customer account files on a daily basis furnishing the credit department with timely authorization information and reports on any unusual activity from the previous day. We were also able to bill customers three days after their closing dates.

The computer made all our jobs easier—from the buyers who no longer had to carry around heavy unit control books to Zelva's accounting department which now had precise figures at the end of each day.

Mac was very cognizant of things around Joseph Magnin that had to be done—things that perhaps I didn't take the time to notice. In her department, for instance, were many Asian girls, Japanese and Filipino, who worked on the accounts receivable ledgers and on inventory control. They were tiny little ladies who sat on telephone books on chairs that were scaled far too big for them. Zelva tried many times to get me to buy adjustable posture chairs, but either I didn't have time to talk with her about it or I just didn't want to spend the money. Finally Zelva, finding me in an open and agreeable mood, just about tricked me into spending the $50 per chair that was necessary so those women wouldn't have to perch on phone books. (I absolutely hated waste of any kind and was beset once by a secretary who insisted that I have fresh flowers in my office every day, something which, at the time, I thought was an expensive and frivolous extra, one which I could do without.)

While Mac was one of the most original and efficiency-minded of all my people, she was also one of the most respected and the most loved. We would do just about anything to surprise her and make her happy. Such was the giant cheesecake caper. She loved Lindy's strawberry cheesecake—absolutely adored it. She had eaten it in New York and had talked about it for weeks after. For her birthday, one year, I insisted that Mac have an entire strawberry cheesecake and I turned the New York office upside-down for two days (I'm not sure they got any Joseph Magnin work done at all) trying to find exactly what she loved. The operation seemed to go off without a hitch but it was important that we get exactly what she wanted. The cake had to be strawberry. Blueberry or cherry just wouldn't have done at all. After Zelva had received her birthday treat, a series of memos were issued chronicling the entire project.

TITLE—OPERATION CHEESECAKE

TUESDAY	Dilemma	How to surprise Miss Mac on her birthday
	Flash	Why not a Lindy's strawberry cheesecake? She hasn't stopped yakking about the last piece she had.
	How?	Simple—find someone who had one shipped from New York.
	Panic	*Who* has? No one.

166

When in distress, Father knows best. Wire to Mr. Magnin:

DEAR BOSS—FAVOR PLEASE—NEED ONE LINDYS STRAWBERRY CHEESECAKE THURSDAY AFTERNOON SURE—SURPRISE FOR MACS BIRTHDAY. BILL US WHEN YOU CATCH US. LOVE.

WEDNESDAY   Must have been simple. Request filled with dispatch, as return wire from Mr. "C"

CHEESECAKE ARRIVING UNITED 6:49 A.M. THURSDAY

(A.M.? Amen!!!!!)

THURSDAY   Mad dash to airport to get cake. Stealthy sneak past Mac's door to resting place under assistant's desk. Picked wrong day—Miss Mac very chummy, wishes to discuss all sorts of problems with assistant. Many gray hairs, staff in utter terror smoke will escape from dry ice under desk.

Miss Mac's composure too much for us to take. Let's crack it, drop a few hints. This really cracks her composure—curiosity killing her. Rest of assistant's day spent pinned in corner. Barrage of questions; finally ran out of noncommittal answers.

Result—party successful; Miss Mac very pleased; terrible anti-climax to all confusion. Assistant collapses.

EPILOGUE   We have sworn off strawberry cheesecake for life.

Then in a memo on Joseph Magnin stationery noted from the New York office at 1440 Broadway, I received a "Case History of A Strawberry Cheesecake":

10:00   Telegram

       to Mr. Cyril from Lody and Phoebe

FAVOR PLEASE. STRAWBERRY CHEESECAKE FROM LINDY'S FOR THE BIRTHDAY OF MISS McMILAN TO ARRIVE IN SAN FRANCISCO THURSDAY FOR THE OCCASION.

11:00 Contacted Mr. Irving Gilbert. SOS Please help. Discoveries. Lindy's no longer makes Strawberry Cheesecake. Only plain.

1:00 Mr. Cyril suggests Rubens; advised available but not advisable. This would dissolve into mush on arrival in San Francisco. Suggestions: Cherry, pineapple or plain.

PROBLEMS

1. How to pack so strawberries don't become mush?
2. What time shall cake board plane for pickup in San Francisco Thursday morning?
3. Delivery to plane?

2:00 MUST HAVE STRAWBERRY CHEESECAKE IN SAN FRANCISCO THURSDAY MORNING
(Signed) Cyril Magnin

3:00 Panic Stricken.

Gilbert cannot accommodate. No refrigeration on their plane. Mr. Pierre Desetelle of TWA contacted. Unfortunately he is tied up in conference all afternoon.

4:00 HURRAH. Gilbert comes through. Mr. Bob Huly after 2 hours of telephoning the air lines saves the day. He will buy HOT ice to preserve the STRAWBERRIES. Rubens will pack in tin. Western Union will pick it up and deliver it to Gilbert. Cake driven to Idlewild Airport for Flight 717 to San Francisco by Bob Huly.

THURSDAY: Arrival of cake (I HOPE)

VERY HAPPY BIRTHDAY MISS McMILAN

P.S.   Don't we have a wonderful boss

As large as Joseph Magnin was growing, we never forgot the importance of the individual, whether it was a member of our organization or a customer. Especially the customer. Then, as now, I paid personal attention to every customer complaint. It was the one area that was sacrosanct—completely mine. I got tremendous input from the customer as to why she was dissatisfied. It was physically impossible for me to handle all the complaints myself, but I hired a secretary whose sole job it was to process all customer complaints. To keep the customer happy, she would write a letter pertaining to the complaint over my signature, then she'd analyze the source of the complaint and keep a complete record for the company. There could be many reasons why a customer complained—merchandise that was not up to our standards, an impudent salesperson, a department where customers thought our fashions weren't up to that of our competitors . . . it was all duly recorded and followed to completion. I would have the complaint secretary send the customer complaints on to the department heads and they would put it right.

I can think of one instance that had to do with our Joseph Magnin brand of stockings. We had them made at a mill that specialized in private-label merchandise. Donald found them because he was afraid to have a company like Hanes make our stockings because he knew that if there was ever a squeeze in the supply line that, naturally, Hanes would be making their own stockings and we would not be getting ours. He contracted with the most legitimate, private-label mill in the country. We sold the JM label stockings like crazy—and only by the box, which was $2.95 for three pair of hose. Priced under our competitors, a good product, nicely packaged. They brought customers into the store. All of a sudden I started getting complaint cards across my desk with more frequency talking about defective stockings. Not only were the cards coming from customers, but the store managers, who were also required to fill out complaint cards, were also sending them in.

I decided that we had to do something so I called Donald in and said, "Hey, the complaints on JM private-label stockings are increasing and that's one product that can't be wrong because our name is on it. We can't blame it on a famous maker—these are Joseph Magnin stockings." Well, when we looked into it, we changed suppliers immediately.

I continued to get input about what was happening in our stores, even when we had more than thirty, from those cards. I think that it was probably tantamount to getting fired if a store manager didn't fill them out and follow up.

Joseph Magnin was growing into the image that our advertising department had set. But it wasn't the only one of my "children" to grow into a glamorous and effective maturity. All of my children—Donald, Ellen and Jerry—became proficient merchants in their own right, although each of them was quite different from the other. None had an easy road just because each was the boss's son or daughter. They, like all my creative people, were given their heads as to how they carried on business. And, since they were encouraged in their creativity, they made mistakes and took their lumps accordingly.

There was a time, for instance, about eighteen years ago, when Donald made a bad call on women's blue jeans. Walter Hass of Levi-Strauss came to see me and said that the company was putting in a line of ladies' jeans. He offered JM a six-month exclusive because Levi's liked what we were doing; we had what they wanted—the young female customer. I told him that I would turn him over to Donald because I didn't get involved in the merchandising end of the business to any great extent any more. Donald had a discussion with his assistant, a woman named Marilyn who had also

170

mentioned that blue jeans, Levi's especially, were going to be very big. Donald said, "Marilyn, leave Levi's to Macy's, will you?" And she said, "Sure," and the matter was dropped. Donald says, sardonically, that the nice thing about retailing is that it's insidious. It's almost like cancer. By the time it hurts, it's too late. Don may have zigged when he should have zagged because Levi's for women became all the rage. The one thing I had always tried to teach my children was not to stand in the middle of the street—get to one side or the other. Don't vacillate. If Don chose unwisely, at least he chose. As retailers we all make mistakes and as I've said, those who make the fewest usually are the most successful.

Donald, however, had a sharp eye and wasn't wrong very often. On one buying trip to Europe all he saw in Paris in the streets was the short, short skirt—and the maxi had gone mini. When he came home, he couldn't wait to get our display department to pin up every single dress we had in the windows. Overnight our clothes were *au courant* with the latest fashions coming out of Paris for the with-it woman. But for weeks we didn't have a single short dress in stock.

Jerry learned his lessons also and some of them were a little tougher than just a judgment call on blue jeans. When he was married to his first wife, Gayle, he was in the air force. When he got out of the service, he was assigned to the Cal-Neva store in Lake Tahoe. He had gone into the service right after he married and was away from Gayle for a while. It wasn't very pleasant. It didn't get any better when he got back because he had to put in long hours in the store. Gayle waterskied and Jerry didn't. Now, Jerry is a very competitive person and swore that he'd learn to ski so they could do it together. He took a few days off to learn to ski and every time he did it, I happened to call and would ask, "Where's Jerry?" The answer was: "Out waterskiing." From Cal-Neva Jerry was to have gone to Sacramento, but when the season ended in Tahoe, I called him back to San Francisco where we had a

171

policy meeting with Donald and Walter. I was very harsh on Jerry, probably embarrassed him in front of his brother and his brother-in-law—men who not only taught him to play softball and to box, but who had probably taught him the facts of life. I reminded him that his name was Magnin, that he walked away from a business which bore his name on the door to go waterskiing, and I told him that I was going to put him in the office next to his brother and all he would do for the next two years was to watch and see how a good business was run. In retrospect Jerry says that I was right.

In the later years I tried to give my children and our bright, young executives more self-sufficiency. Often there were jurisdictional squabbles—things I tried to keep out of completely. Ellen, for instance, was making her orange, lemon and lime coats, tying up all the fabric and a small manufacturer to make it especially for JM, and one of our more zealous buyers was also making the same coat, competing with Ellen for the material. The buyer had found some seamstresses in Chinatown who were zipping out the coats—a competition that Ellen felt wasn't good for the store. Another little skirmish pitted Jerry and Donald against each other in the matter of the daisy plates.

Don had started what was to become a very lucrative gift business in the store by putting a few ice buckets on the scarf counter in a year when scarves weren't moving well. Jerry took it over and the gift department became his baby, his pride and joy. He nurtured it, built it and developed it into one of the most exciting parts of Joseph Magnin. Donald at the time was general merchandise manager and, unbeknownst to Jerry, he bought some inexpensive pottery plates in the shape of a daisy. Jerry hated them with a passion because he felt they were, as he put it, "cheap, garbage merchandise." Still, we were selling them like hotcakes. Jerry came back from a buying trip and was told that the plates had sold out and that the branches were screaming for more. Jerry refused

172

to reorder because he felt the merchandise was too shoddy for the Joseph Magnin concept. Donald called Jerry into his office one afternoon and told him that he'd received a memo from the manager of the Palo Alto store, one from San Jose and so on—all asking for daisy plates. We needed at least a thousand pieces to satisfy the demands of our stores. Jerry said, "I think they're garbage," and Donald said to my twenty-three-year old zealot, "Look, young man, don't you ever forget that the final judge of how good or bad anything is in your store is your customer." I always tried to teach that to my children— that not only is the customer always king, he has the final word as to whether we have bought the right merchandise. Though the customer is right, his taste may be terrible—I also taught my children that. (I remember one occasion where Al Duarte had helped us design a raincoat styled along the lines of a French butcherboy's coat. I told Al when the customers had turned us down completely, "The customer has no taste." But they certainly have the money to buy whatever suits them—daisy plates and all.)

The end result of my children working in the store was that three great merchandisers were developed. Perhaps with the genes they inherited from their talented mother and grandmother and even great-grandmother—and, incidentally, from me—they could have become good merchants; but with the experience they gained directly on the firing line, they became *great* merchants.

My children may have been the boss's kids, but they didn't get any favorable treatment. Perhaps I was harder on them *because* they were my children, depriving them of a normal upbringing and making it necessary that they become an integral part of the growth of Joseph Magnin. I think that I am very fortunate. That it is a gift from God that my children have all become excellent in business. When Jerry went to Southern California to run that operation, he developed a menswear business that became second to none. Today, as the proprietor of Jerry Magnin on Rodeo Drive in Beverly Hills, he is the innovator and taste-maker that his great-grand-mother, Mary Ann Magnin, was in her time. My daughter Ellen is the mother of three boys. Her middle son, Robert, died on the first day of Spring, 1981, of brain cancer. She has a successful consumer-oriented consulting business for major corporations. Through her management ability Ellen has become a director of several major companies including the Wells Fargo Bank, Kaiser Aluminum and Macy's San Francisco. Her drive and determination have made her one of the most well-thought-of businesswomen in San Francisco. And Donald, who has two daughters and a son, has opened an import business called Domain Imports at which he is excelling. To get where they are, all of my children had to make their mistakes and learn from them before they got to be any good at what they did.

Joseph Magnin, by 1959, had become a fabulous success. We had to think about the expansion of the business out of California and into major markets. It was necessary to generate some working capital, and as we consolidated all the family stock, we also made plans to go public. I was beginning to do other things once I knew I could turn over the day-to-day operation of the company to my children and to my capable executives. I had to decide—where to, next.

The "Lucky Thirteen" Joseph Magnin store makes its
debut in Las Vegas, Nevada, in January, 1957, with
Jane Powell cutting the ribbon

Three examples of Joseph Magnin's distinctive advertising style—unique in retailing and attention-getters wherever they appeared (BETTY BRADER ASHLEY)

LEFT: *At the White House with President Johnson, July, 1968.* BELOW: *During the unofficial visit of Ambassador Huang Chen of the Liaison Office of the People's Republic of China, a tour of the Napa Valley wine country was on the itinerary. A wine-tasting at Inglenook Vineyards topped it off* (KEN ARNOLD)

Rehearsing for the motion picture Foul Play *with director Colin Higgins*

Is the Pope a Catholic? Not when he's Cyril Magnin, robed for Foul Play, 1977

As chief of protocol for the city of San Francisco, Cyril Magnin gave the Prince of Wales the grand tour on October 28, 1977 (**WIDE WORLD PHOTO**)

Cyril, Bob Hope and a bevy of beauties, 1976, at a U.S.O. dinner in Los Angeles

Cyril and his favorite diva, "Bubbles" Silverman, a.k.a. Beverly Sills

The opera buff with Katia Ricciavelli, Maestro Kurt Herbert Adler and Placido Domingo, 1978

*Magnin and his dog Tippycanoe at the Elegant Cele-
bration of Christmas benefit for the American Conservatory Theater, November, 1979* (RAY DE ARAGON)

*The Magnin Jade Room at the Asian Art Museum in
San Francisco. It is dedicated to his parents and his
late wife, Anna* (FRED LYON)

Cyril and George Burns: The Pope meets God
(GREGG COBBAR)

CHAPTER NINE

Mr. San Francisco, Step One—"I Do Not Choose to Run"

MY FATHER WAS A VERY ASTUTE, conservative businessman who loathed controversy. He did not trust politicians. He felt that if you were in public office, sooner or later, you were going to fall prey to bribery or do something dishonest. Politics, for Joe, meant taking sides, being controversial. In some ways Joe was of a contradictory mind. In his office he had a plaque on the wall which read, "Profit is the by-product of service to the community"; and while service to the community implied getting involved with things and taking a position, it was contrary to what both Joe and most retailers would prefer—keeping a low profile and not taking any kind of stance that would insult and scare away a potential customer. Joe also felt that people who headed civic committees had some kind of motive other than the benefits to the city—dedicated self-interest. He was, therefore, not happy with me when I started to get involved in politics and civic affairs. The most he could extract from me was the promise that I never run for office.

Given the limits placed on my outside interests, I found that my skill was to take the dedicated self-interest of others and use it for the good of the city or for the benefit of some of my political interests, *without* assuming a visible posture myself. In effect I became a kind of political kingmaker. I have often thought about the power that has been ascribed me by others, and all any of us in the political inner circle thought we were doing was taking care of our friends. Naive? Perhaps, but we were very effective.

Very early the powers-that-be found that I was skilled at raising money, and more often than not I was asked to be treasurer of fund-raising either for a political campaign, a bond issue or charitable or civic causes. I seldom took chairmanships in those days because I felt that when you get too far out front, you get vulnerable and lose some of your clout. I did feel that I was adhering to Joe's wishes, that merchandising in private industry was to be my vocation and that public service was to be my avocation. And as long as I was actively involved with Joseph Magnin, that was the way it continued. I intended to keep the two entities separate and time and again, when I was approached to run for office, especially for mayor of San Francisco—something which happened to me with regularity over the years—I, like Silent Cal, said, "I do not choose to run."

In the midst of a traditionally Democratic, heavily Irish-Italian-Jewish-Labor town, I began my political life as a Republican. I've always taken a liberal point of view and in the 1928 presidential election, the cat fight between Catholic Al Smith and Herbert Hoover, I changed my political affiliation because of the prejudice against Smith. The Democrats, also, had traditionally been the party of the young and the disadvantaged, the underdog, and that appealed to me probably because my Grandfather Isaac had always been the champion of the downtrodden—it was in my genes. So, in 1928 I went down to Democratic headquarters and asked if I could help. I was told that I could go out and raise money and ever since, I've been in Democratic politics, helping fill the coffers and ofttimes making policy. Of course, after Joe died in 1953, I could have gone back on my promise to him, but by that time I much preferred playing the role of political powerbroker instead of political candidate.

Throughout my adult life I have tried to be of service, doing those things that were asked of me, whether it was chairing a Jefferson-Jackson Day Dinner, raising monies for earthquake relief, eliciting funds from the city to buy badly needed ambulances . . . or the time I took part in an outrageous stunt when I rode in a horse-and-buggy with two assemblymen and a prominent San Francisco matron trying to call attention to an amendment in the city charter to raise the city supervisors' salaries. I find that today I am loathe to refuse any responsible request for assistance or funds, although there are as many as five or six letters or calls asking for money or aid that come across my desk every day. Back in the late forties and early fifties I acquired a reputation for accepting just about any job, no matter how big or small, if I felt that I could support the project not only with money but time. I was a member of the Draft Review Board during the war, and shortly thereafter, chaired money-raising projects for Ecuadorian and Greek relief, Catholic charities, brotherhood committees—things I believed in. I always made a point of finding out what the funds were going to be used for and I had one rule of thumb: I wouldn't go out and ask anyone for money if I didn't think it was going for a useful purpose or if the monies collected were going to be used mostly for expenses instead of going directly to the cause. I felt that someone must take responsibility and that the greater your stake was in the community, the more responsibility you had to assume.

My fund-raising efforts knew no party lines, although, I must say, I've probably raised thousands of dollars for

Democratic candidates over the years. If I thought that a man was best-suited for the job, he not only got my vote but my full support. I could not in good conscience support Jimmy Carter in his run for the presidency and remember telling a close friend of mine, Bill Moyers, President Lyndon Johnson's former press secretary and host of "Bill Moyers' Journal" on public television, that although I thought Carter was an excellent campaigner, he was not going to be an excellent president. And in both the 1976 and 1980 campaigns, I could not in good conscience support him with either my money or my vote. When I voted for Gerald Ford, it was the first time since before 1928 that I had ever voted for a Republican presidential candidate.

One man who did get both my money and my vote, however, was George Christopher, the mayor of San Francisco from 1956 to 1964. George was Greek-born and came to the United States when he was two. Christopher was a name tagged on him in the first grade when a teacher couldn't spell his father's surname. George's father had an eight-stool hamburger stand in San Francisco and died from years of inhaling greasy hamburger smoke seven days a week, fourteen hours a day, when George was still a boy. George left school at fourteen and went to night school for the next nine years getting a degree in accounting. He never missed a single session. He became an accountant and later bought a broken-down little dairy company for $3,000 which was to become Christopher Dairy Farms, one of the Bay Area's largest independent dairies.

As a Greek George found that he couldn't get a political appointment because of what he called "resentment from entrenched politicians." He ran for city supervisor with no political endorsements from either business, labor or the press. All he had was an army of dedicated people who plastered stickers and posters all over town. He got into office, barely squeaking through, but after that, he gained such a fine reputation as an honest politician that he headed his ticket each time he ran. He made his first run for the mayor's office against Elmer Robinson, the incumbent, and lost by only 1,200 votes. It was such a close election that the outcome wasn't known until the absentee votes were counted. Because he had been beaten by the incumbent by so few votes, George and his people knew that he would make it the next time. He did.

I met George back in 1945 when he was first elected to the Board of Supervisors. He was a stocky man with a powerful, athletic build. He had a full head of wavy hair, a broad, ruddy face and was a strong, handsome man. Today at seventy-four, he looks fifty and has the stamina of one half his age. Anyhow, he was always open and believable. He tried to do everything aboveboard and could be very convincing, which made him one of the most effective politicians I've ever met. He was also very savvy and could be counted upon to come up with the proper response in just about every circumstance. He tells of the time when he was first elected mayor that "the mob" sent a "representative" to feel out the territory—something they did, George explains, with every new mayor. George had the man met at the airport by the chief of police and a couple of uniformed officers who were there to "escort" their visitor around town as a courtesy so that nothing would happen to him. There was a police guard posted outside the man's hotel room around the clock and after days of such personal service, Mr. Mobster took his leave of our fine city.

As president of the Board of Supervisors, it was George's responsibility to appoint various citizens to small committees. I was always interested in "do-good" work, as George called it. Usually, if he needed help or funds, some of the money came from my own pocket. He still calls on me occasionally as in the case of ambulances and medical supplies needed a few years ago in Cyprus. At the time I was heavily involved with

179

my business, and although he offered me many jobs, I wasn't interested in a permanent commission appointment. I managed to evade George, who, as I've said, could be very persuasive. But when George had something big that had to do with extracting money, he called on me. We always got along because we understood each other's thinking, realizing that no one group, no two people can agree on everything.

I have always considered myself a pretty fair negotiator, and in politics I tried to exercise that quality. During my more activist days—especially during the Kennedy and Johnson campaigns—I worked closely with a good friend of mine, Adolph Schuman, chairman of the board and founder of the Lilli Ann Corporation. Adolph, at seventy-two, is a virile, ebullient, almost macho sort whose passion is scuba diving. Adolph sports a year-round tan and is one of the more opinionated charmers extant. We seem to be opposite sides of the same coin. Both Adolph and I were very active in the Jack Kennedy and Bobby Kennedy presidential campaigns . . . but we did our respective jobs quite differently. When Robert Kennedy wanted a particular job done with care and finesse, sometimes a so-called hatchet job, he called on me; and, as Adolph is fond of putting it, "when Bobby wanted blood to run in the streets," he called on Adolph. It was a matter of style.

Probably the first time I took on a major position as chairman of a large project was for the 1948 Portola Festival commemorating the discovery of San Francisco Bay in 1769 by Don Gaspar de Portola. In mid-July, 1769, Don Gaspar and sixty-three men left the pueblo of San Diego far to the south in search of the port of Monterey, 159 leagues distant. By October 28, after camping on the present sites of Los Angeles and Santa Cruz, they had made it to Half Moon Bay, and in another month they found our beautiful, protected harbor guarded on one side by the green hills of Marin County and on the other by the craggy promontories of the ocean cliffs west of what is now San Francisco.

It was a long and arduous trek and quite an accomplishment, the anniversary of which was celebrated in 1911. At the time, all the men in the city were requested to grow beards and the entire town turned out to commemorate what was basically the founding of San Francisco. The idea to revive the 1911 celebration was Marvin Lewis's—something we had discussed on one of our long walks from Sea Cliff. He was on the Board of Supervisors then, and he said that Mayor Roger D. Lapham wanted me to co-chair the festivities which would also celebrate the centennial of the gold rush and California's statehood. There were even long-range hopes that we could turn the Portola Festival into an annual event like the Mardi Gras in New Orleans. Per usual, I couldn't say no. When I took the job, I couldn't realize that it was to set a pattern that followed me my entire life.

The festival was scheduled for the entire month of October, 1948. Ann had passed away the previous July and I threw myself into the final arrangements to help assuage my terrible loss. The festival was well over a year in the planning. Our intention was to involve the entire city in the project with ethnically inspired events which included everything from a salmon derby in the Bay at Aquatic Park, to a tennis tournament, to a performance of *Boris Godunov* at the Opera House conducted by Eric Leinsdorf, to a South American music concert and a pageant. We were planning an enormous parade and a city-wide production called *The Shining Trail* at the Cow Palace which was to be admission-free. We filled that enormous arena to capacity three nights in a row. We ran a city-wide contest to elect a Portola Festival Queen and we even had a man portray Don Gaspar in full conquistador regalia for all press functions and public appearances. It was important that not only San Francisco but the entire country know about our festival so that vacations could be planned and the city could benefit from all the excitement with increased tourist revenues.

I convinced American Airlines to loan us one of their DC-

6s to fly around the country and visit nine key cities to promote San Francisco tourism and the upcoming fiesta. The airline paid all of our expenses, hotels and everything. They had just started service to San Francisco and they wanted the media exposure. We would take Don Gaspar, in reality Mike Dessiano, a Brooklyn-born San Francisco plumbing contractor, several queen candidates, Ann Curtis, an Olympic swimmer, a number of prominent San Franciscans and a full crew, including a pair of twin stewardesses. About thirty people in all. At the last minute two seats opened up. Donald was attending Stanford and was on his summer break. I called him and said, "Can you be ready to go in four hours? You're coming along as my administrative assistant." Donald dragged his feet because he thought the plane was going to be loaded with a bunch of boring, cigar-smoking politicians. I told him that he could bring his own "administrative assistant" to keep him company and he asked a friend. In midsummer we were off, but not exactly on time. The plane was delayed by smog in Los Angeles.

Before we arrived in each city on the tour—Dallas, St. Louis, Chicago, Detroit, Cleveland, Philadelphia, Washington, D.C., Boston and New York—we sent chef Don Lischetti ahead. He had the major task of teaching chefs in our nine host cities how to prepare the typical San Francisco dishes we were serving at our luncheons and dinners. We dined on meals of Monterrey sand dabs, cracked crab, tiny Bay shrimps, Oscar pancakes and Ghirardelli and Blum chocolates until we couldn't stand it any more. Boston's colorful mayor, James Curley, was kind enough to serve us a bean dinner which relieved the boredom. Chef Lischetti must have winced at the way the citizens in the host cities attacked our epicurean delicacies. In Dallas, for instance, someone ate the baby shrimp, shells and all, and tore the delicate sand dabs to shreds trying to pick out the bones. Our best meal, however, was hosted by the airlines at the Waldorf in New

York. It was an enormous groaning board buffet honoring Mayor Elmer Robinson and what the press was calling the 20th Century Conquistadors . . . us. There were whiskies and liquors from all over the world; we were served Icelandic shrimps, Scottish smoked salmon and Norwegian herring, Mexican tortillas, Virginia hams, Texas turkey, Boston baked beans, New England lobster, Danish bleu cheese, English cheddar, French petit fours and California fruit.

We were received royally in each city, but the trip was not without incident. In Philadelphia, for instance, we were late getting into town and the host cocktail party had been in progress for some time. By the time we got there everyone was so high, they could not have cared less about the Portola Festival. It was a very noisy group and one of our number got up to tell a joke to get their attention. The joke was in poor taste about someone with a speech impediment. When the man finished the story, there was an embarrassing silence and some nervous laughter. Someone from the *Philadelphia In-quirer* approached him and said, "How could you tell a story like that? Don't you know that our mayor has that affliction?" It was the classic blunder, one which has not been repeated by that particular man since.

In Boston we were met by a fifty-motorcycle escort. Mayor Curley was a brusque, tough sort of fellow who spoke his mind and he warned one of our visiting politicoes, "Young man, get out of politics; you'll either land in jail or in the poorhouse." His words were prophetic. Soon after he went to the penitentiary. And in New York, in spite of a truckers' strike that crippled Manhattan, we were escorted to City Hall with much wailing of police sirens to meet Mayor O'Dwyer and the city's official greeter, Grover Whelan. It was red-carpet treatment all the way, with a parade staged at noon so thousands of New Yorkers could gape at Don Gaspar, the San Francisco businessmen, the Portola queens and Ann Curtis, the Olympian.

183

Since I was co-chairman of the whole shebang, I was asked to ride a horse in the Festival parade. I've never been closer to a horse than perhaps the $2 window, so I turned that dubious honor over to Marvin Lewis, who, garbed in velvet with a sword and plumed hat, looked every inch a conquering Spaniard on his horse. During the parade it had begun to rain and the trolley tracks in the center of Market Street made the going hazardous. It was then that Lewis's horse decided to make it a horserace and took off down Market Street with a latter-day Don Quixote on his back—Lewis with his legs, hat and rapier flying. The only thing that stopped that nag was the Ferry Building at the end of the street.

Meanwhile, Don Gaspar—Mike Dessiano—was about as familiar with horses as I, and right in front of the grandstand he fell off his steed, just the same as the man who had played the Don in 1911. It was as if it had been rehearsed. More than 750,000 turned out for the parade which was staged by Norman Manning, a Los Angeles showman who put on parades for a living. He said that ours was as grand as the Rose Parade, the Philadelphia Mummer's Parade and the Mardi Gras combined. There were 218 units of marchers, 29 bands, 39 drum and bugle corps and 82 baton twirlers, not to mention flower-bedecked floats, city officials, queens and horses—65,000 participants or more in all.

We came up about $25,000 short on the Festival. Although we did have city-wide cooperation, there were feelings after that that perhaps we should reconsider sponsoring Portola as an annual event, especially because of the deficit. I said at the time, "It was good once a year if people let their hair down, although there are limits. . ." Apparently the good people of San Francisco, known then as "the city that knows how," thought that once was definitely enough. The Festival has not been revived since.

By the mid-1950s, I had a very good organization at Joseph Magnin with my family taking an active part in the business. I figured that I wasn't going to be around forever and began to give them more and more responsibility. I wanted to take more of an active part in the city, perhaps remembering the plaque on my father's wall. When Mayor Robinson approached me in 1954 to accept a job on the San Francisco Redevelopment Agency, I accepted. It was a four-year appointment. About that time I backed Goodwin Knight, a Republican, for governor of the state, which was duly noted in Herb Caen's column along with the fact that I was a lifelong Democrat. When Knight won, he asked me to take a position on the State Harbor Board. He knew I wasn't anxious to have the job, but he said he trusted me and appealed to my sense of public duty. In the political arena, to the winners go the spoils, and while I was probably being considered for the appointment because of my fund-raising work for Knight, I wouldn't have taken the job unless I thought I could devote the time to do it right.

When I was appointed to the Harbor Board, I didn't know a thing about shipping. "You'll learn," promised Goodie Knight. I guess he was right. I spent night after night reading about shipping, cargo handling and other pertinent data. It didn't take me long to see that our Port of San Francisco was in trouble. We had no tax subsidy and no oil revenues like Long Beach, so we weren't in a position to compete for maritime business. For years San Francisco had given over the control of the port to the state—we were one of the few ports in California that was not city-owned. A bond issue was the answer to raise money to save one of the best deep-water ports in the entire world. The scoffers said that we wouldn't have a chance of passing a state-wide bond issue without state-wide help, and traditionally Southern California cared not two figs and a navel orange for what happened in "The City." I headed the campaign to raise the $50 million needed to put our port back on its feet, by traveling up and down the state, city to city, visiting with mayor after mayor.

Los Angeles agreed; San Diego, Long Beach and Sacramento agreed. Even Oakland, whose own port was beginning to compete with ours, agreed. I went to Joe Knowland, who owned the *Oakland Tribune.* He was a crusty old boy; a very reliable, honest man. He was opposed to putting a freeway in front of the Ferry Building, a point upon which we both agreed. He said that if I would oppose that project, he would go along with our bond issue and would recommend it—on the front page in big, black letters—to his readers. We struck a deal and he was good to his word, lobbying for the passage of Proposition Five, $50 million for the Port of San Francisco. All I did was sell the idea, using merchandising techniques I'd learned my whole life in the business. Also I think that I've been lucky because I was born with the ability to make people see things my way.

By September of 1955 the port was making money for the first time in years. When I joined the Harbor Board, the port was $200,000 in the hole, and after instituting a more aggressive policy for soliciting business, we were, all of a sudden, $66,000 to the good. Governor Knight named me to head a reorganized San Francisco Port Commission. Subsequently I was reappointed by Governor Pat Brown, and then, when San Francisco took over operation of the port from the state, a move I never felt was wise, Mayor Joe Alioto (who as attorney Joe Alioto replaced me on the Redevelopment Commission) also reappointed me. I served as head of the port for nineteen years. They were eventful ones, because the port became embroiled in some of the more emotional issues of the times.

One of my first acts as head of the port was to get the restaurant owners on the famed Fisherman's Wharf to ante up more rents. When I became Port Commissioner, all the restauranteurs were paying a flat and antiquated rental. I told them, "The party's over, boys," and the hue and cry could have wakened Don Gaspar. I think I proposed an eight percent raise in rents and a ten percent percentage rental on food and liquor, leaving room for negotiation. I could see that regardless of what it cost to operate (even if the port was making a lot of money), we'd be in the red very soon and these people were not paying anything compared to what they could afford. They were furious. They said they'd inherited the restaurants from their families and that they shouldn't have to pay any higher rents or any tax. I pointed out to them that when Joseph Magnin was first on the corner of Stockton and O'Farrell in the early days when nothing else was there of any value, the property was improved, and in the course of years, the land became more valuable. As the city grew and prospered, so did we and we paid more rent and taxes. I asked them why should their locations make them any different. My father built his business and increased the value of his property just the way their fathers had—why should being a pioneer exempt them from their civic duty?

Still, there was a terrible stink and not just from the fresh fish they were serving. The Alioto family, who own a huge seafood restaurant on a prime piece of Wharf real estate, never forgave me. Every month when Frank Alioto would send in his rent and percentage rental check to the city, he would write on it, "Paid in Protest." Today, the city gets nearly $3 million in rentals from the Wharf properties but back then, when the city was earning only $300,000, I was the most unpopular man around Fisherman's Wharf for years. Parenthetically, I'm not sure everyone has forgotten and I find it too coincidental that on one trip to Sabella's restaurant, I was bitten by a crab owned by Angela Sabella.

There was a revolution going on in the shipping industry that eventually snatched most of the shipping business away from San Francisco—containerization. Something I noticed as long ago as 1957. The Japanese, whose ships were the most numerous in our harbor, were starting to convert their ships to containerized freight instead of loosely loaded, breakbulk

187

cargo. When goods are containerized, prepackaged in huge lift-on, lift-off containers, a ship's turnaround time in port is much faster, enabling it to be on the high seas much longer. A shipping company loses money if a ship is in port too long. San Francisco had finger piers, long, skinny "fingers" that reached out into the water for off-loading of breakbulk cargo which had to be stored in sheds alongside the ship. Turnaround time was four or five days—not economical vis-à-vis containerization where cargo could be off-loaded, stored in huge sheds and then loaded onto trucks and flatbed railroad cars without being unpacked. Containerized cargo required acres of dockside land for storage and the Port of San Francisco was short on land and long on excuses as to why containerization wasn't possible. Eventually, in the years after the war, Oakland geared up for containerization and literally plucked eighty percent of the cargo business away from San Francisco, not only because they had the land, but because Oakland was much more convenient to the railheads and the interstate trucking firms.

The Port Commission had six different studies made over the years to find methods to revive the port, given our loss of cargo vessels to Oakland. The reports indicated that the city should cease all maritime activity north of our Ferry Building and turn it into a revenue-producing area with hotels, motels, restaurants, parks, plazas, offices and shops. All areas south of the Ferry Building could take the tax revenues realized from northern waterfront development and build piers for containerized shipping. One report by the Arthur D. Little Company predicted that San Francisco would eventually house the very rich and the very poor. The rich would live in high rises and condos, the report said, and the poor would take over the outlying district neighborhoods. The city would be a financial center—a headquarters city (which it is)—for banking, brokerage and home office interests rather than a center for heavy industrialization. There was also a prediction that shipping would fall off in the seventies and then pick up in the eighties because of trade with the Peoples' Republic of China. The only hope for the port, said the Little report, was to develop nonmaritime, revenue-producing projects to provide enough income to rebuild rotting piers and to build new facilities elsewhere convenient to rail and truck transportation. The only question that remained was what to build.

Several projects were suggested including one called Embarcadero City, a complex of hotels, office space and sailboat marina. There were also two proposals to develop 8½ acres of bayside area at the Ferry Building that were given short shrift. So far, nothing was happening. But under Mayor Alioto there was an all-out drive to regain city control of the port which the state had owned since gold rush times. I was not, as I have said, in favor of it. I warned that the port would be worse off under local ownership if the Board of Supervisors was allowed to control the port's finances. I thought that the port would become a political football. Besides, if the city took over the port, it would have to assume its debts which I felt we couldn't afford. For years the port received no outside help other than what it earned in tax monies. Neither the state legislature nor the local community did anything to help it. So the port had to exist on its own revenues. State ownership had a deadening effect on the port and we were caught napping as all major shipping lines began to containerize in earnest in the mid-sixties. Although I thought city ownership of the port was a bad idea, I had to go along with it because I was outvoted.

Given the city's ownership and what the commission-sponsored reports said, we had to begin to generate tax revenues not only to revitalize the deterioration of the waterfront, but also to inject new business into the area. In November, 1968, Mayor Alioto and I, along with twenty other business and civic leaders, flew off to New York to urge fifteen Fortune 500 firms to set up their Western headquarters in San Francisco and to submit plans for building directly on the waterfront on the sites of the outmoded piers. Of the corporations solicited, only the Ford Motor Company and United States Steel responded with plans for complexes which would not only house corporate offices, but in the case of U.S. Steel, would contain a badly needed passenger terminal. The existing one in San Francisco, the Queen of Harbors, was a rundown corrugated iron shed. The U.S. Steel building was the most acceptable because fifty-five percent of its planned space would be a people-oriented open plaza designed with view corridors so as not to impede the waterfront panorama.

Skidmore, Owings and Merrill, a national architectural firm with its main office in San Francisco, came up with a workable concept—a set of plans which cost them $75,000 out-of-pocket. It was just a schematic, not a total plan, but when it was submitted to the various commmissions for approval, the fight began. The building included our passenger terminal, 1,000 feet of front footage between Howard and Folsom Streets on the area occupied by Piers 14 through 24, and a 550-foot-high rise built adjacent to the south tower of the San Francisco–Oakland Bay Bridge, which was 470 feet high, a fact that aroused the ire of powerful *San Francisco Chronicle* columnist Herb Caen, who hammered away at the project in columns that dated from December, 1969, to January, 1971. Caen's feeling, which reflected the complaints of most of those opposed, was that United States Steel had the temerity to build a monolith and destroy not only the view but the proportion of the bridge. He was to become not only vocal in print, but an active participant in a protest march headed by actor Paul Newman.

The Steel building was a *cause célèbre* that galvanized the city into action against big business, big developers and in some cases, me. The fight involved not only environmental groups but also publicity-seeking businessmen, including a young dress manufacturer who had plans to run for office and

190

needed the publicity; newspapers whose editorial departments were moderately in favor but whose columnists, Caen
and Charles McCabe of the *Chronicle* in particular, were
vehemently opposed; the Board of Supervisors, the Planning
Commission and the Port Commission of which I was the
head. Since the port was pushing for the go-ahead, I took
most of the flack because of my position as head of the
Commission. The loudest complainers, however, were a vocal
group of people who lived on Telegraph Hill who objected to
having their view of the waterfront and most of the East Bay,
Fremont in particular, impeded by what they thought was
going to be a steel, concrete and glass horror. I must say that
concurrent to the Steel project, another called the Ferry Port
Plaza, a stunning design put forth by Skidmore, Owings and
Merrill for the Oceanic Development Company for a Milan-
style galleria, shops, office and hotel space, was also at the
mercy of the Board of Supervisors and the lobbyists, some of
whom lived perched atop Telegraph Hill. Both projects from
start to finish were not only the subject of messy controversy,
but they were doomed. They were never built. After months
and months of delays, mostly over the Steel building height
restriction, U.S. Steel pulled out.

The original height of the Steel building was cut down to
an "acceptable" 125 feet which would have made it economi-
cally unfeasible for Steel to build. A beleaguered U.S. Steel
released the following communication to the press which
reflected some of their growing impatience and frustration
with the city fathers. It was a carefully worded press release
which said, "United States Steel is not presuming to tell the
people of San Francisco what kind of building or development they should want for their waterfront. This is a decision
which rightfully belongs to them and their elected officials.
Frankly reasoned public discussion of that issue is highly
desirable to the end that appropriate zoning may be established for the Port as a realistic basis for any future develop-

ment . . . That discussion, however, should not be confused by continuing public misunderstanding as to the role United States Steel played in the past or that which it may—or may not—play in the future." We had indeed solicited United States Steel to build a building and to relocate in our city and ever since the project had been announced, there had been nothing but baseball bats thrown at the shins of progress.

After the concurrent defeat of both Ferry Port and U.S. Steel, I was feeling terribly discouraged. I like to win, and in my entire public and personal life I'd never experienced anything quite as frustrating. Both projects would not only have provided a beautiful complex of shops, hotels, a marina and a passenger terminal, but a lot of jobs and tax revenues for the city. But the times were very much against us. It was a period when the war in Vietnam was winding down and when public protest had become a way of life. United States Steel and the other developers were looked upon not only as giant, gobbling corporations, but as enemies who were going to subvert our glorious skyline and view. The Steel building would have been the first of its kind in that area, i.e., a high rise directly on the water. It didn't matter that Southern Pacific was building two towers not 100 yards distant on the other side of the street which managed to block the Telegraph Hillers' precious views . . . or that eventually, the "Manhattanization" of downtown San Francisco would become *fait accompli* in just six years.

I don't give up so easily and although we were getting thwarted at every turn by selfish interests, I thought I could accomplish something. But there were too many blockades in my way. The environmentalists didn't want development of the port at all. I still can't understand their reasoning . . . they kept saying that we were tearing San Francisco apart. It's the same with Neiman-Marcus wanting to go into the old City of Paris building, which was empty for several years. With Neiman's it is a question of a stained-glass dome. The historical society boys wanted the dome incorporated into the building exactly where it was in the first place and Neiman-Marcus wanted to move it into a corner and design the downstairs for a better traffic flow. You can't have a hole in the traffic pattern like there would be if the dome were in its original place. The cost of running salespeople from side to side would not be feasible or profitable. But for the five years the fight went on, the city was out taxes and sales taxes, not to mention jobs. Downtown San Francisco would be improved with the addition of another competitive high-fashion store—the more stores in this district, the more important San Francisco becomes as a shopping mecca to attract people to the area. And it has been the same kind of people who stopped Ferry Port and the Steel building that tried to delay the beginning of construction on Neiman-Marcus. I'm sure these people believed in their course, but I'm not sure they realized the long-term consequences of their opposition.

I finally quit the Port Commission after nineteen years of service, ostensibly over a jurisdictional dispute. Behind our corporate offices at Joseph Magnin at Harrison and Spear Streets (right under the Bay Bridge south tower) is a tiny strip of land which we leased from the city at the going rates for our car and truck park. It was thought to be a conflict of interest that I be a Port Commissioner (i.e., the landlord) and also a tenant. It was a convenient excuse to get out of a disappointing, frustrating situation. I don't like to walk away from a fight without accomplishing what I'd started out to do, but in this case, it was the only practical way I could think of to extricate myself and I did it.

I think that ultimately my position that the waterfront should have been redeveloped with sensibility has been vindicated over the years. From a strictly mercantile point of view I considered myself a futurist—that for the continuing health of the city of San Francisco, we had to override a noisy minority who were clinging to the status quo. I must make it

193

clear that I was not in favor of development for development's sake and that the new structures that I favored would have been aesthetic improvements over rotting piers. But I also wanted to add a substantial tax base and more jobs to the city of San Francisco—things which, ten years later, are beginning to happen.

While I was Port Commissioner, I was in favor of putting all the Bay Area ports and terminals under one authority. The San Francisco Chamber of Commerce had taken a short-sighted, obstinate view of the project. They weren't willing to go along with the amalgamation of the ports and terminals unless they had unreasonable concessions. I would have made a reasonable settlement if there was a chance—that eventually all the ports in the state could have been put under one aegis (and that was my long-term hope), but our Chamber stymied me. In its favor, however, I must say that we had the Chamber support on both the Ferry Port Plaza and the U.S. Steel building. However, I never had much respect for the Chamber. At the time, they weren't as good as the Southern California Chamber of Commerce which had made such great strides for the Los Angeles area. I say all of this as some sort of background for the fact that eventually I became very involved with the San Francisco Chamber, not under duress, but with reluctance.

By 1966 a man named Bill Dauer had come to San Francisco from Kansas City to head the Chamber. We had met briefly at a dinner where he confused Joseph Magnin with I. Magnin (he was so new to the city, he hadn't yet learned the difference), and I'm afraid that from that time on, I did not think too kindly of either him or his organization. Dauer was, however, a hard-working, astute person who realized that it would be perhaps advantageous to have me and the Joseph Magnin organization in his corner.

Jim Rudden, a fellow Port Commissioner and good friend—we have walked to work together for the past seventeen years—was visited by Dauer and one of his people who wanted to set up a foundation through the Chamber. Rudden had done similar work with the Loyola University in Los Angeles and explained to Dauer that the Loyola Foundation had gotten the aid of two or three prominent, wealthy people. In the course of the conversation my name came up and Dauer told Rudden that I was a Chamber-hater. Rudden asked Dauer, "Do you want him if we could get him?" and of course, Dauer said yes. Concurrently I was approached by Gwin Follis, then chairman of the board at Standard Oil, who was very active in the community. We were friends, not socially, but when I wanted anything for the community, Gwin always came through. I always went to the top although others, when dealing with a company like Standard Oil, would work through the public relations department. Gwin always asked, "Why do you come to me?" and I told him the homily my father repeated to me, "If you want to go to heaven, talk to God, not the angels." Over the years he was always kind to me and supportive of my causes. Then one day, after never asking anything of me, Gwin said, "Will you do me a favor?" I couldn't say no and when he asked me to be a director of the Chamber of Commerce, I told him quite honestly that I didn't have much faith in that body. The previous management before Bill Dauer was weak and although I didn't remember meeting Dauer, I re-emphasized that I didn't have much regard for his organization. Perhaps I was double-teamed by Follis and my friend Rudden, but reluctantly, I agreed to go on the Chamber for six months.

I am not the kind of person to do things by halves, and thus committed to six months on a board for which I had little respect, I resolved not only to make the best of it, I found myself taking an active interest. I became quite enthused because the tone of the Chamber was changing. They were acting in the best interests of the city which they hadn't done in the past. They were making progress, not standing still.

195

When I had served my six months, Gwin came to me again and asked one more favor—would I consider becoming president of the Chamber and I said, "Me?" I told him I thought they were making a big mistake, but in six months I had come to admire Dauer and his ability. He was effective because he had a stubbornness and a tenacity. If he thought he was right, he stuck to his guns. The position of president of the Chamber of Commerce is a volunteer one and I think that it was probably one of the most exciting and rewarding things I've ever done—the most fun, too. I was the only three-term president the Chamber has ever had and at the end of my tenure, I was made a lifetime director.

At the time journalist Kenneth Rexroth wrote, "[Of Cyril Magnin], the number of boards and committees he is on is not as important as the fact that he is usually not just window-dressing but is an active and leading member who does real work. How he gets the time, nobody knows. It so happens that a lot of these responsibilities lie in the general field of culture and urbanism. He is even on the board of Ann Halprin's dance group, so nobody in this highly cultured city can claim we've got a lowbrow Babbitt at the head of the Chamber of Commerce who stands in our way of becoming a new Athens."

As president of the Chamber of Commerce, it was my job to revitalize the work of the organization. I wanted to give it a social conscience as well. We had to work hard to ameliorate racial discrimination. The Chamber was helpful with a summer-job program. Any black person who wanted to go into a small business was given assistance by the Chamber. Joe Alioto, who was mayor at the time, mentioned that President Johnson had said, "San Francisco came out of the urban crisis better than any other city," and I'd like to think that it was in part through the efforts of the Chamber and certainly, through the unfailing efforts of Joe Alioto himself, who was dedicated to the cause of minority employment. Ultimately our job was to improve the business climate of San Francisco, and instead of my taking hold of a situation and bulling it through, my major strength as negotiator came in handy. We were able to build a workable consensus between two opposite factors—in many cases, bringing cooperation between labor and environmental groups.

But my principal job was fund-raising, which is really my hallmark. On Monday through Friday of each business week I would make an appointment with a company—one each morning and one each afternoon—and talk to them about a heavy reevaluation of their dues. I would send my car for Bill Dauer and together we'd make the calls. We got the system timed down to one and one-half hours per call or three hours a day, and at the end of three years we had added $300,000 in new money to the Chamber's coffers on an annual basis. My method: pure salesmanship. I had a fairly big name in the community and the heads of the companies we visited were pleased that I would come to pitch them in person. When I was president of the COC, I came to adore the people on the staff. I was the only outsider consistently invited to the staff parties and special events. I loved putting on dinners at different restaurants or the World Trade Club for the chamber staff. Money was never a large consideration. Each year the annual party would get more and more elaborate, and at the end of my second year I threw a party in the champagne cellar of the Blue Fox restaurant that started at 5:30 P.M. and ended up at two in the morning. Four of the Chamber staff were arrested for drunkenness and operating a moving vehicle while intoxicated, i.e., drunk driving. Dauer says that he would have been picked up himself had he not driven home in the other direction.

During my final year I wanted to do something very special. At first I asked Dauer if he'd let his people off for a half-day. The plan was to go by Matson ship to Long Beach for an overnight trip and then fly back the next day. Dauer told me that he had both single and married people on staff and that the wives and husbands would object to a private staff-only party under those circumstances, so I came up with another plan. I decided I wanted to fly everyone to Las Vegas for the evening and sent them in limousines to a supper club for dinner and a show. I gave them all money to gamble with ($25 apiece) and got them back into the limos onto their plane and back in the Bay Area by midnight—as if they would turn into pumpkins or something. The whole caper was written up in a national COC publication and Dauer was the envy of all other national chamber heads for years after.

Often I would represent the COC at out-of-town functions and I remember once, Dauer and I went to Los Angeles to attend the Los Angeles Chamber's meeting. It was a black-tie affair at the Century Plaza, which, by the way, is located right near our Century City Joseph Magnin store. After the dinner we went into the bar on the lower level where there was live entertainment. I was fairly well-known in those parts not only because of the store but because my son, Jerry, was active in the L.A. area as both merchant and restauranteur. We wound up sitting at a table with Nat "King" Cole's widow, Tennessee Ernie Ford and Claude Jarman. There were twelve in the party. Pretty soon the band was playing things just for us. The only person who didn't know who I was was the waitress.

Now, I must preface this by saying I am a notorious check-grabber, and when it came time to ante up, I decided to have some fun with the waitress. I said to her, "Tomorrow, I'd like to buy a fine handbag for a lady friend . . . what shop should I go to?" She said, "Joseph Magnin's." But I was insistent. I told her I wanted something *really* nice and she said, "Well, if you want something that good, go to . . ." and she named another store. Then I handed her my credit card, and she got very flustered. I told her, "You're still going to get a nice, big tip, but if you hadn't changed your story, it would have been bigger." When Dauer tells the story, he also adds:

"The last time I saw that waitress, she was going down the hall to Cyril's room with him." Well, sometimes, rank does have its privilege.

In January, 1971, I stepped down as an active member in the Chamber of Commerce. I had spent three years as president and two years as a member of the Board of Directors. At the time I said, "I came to the Chamber with reservations because I never realized the fine work the Chamber did, and what it contributed to the welfare of San Francisco, not alone the business community, but the community as a whole. I don't think any organization or chamber, United States or otherwise, has a stronger, a better, a more dedicated staff than here (in San Francisco)." Perhaps what I didn't say was what we had been able to accomplish working together all those years. We were able to get federal support for some of our projects to the tune of $38 million; we increased our membership and monetary support by over a quarter of a million dollars and we helped bring in business which ultimately alleviated some of our unemployment problems.

My rewards for the work I did with the Chamber have been many. But the most fun, I think, was the dinner given in my honor in the summer of 1979 to celebrate my eightieth birthday. It was the Chamber's annual meeting—a sell-out crowd of 2,000 in the ballroom of the Fairmont Hotel. Steve Silver of *Beach Blanket Babylon,* a marvelous and long-running review, and Bing Crosby's widow, Kathryn Crosby, wrote the show which starred 150 members of a Chinese drum-and-bugle corps; San Francisco's fourth most talented violinist (if you count Isaac Stern, Yehudi Menuhin and Ruggero Ricci before him), ex-mayor Joe Alioto; and diva Beverly Sills, one of my favorite people who flew in from Haiti to take part in the evening. There were all sorts of performers including some young women from the American Conservatory Theater and our own California governor, Jerry Brown.

Now, I think that Steve Silver is a very inventive guy—I call him "the Ziegfeld of the eighties—but he could only rehearse his performers when he could get them. He says that ten minutes before the show he was still auditioning the drum-and-bugle corps. When Beverly Sills came out to rehearse, she went to Steve's club, the Fugazi, which is a rebuilt Italian opera house in North Beach. She walked up to Steve's office which has a balcony overlooking the street. Across the street is a funeral parlor and there was a Chinese funeral in progress, complete with a band playing an appropriate dirge. I happened to drive up in my car while Beverly and Steve were standing on the balcony and with the Chinese dirge in the background, Beverly and I did an impromptu "Romeo, oh, Romeo," our own Shakespearean balcony scene.

The evening of the dinner and special show was completely videotaped, something I wasn't aware of at the time. A few weeks later I was invited to the home of a local developer who not only gave me the tape but the cassette recorder on which to play it. It was like seeing everything for the very first time. It was a completely new experience for me because while it was happening, I was too caught up in it to remember anything.

CHAPTER TEN ❧

Lyndon and Me

❧ TRADITIONALLY, when you're active in party politics, you usually get to meet the politician you've been supporting. A handshake, perhaps, at a political function or a quick "hello and thank you" from a blurred face between two Secret Servicemen. But as a major fund-raiser for supervisors, mayors, congressmen, governors and senators, I have been more fortunate than the usual $10 giver. I have supported most of the Democratic candidates for president since Al Smith in 1928, and more than one of them from Franklin Roosevelt on have, indeed, called me Cyril.

I have been invited to presidential inaugurations for years, including FDR's final ceremony in 1945. Ann and I had been included in all the festivities from the pre-inaugural party, to the swearing-in in front of the Capitol Building, to the Presidential Ball afterwards. We had one problem. No hotel reservation. Washington was more booked than New Orleans at Super Bowl time. We were about to refuse the invitations with great regret when the President heard about it from an aide. He not only invited us to the inaugural, but asked us to stay overnight in the White House, which we did. When FDR passed away, I became friendly with Harry Truman. When he was nominated at the 1948 convention, I was a member of the California delegation along with Will Rogers, Jr., Edmund "Pat" Brown (who would become attorney general and then governor of the state), and John "Jack" Shelley who would eventually be mayor of San Francisco. While they were regular delegates, I was selected to be an alternate. When Truman was elected, another invitation to another inaugural ball came to me, and when he went out of office in 1953, I was asked to co-chair the Northern California fund drive for the Truman Library. Eventually I became one of the trustees.

But I was never more active and close to a president than I was during the Kennedy-Johnson years when I served on a citizens' advisory committee for both men. You might call it a patronage appointment—I won't quibble with that—but I could have said no, as I had done time and again, previously. But I was a good Democrat and considered myself a patriotic American. So when President Kennedy wrote to ask Governor Pat Brown to recommend someone in whom he had confidence for an appointment, Pat called me and said, "How'd you like to go to Washington to help the President?" I thought, "Now who could turn that down," but I told Pat that I didn't think I was qualified. He reassured me by saying, "I have faith in you and know your dedication to anything you get involved with. You're the first one who came to mind for this appointment."

The commission came in May, 1963. I was to be a member of an eight-man group headed by former Pennsylvania governor and long-time mayor of Pittsburgh, David Lawrence, and included people such as Roland M. Sawyer of Pittsburgh, housing consultant to the United Steel Workers' Union; Ferdinand Kramer, a Chicago builder, broker and mortgage banker; Charles Keller, Jr., president of a New Orleans construction company; and Jack Conway, who had been assistant to the AFL-CIO's Walter Reuther. I received a telegram from President Kennedy which read, "I shall shortly sign your commission appointing you to be a member of the President's Committee on Equal Opportunity in Housing. It gives me a great deal of pleasure to do this and I want at the same time to send you this message to tell you how delighted I am that you are going to be able to serve." It was a gracious message, one that I have cherished over the years. As civilian advisors it was our job to research the problems of discrimination in housing which we did through a competent staff that would draw up the reports we submitted to the President. We were in Washington generally two or three days a month and when it was necessary, we met with the President. I would fly to Washington to join the other members of the commission and we'd have our luncheon meeting often with JFK. I hadn't been on the commission very long before that awful, but memorable day in November, 1963, when we got word that President Kennedy had been assassinated in Dallas. The entire country went into deep mourning, including San Francisco and our Joseph Magnin stores. In memorium our windows which had already been decorated for Christmas carried a plainly lettered inscription in large white print, "Joseph Magnin Deeply Regrets and Mourns the Loss of President John F. Kennedy." We also closed all the stores for a day to pay honor to our fallen President.

After Kennedy's death I figured that my services on the housing commission would no longer be needed. New presidents usually clean house and appoint their own people, but President Johnson personally asked us to stay, saying, "I know you're starting a very important assignment, one that is an important service to your government and I'd like you to continue." So, each of us continued.

Our office was in the building directly across from the

back entrance to the White House. During the course of my tenure on the committee Mr. Johnson and I got to be friends. I had met him years before when he was campaigning for President and I liked his spirit and personal magnetism. He was a negotiator in the Sam Rayburn tradition—all cards on the table, deal straight from the shoulder. As we worked together, we became friends and often I was invited to lunch with him in the Oval Office on a purely social basis. I always felt that President Johnson was a wonderful, great man—a man very much maligned. Our lunches became dinners in his private quarters. They were times when he could relax and get away from the pressures of office. Soon I was no stranger around the White House.

People often wondered what a rough-hewn, sage old politico like Lyndon Johnson would have in common with a seemingly urbane Jewish merchant from San Francisco like me. As Bill Moyers, Johnson's former press secretary and now dedicated journalist, explains it, "You meet a lot of people in politics who are financial supporters whose relationship (with the candidate) is only emphemeral and perishes very rapidly, but there was about Cyril a quality that impressed Mrs. Johnson, then me and then LBJ. It is a certain kind of old-world charm about Cyril, a certain kind of grace amidst wealth that some people of fortune do not have." I found Moyers's words to be very complimentary, but he perhaps more than anyone else understood LBJ and could put into simple sentences just what the two of us shared. LBJ was a complete negotiator—he believed in one hand rubbing the other, in having one's back scratched in return, and as Moyers pointed out, we probably got along well because we understood the rogue deeply imbedded in each of us—not a negative quality, but at least the part of us that harkened back to simpler times when pioneering men of vision saw what they wanted and reached for the stars. Finally, perhaps one of the most solid things about our friendship was that I never really wanted anything from President Johnson. I simply wanted interesting conversation and a chance to drop by and talk to someone about my views. While there were some favors we could do for each other, they really never amounted to anything except the good deeds one does for one's friends. The President and I spent many casual lunches just chewing the air about the things we believed, whether it was economics, business, the price of oil or the latest ball scores. He, like just about any other American, loved sports.

Occasionally we were in a position to do each other small favors. In May, 1964, just as his campaign for re-election was heating up, he donated a 1,260-pound steer named LBJ from his Texas ranch for a fund-raising auction at KQED, the local public broadcasting station in San Francisco. The steer sold for $1,425 to a family in Sonoma. It was a very handsome beast and I thought it was a shame to turn him into hamburger.

In 1964 I was a delegate to the Democratic convention along with hotelier Ben Swig, Mrs. Ruth Berle and Adolph Schuman. I was the state co-chairman for finance for the California Committee to Re-elect President Johnson, so it may seem curious to some that I also attended the Republican National Convention which was being held in San Francisco. But party lines meant little to me at the time and the mayor had asked me to be chairman of the entertainment committee—so my presence at the Goldwater convention was purely ceremonial. It did, however, afford me some of the best seats in the house.

When President Johnson was re-elected in the landslide of 1964, we became even better friends. Probably never were there two more outwardly different men. He was tall; I am not. Johnson had a native exuberance that flowed over into a physical dynamism. He was consistently on the go. He radiated animal energy. I, on the other hand, am a fairly calm person, physically, and where Johnson would be up and

205

active, I could sit in one place quietly, taking it all in with an intensity that I kept inside. LBJ was a complex man, not very cosmopolitan, but wily. He was a good infighter with street smarts. While I wasn't conversant with the world of foreign policy and diplomacy and he wasn't particularly knowledgeable about the arts and philanthropy or the rag business, we did have our love of politics in common. I adored politics—smoke-filled-room deals and closed-door fights. So did President Johnson—it was a quality that had made him such a successful and persuasive party leader. Politics was a link for us in the beginning of our friendship. We could talk politics for hours, and from there we began to talk about business and the economy. Then we started talking about our families and I guess in that kind of shared intimacy we became friends.

On occasion I would be invited to the White House for dinner. The invitations came on elegant, gold-engraved cards. Dinner itself was a plush affair with good, substantial American food gussied-up with French names on the place cards for the sake of elegance. One dinner in September, 1965, consisted of crabmeat crepes, filet mignon Rossini (good 'ole American beefsteak), Jackson potatoes, peas White House, a green salad, fruit and cheese. The wines served in the White House during the Johnson tenure were usually Californian—a Charles Krug Johannisberg Riesling, a Beaulieu Pinot Noir or Cabernet Sauvignon and Almaden Blanc de Blancs champagne—simple little wines for simple little dinners.

My son, Jerry, had been married about seven years to his first wife, Gayle, when I called him up with a surprise. I knew that Ellen and Walter and Donald and Elaine had been to inauguration ceremonies and I felt that Jerry's wife hadn't had the pleasure. I mentioned to Jerry that the President wanted to do something nice for me and the only thing I could think of was for him to have Jerry and Gayle to a White House function. Jerry said that he really didn't care about those kinds of things, but lo and behold, the Jerry Magnins received an

invitation in the mail to attend a dinner and ball given in
honor of Ayub Khan, President of Pakistan. They were both
terribly impressed and scared to death. Gayle fussed that she
had nothing to wear and Jerry was just embarrassed by the
whole thing. They did, however, decide to go.

I got them first-class airline tickets and put them up at the
Madison Hotel in Washington. I also arranged for them to
have lunch with Bill Moyers, for whom I had great admiration
and respect and with whom I was developing a close friendship. They were having lunch in the White House dining
room which was catered by the navy mess when Moyers
turned to Jerry and in his soft Texas drawl asked, "How do
you feel about having dinner with the President tonight?"
Jerry told Bill he was scared to death, that this wasn't dinner
with just anybody. Jerry said, "Look, I'm here because my
father wanted me to go and I feel like a jerk."

During lunch the President had summoned Moyers and
Bill had a phone brought to the table; he told LBJ that he was
having lunch and that when he was finished, he'd call him
back and come over to the Oval Office. Moyers was famous
for that sort of thing. I think he was one of the few people in
the entire Johnson administration who would not kowtow to
the President, which was probably all right with Johnson
because he hated yes-men. Anyhow, Moyers returned to his
conversation with Jerry without skipping a beat and said, "Let
me tell you something. When the President gets up in the
morning, he puts his pants on, one leg at a time, just like you
. . and don't ever forget it. You go tonight and have a good
time and don't you be nervous. It could be you standing there
someday as the President of the United States, and you
wouldn't want anybody to be nervous. Don't ever feel that he
is any better a person than you are." To this day Jerry says
he'll never forget that conversation. And oh, yes, he and
Gayle went to dinner with the President and had a wonderful
time.

I have mentioned that one of the more important things

between political friends is the ability to do favors, and while I never asked President Johnson for much more than a dinner at the White House for my son, LBJ called on me to help him with several pet projects. One concerned the IRS form and the other had to do with his daughters, Lynda Bird and Luci Baines.

Say the words *"Internal Revenue"* and most people start quaking in their boots. Our IRS 1040 forms are very intimidating, but one day, I had a brainstorm. I thought the forms scared people and I also thought the government and the Internal Revenue office would have a better image with better graphics. I talked with Bill Moyers about it and he relayed my thoughts to Mr. Johnson. During one of our private tête-à-têtes I had told him about Joseph Magnin's prize-winning ads and attractive graphics—how much they had contributed to the positive image of the store—so he asked me to come up with an improved design for the yearly tax form. I called Walter Landor, a graphic designer who has an office in an old ferryboat at Pier Five on San Francisco Bay, to help me together with our graphic artists at Joseph Magnin.

Now you can't make a thing like a tax form that simple, but you can clean it up so a person doesn't panic the moment he sees it. That's what Walter and I tried to do. There were some conflicting reports in the press—mostly humorous ones. Charles Denton wrote a column in the *San Francisco Examiner* (tongue firmly planted in cheek): "The news that Cyril Magnin and Walter Landor have succeeded in brightening up this year's federal income tax form is truly as heart-warming as boardinghouse stew. It will not, of course, alter the fact that we're all about to get gored worse than a cross-eyed bullfighter. Because all they've really done is change the bull." Denton went on to say that our new form was supposed to have more "eye-appeal . . . And that must have been tough to do because personally, I cried pretty good over the old one . . . I mean, trying to remodel the IRS image just by changing the tax form is like trying to improve Count Dracula by making him use a straw." Well, we tried.

Lyndon Johnson and I shared a lot of confidences about business and politics, but another thing we had in common was our love of pretty women. He always noticed when a beautiful woman walked by. With his great eye for a well-turned leg or fashionable figure, he noticed that Ann Hand, the wife of his protocol chief, Lloyd Hand, had changed her image. When Hand was appointed, Ann had been a typical Southern belle—all she would have needed to go along with her honey-and-magnolia accent was a hoop skirt and a parasol. But she began shopping through our New York buying office with the aide of Rita Wohlman and Selma Gross. Together they helped her reshape her entire image, making her into a very chic woman. The President complimented me on the work my staff had done with Mrs. Hand and wistfully (if you could attribute that emotion to a man as large and blunt as LBJ) he mentioned that he was a little unhappy about the way his own daughters were looking—could I have my people help them the way they'd worked with Mrs. Hand?

The President wanted nothing but the best for his girls, but he didn't expect any favors and was always insisting that he pay retail, and usually on the spot, for the clothes. He even tried to give Rita a check for some of the things they'd picked out and she had to remind him that she wasn't a salesgirl. Moyers would tell me later that the President was very conscious of appearances and of any potential favoritism that might be harmful to either himself or me (with memories of Sherman Adams and his vicuna coat in the Eisenhower administration around to haunt everyone). What Johnson wanted was the counsel and the taste from an organization that had the reputation of being the liveliest, most stylish store in the country for youthful women. He wanted his daughters dressed by someone whose style and taste he admired, but he wanted to pay for it. Nothing would be a gift.

And we did our jobs and did them well. Joseph Magnin turned two fresh-faced school girls into glamorous young women; we were even responsible for getting Lynda Bird on the Best Dressed List, something for which she's given us full credit.

When Lynda first walked into our New York office, she was wearing a Villager dress which hung midway to her ankles, an old, fur-trimmed red coat, a flowered tapestry bag and a wig. Rita and Selma looked at each other and said, "No way could we help this girl." But Lynda had a beautiful face with magnificent skin, terrifically expressive eyes and good carriage. There were, as Rita says, "possibilities." Mrs. Johnson was always well-groomed in a classic way, but she wasn't a clothes-horse and fashion bug in comparison with Jacqueline Kennedy; her concern was that her daughters always be neat and clean. Lynda Bird's attitude was that any old thing would do as long as it was clean and tidy. At the time she admits to having no feeling for clothes. High fashion was not high on her list of priorities. But over the years she became very cognizant of what looked good on her and what didn't.

Lynda Bird is a tall woman, about five-feet-nine, and she is long-waisted, which was a problem for her during a period when designers were making clothes for shorter-waisted women. She also felt that she wasn't perfectly proportioned and that she wanted clothes to camouflage what she called her "sins." No pleats, nothing that was cut low in front or back. She also wanted to buy practical things—clothes which were packable and didn't require too much ironing or alteration. At the time we were consulting with her, she was on the campaign trail for her father and needed go-everywhere clothes. As the daughter of a president, she also had to be careful about offending people. She couldn't be seen, for instance, in a sleeveless dress in a part of the country where it was considered unladylike or rude to be seen in bare arms; she was, in effect, to be a role-model for women her age throughout the entire country.

While dressing the President's daughters was a tall order, Rita and Selma did their jobs well—well, that is, after their initial meeting with the Great Man himself, which had Rita scared "spitless," as she is fond of saying. The President often had occasion to be in New York. Once it was for a meeting with the Pope and he wanted some new clothes for his wife and daughters for the historic event. I called Rita and told her, "You're going to meet Mr. Johnson," and all she could scream was, "I didn't have my hair cut." Ann Hand was to take Rita to meet the President and she was very nervous. Her only memory of the meeting was the President's size. "He was enormous," is all she can say. But the first time Rita ever went to the White House, the first visit of quite a few, she dressed elegantly, and in her haste she fell flat on her face getting out of the car. When dealing directly with Luci and Lynda Bird, however, both Rita and Selma were cool and kind professionals.

The girls favored American designers such as Malcolm Starr, Donald Brooks, Kaspar for Joan Leslie, Harvey Berin (who Lynda liked especially for his beaded evening dresses) and Geoffrey Beene. Lynda's wedding gown was by Beene who also did the rest of the gowns for her bridal party. Luci liked the Beene designs so much that although she had bought a dress in Texas for her sister's rehearsal dinner, she was insistent that Beene design a dress for her. The rush order was cut and stitched in four hours. I nearly had to stand over the seamstresses myself to snatch up the finished dress and fly to Washington to deliver it. While I personally didn't do the sewing, I certainly did some heavy needling to get it done on time.

Of the 500 people invited to the wedding, I was one. My New York staff, meanwhile, was asked to help coordinate the clothing end of the wedding. It was Rita's job to move into the White House to bring everything together. Lynda spent lavishly on her trousseau—I think that the *Washington Post* put the figure at $4,000—which was a gift from her father who insisted again on paying retail for everything. She had ordered twenty-five coats, suits and dresses from major American designers. The night before Lynda's wedding to Charles Robb, as Rita was checking to see that everything was in order, she discovered amidst the tissue paper and hangers that were strewn all over every space of the girls' bedrooms that a part of one of the bridesmaid's ensembles was missing—a jacket, I think. She called New York in a panic—the missing piece had to be airfreighted immediately. She was lying down on one of the beds upstairs in the White House with her shoes off when an aide knocked on the door and said, "There's someone downstairs to see you. He says he's from Joseph Magnin." When Rita ran downstairs to get what she thought was a package from New York, she found me standing there with Luci's dress and the missing jacket. Still a delivery boy after nearly fifty years in the business! I just thought it would be fun to make a delivery to the White House.

I was very fond of the Johnson girls and they of me. We would exchange good wishes at Christmastime, although one of the most poignant notes I received during that time came from Luci and Pat Nugent. It was a picture of Luci alone, standing in a red dress in front of the White House holding her baby son, Lyn. Pat was in Vietnam, and during one of his "R-and-R" leaves Luci had met him in Hawaii; first, however, she'd stopped off in San Francisco and had gone shopping at JM for some new clothes for their reunion. While I'm sure the picture of Luci and her baby was to have been a happy one, she did look a little forlorn. The message was warm and sweet: "May the peace of Christ be with you now—and always. You have done so much to make our White House years the joy that they have been and we shall always be grateful. I could not close a Christmas wish without thanking you for all you did to make our reunion so truly perfect. Your personnel were delightful, helpful and sparked my trip off with a huge gold star. My only regret is that I couldn't thank you personally for bringing such ecstasy in my life. With affection, Luci."

Lynda and Chuck Robb came to San Francisco on their honeymoon. Chuck was on his way to Vietnam as a newly commissioned officer and both were campaigning for the President's re-election. I organized a large gala in their honor at the de Young Museum—a real dress-up affair. As with most visiting dignitaries, and Lynda and Chuck were no different, we also planned a little sightseeing tour of San Francisco for them. It wasn't exactly like taking a friend out to see Coit Tower, Fisherman's Wharf or Golden Gate Park— not with the amount of Secret Service people along for the ride. One point of interest for most San Francisco visitors is our cable cars, and Lynda was no different. We were riding in my car, accompanied, of course, by her Secret Service escorts, when we got to Hyde and Union Streets. We decided that we wanted to hop a cable car and ride down to the Hyde Street Pier with the limo following behind. There was a Swensen's Ice Cream Parlor across the street and we stopped in for an ice-cream cone—it was one of those rare hot days in San Francisco and we were all feeling a little parched. Lynda was eating a large butterscotch cone when this big, burly conductor comes back to collect our fares and says, "You can't get on this car—there's no ice cream allowed. You'll have to get off at the next corner." He not only failed to recognize the President's daughter, he was obstinate and insistent. A Secret Serviceman started to tell him who Mrs. Robb was, but I said, "Let's not make a fuss; let's get off before we get into the papers." Well, it made the papers anyhow and the conductor, who was very embarrassed, claimed he didn't know who we were. Afterwards, Swensen's sent Lynda some butterscotch ice cream.

It was a sad time for all of the Johnson supporters when he decided not to run in 1968. I felt that his involvement in

Vietnam was unfortunate, that perhaps he had no choice but to do what he did, given the futility of the whole conflict, and that to bow out gracefully was perhaps his only option. With Johnson out of office, we still maintained our friendship. He was extremely interested in building his own Presidential library and asked me to help him raise funds for it. My family and I had been invited down to the LBJ ranch on several occasions. On one trip, I took my sister-in-law, Adele Simpson.

As I've mentioned, the President had a way with the ladies. He was quite a wag and quick with a quip. He invited Adele to come with him to tour his home. When he got to his bedroom, he said to Adele, "Now I want you to lay down on my bed and I want you to see how comfortable it is." She did as she was asked and he smiled at her. As tough as he was, he could be an engaging charmer and he told Adele, "I want you to tell all your friends that you slept in the same bed as the President of the United States."

The LBJ ranch on the banks of the Pedernales River looked like it belonged to just plain folks—it was a comfortable white-painted frame ranch house with rolling lawns, bushy green trees, neatly clipped shrubs and marvelous flowers, especially the Texas bluebonnets which colored the hillsides. The ranch stretched for miles and the President was very fond of touring his acreage in a little electric golf cart although there were plenty of horses on the property. Johnson had his own airfield and we would fly in from Austin on a private plane. He was also a car nut, and instead of horseflesh in his stables he had horsepower under the hoods of several classic cars, an old fire engine and a powerful Lincoln Continental. There were also television monitors all over the house in threes, one for each of the major commercial networks. He had them in his office, his bedroom and his library. He always had on all three sets at the same time. On one trip down to the ranch I brought Jerry and my grandson,

Ronald, who had not been invited to have dinner with the adults. He was, however, allowed to sit in the next room at the President's own desk with all three TV sets going, and at that point he said to his father. "Dad, I don't want to go to dinner with you when I can sit here."

Before President Johnson could see his library completed, he died. Lady Bird responded to my telegram of condolence with a gracious letter: "Your sympathetic telegram and generous prophesies about Lyndon's presidency meant so much during these difficult days. Thank you for giving him your help and friendship always . . . and for giving us comfort and courage now." When the library in Austin was completed, my family and I were invited down for the dedication by Lady Bird Johnson. The library is quite striking, not for its architecture which is clean and modern, but for the honesty of its content. One of the first displays inside is of the Vietnam war with no holds barred. There are pictures chronicling the entire conflict—the bloodshed, the tragedy. But there is nothing in the library which even indicates (as is often the case in buildings of this sort) that Lyndon Johnson was a great man. I think that eventually history will vindicate Johnson and show that he was a victim of his times.

If it hadn't been for my association with Lyndon Johnson, I'd have probably never met Bill Moyers, one of the most capable and astute people I've ever known. I met Bill in 1964 when he was a special assistant to President Johnson and I was an activist, liberal Democrat who was supporting LBJ. We had already met briefly prior to that in 1960 when Moyers and Johnson were enroute to the Democratic National Convention in Los Angeles; they had stopped in San Francisco for a fund-raiser given by Ben Swig who owned the Fairmont Hotel and who was a great Johnson supporter. We had a cursory conversation as people are wont to do at cocktail parties, but we did not become friends until I started working closely with the Johnson administration.

215

Bill was a fifteen-year-old high-schooler when he went to work for a newspaper in Marshall, Texas, his hometown. He decided he wanted to be a political journalist at college, North Texas State, and he wrote a letter to then Senator Lyndon B. Johnson, who gave the nineteen-year-old Moyers a summer internship on his staff. Bill says it was a stroke of luck—that somehow his letter impressed Johnson enough that Bill was hired; they got to like each other and Johnson called the publisher of the newspaper Moyers was working for and gave him a good report. Johnson suggested that instead of Bill going back to North Texas State, he finish up at the University of Texas. There Moyers worked at the Johnsons' family-owned radio and TV station to make enough money to get married. When he was a junior, he went off to study for the ministry, but when he graduated, he didn't want to be a clergyman. Then the phone rang. It was Johnson who told young Moyers that it was his intention to run for the Presidency in 1960, would Moyers come to work for him. A six-month appointment stretched into a year and when Johnson got the vice-presidential nod from Jack Kennedy, Moyers persuaded both of them to let him go with the Peace Corps as deputy director, where he stayed for three years. When JFK was assassinated, Moyers joined President Johnson as his press secretary. Bill stayed on for four years and left in 1967 to become publisher of *Newsday.* When the Long Island weekly was sold in 1970, he put on his working journalist cap again and wrote a book called *Listening to America.* Someone at Public Broadcasting was looking for an anchorman for a series they were starting and Bill joined them until CBS came after him and made him the principal reporter for "CBS Reports." It must have been a frustrating time for him because I remember talking to him on the telephone and commenting to him that perhaps CBS wasn't the place for him. I had a habit of picking up the phone and dialing him up just to talk. Our conversations ranged to many things, including my insistence that he run for office some day himself. With his political and journalistic background he's probably more capable than half the men parading around the Capitol—but Moyers is a dedicated journalist and feels that he is much more effective where he is.

I did tell him that I thought it was time for him to go back to PBS just before he made the jump and started "Bill Moyers' Journal." Now, I'm not sure that the public broadcasting audience is a big enough platform for him. Bill and I have become very closely associated and he says that for the past ten years he hasn't made a career move without first talking it over with me. In 1979 Bill was in Colorado for a month around the time of my eightieth birthday. He called me to wish me happy birthday and the moment he hung up, the phone rang for him. It was President Carter asking Moyers to join the White House staff as a policy special assistant. Bill turned it down and eventually Lloyd Cutler took the post. Bill talked to the President for about a half-hour and then called me back. I told him, "If anybody could make a difference, I think it could be you, but nobody can make a difference at the White House now; it's too late." I also told him that as a matter of public duty, he should consider taking the position but as a matter of peace of mind, I thought that it would be a source of frustration for him. Bill told me that he made the choice for both personal and professional reasons: "I'm a journalist," he said, "and I didn't want to go back to the White House and have the credibility that I've worked at over the last ten years be diminished by being seemingly a partisan again."

The matter wasn't finished yet because Moyers also agreed with me and said, "It is a matter of satisfying my personal sense that when the President calls, you have to answer." It was a sense of duty that he was born with, that he was nurtured with down in East Texas, and Moyers was in concert with me that he should at least think about it. He called the President back and told him he'd think about the offer again, and then he called me back and we talked it through some more. I was careful not to tell him what he ought to do but helped him analyze the problem. Eventually he decided that his original decision was correct and I said, "Well, I'm sorry for the country, but I think (the decision) was right for you." Three months passed and President Carter called him again and asked him if he wanted to be Secretary of Education. Again Bill called me and we talked. I pointed out to him that I thought it was an inconsequential job, that you couldn't weld a new bureaucracy onto an old one and that he was teaching more people through his program than he would ever reach as a member of government. I did say to him that if he decided to go back into government service again I would like to help him send his three children through college, but he declined with thanks. A true Texas gentleman and a fine friend whom I never would have met had it not been for my love of politics.

CHAPTER ELEVEN ❧

Joseph Magnin IV— the Sale to AMFAC

❧ BY 1958 THE JOSEPH MAGNIN STORES had far sur-passed my wildest dreams. We were a viable and exciting company, but in the midst of our innovation and success we had gone just about as far as we could go as a family-held company. We had put all of our eggs into one fairly fashion-able basket, but there comes a time when even department-store magnates start working for the government. On a personal level we could have drawn higher salaries as officers in the company but Uncle Sam would have taken an even larger share of our income. We needed to diversify our holdings. We also realized that in order to build new stores, we needed the cash, the liquidity, to build in more markets.

While I never expected to sell Joseph Magnin outright to a conglomerate or to a group of stores like Federated, which owned Filenes in Boston, Lazarus in Columbus, Ohio, I. Magnin in San Francisco and Bullock's in California, or Carter Hawley Hale, which owned the Emporium-Capwell stores in the Bay Area, I knew that the company would have to unload some of its stock and offer it for public sale to get the cash we needed for expansion. We started to make plans to go public in late 1958 and by March, 1960, when JM consisted of fifteen women's specialty shops, the family sold 43,000 of 78,000 shares in a combination offering of common stock and convertible debentures totalling $3,200,000. Our initial stock offering sold for $25.25 per share of common stock and the value never dropped beneath that. The family, of course, retained virtual control, but as a public company we now had a board of directors with outside-the-family members. For nearly ten years more the family held on to Joseph Magnin, expanding through Southern California and Nevada until, in 1969, we had thirty-two stores.

When a company wants to go public and to offer common stock, it is not simply a matter of calling up your friendly neighborhood brokerage firm and telling them that you have "X" number of shares to sell. You must shop for a reputable firm which will fit your needs just as carefully as you'd shop for a pair of shoes, a fine diamond or a new home. And when you're dealing with millions of dollars and thousands of shares of stock, it is not a decision to be made in haste. We sent out our feelers into the brokerage industry and were soon besieged with inquiries from all sorts of brokers, men who call themselves investment bankers. We were being romanced by a company named Blythe—eventually Blythe, Eastman, Dillon—and when they spoke to us, they were also representing I. Magnin. (It is common practice that when one company is trying to buy another, the company on the block doesn't always know who is trying to acquire it.) The representative from Blythe indicated to me something we already knew, that Joseph Magnin was worth a lot of money; and at the time, in haste, perhaps, I made the statement to them that if I could get book value for my company, I would sell.

Immediately Blythe said they had a buyer—Bullock's, a

company which had, incidentally, just bought I. Magnin. But not all of this was out in the open when Blythe arranged for a top-secret meeting in the VIP lounge of Pan American at San Francisco International Airport—real cloak-and-dagger stuff between arch competitors. It was, as Walter Newman is fond of saying, "kind of like having the Germans and Americans together in one room while World War II raged outside." On our team were Donald, Walter, Tony Nocita, our financial vice-president and myself. We arrived first and were just sitting down when the door opened and in walked the people from Blythe with Walter Candy, the head of Bullock's, Hector Escobosa, president of I. Magnin and Eric Stanford, executive vice-president of I. Magnin. With the people from Blythe acting as moderators, I. Magnin indicated that they were there to accept my "offer" and to buy our company at book value, a ridiculously low price. Walter Newman was steaming because he had talked to a broker who had said that JM was worth considerably more than the proffered figure. And then he stepped in and saved the company millions of dollars by preventing us from making a terrible mistake.

Later he told me he was thinking, "I could get killed for this;" but he was representing Ellen and Jerry and he knew that I would speak for myself, so he had to speak for the others. He said point-blank that he thought these people were trying to steal our company. He said that he knew there were much higher numbers in the marketplace for our stock and he recommended on the spot that we not sell. Then everyone looked at me and I said, "I guess there's a difference of opinion," and they folded their books and went away.

In our search for a broker we received a suggestion from one of our store managers, a man named Jack Hughes. His father owned a company in the East Bay called Hexel, and a New York firm with a San Francisco office had taken them public. The company was named F. S. Smithers. During the fifties they'd been primarily a bond house, but they felt that the sixties would be more important for stocks than bonds and they were gearing up to get into the common stock market. The senior Mr. Hughes remarked to me that he was very pleased with the manner in which Smithers had handled the whole transaction, and at that point we met with a man named James Felchlin of F. S. Smithers. Not only did Smithers and Felchlin take us public, they also connected us with a large insurance company, Northwestern National Life of Minneapolis, which lent us the money to expand, in the mid-sixties, into Southern California.

Over the years I had flirted with ideas of selling Joseph Magnin, but they had been fleeting thoughts, some of which were looked upon as bad ideas by my family. When Ann died, for instance, I suggested that perhaps I should sell to I. Magnin and Ellen was so incensed that she quit Stanford to go to work full-time at the store—probably to babysit me so I wouldn't sell. But I think I have a tremendous sense of timing, and I could see that by 1960 the retailing business, not to mention the direction of our country's economy, was changing drastically.

When JM started its big push right after World War II, it was a time when consumer industries were in their infant stages. Raw materials that had been tied up in the war effort were again available to the public and there was a tremendous boom in soft goods, especially clothing. We were in a period of tremendous growth in the fashion industry. Clothing was an easy item for people to buy. It didn't have high capital cost and it dealt with style, a commodity people thought they could purchase. There were lots of places built during the war that had made uniforms; now they were retooling to make finely tailored clothing. And when you have a buying public which hasn't been able to spend its money on anything nice in five or six years, there is a real boom situation created.

Over the next twenty years all sorts of things came onto the market for people with disposable income to purchase—television sets, cars, stereo components, as well as clothing.

Meanwhile the price of ready-to-wear started to escalate and where a person could have bought a fine suit or topcoat for $150 in 1960, today it would cost him substantially more—the same amount of money he'd pay for a good quality color television or microwave oven. You could also buy a nice piece of art for $500 or start a small wine cellar or take a vacation or do any number of things that no one thought of doing back in 1946. The point is, the number of things on which a person can spend money that appeals to a broad consumer base is so much greater these days, and given the fact that our incomes had not grown at an equivalent rate, our consumer is forced to make choices as to what he should do with that same money. Should he spend it on a TV set, a vacation, car repairs or a topcoat?

As long ago as 1966 and 1967 I could see that our economy was deteriorating. I realized also that the heyday of women's apparel was over, that twenty years of sustained growth was finally coming to a halt. And, in 1968, I also realized that even with the placement of new stores throughout Southern California, we were running out of room to grow. Perhaps we had space for ten more stores in effective locations. We had pretty much saturated the market in California and Nevada. All we could do at that point was to hold our position and wait for the others to catch up to what we had known for so long—that the youth market was the fashion market. Except for a few stores that thought young like JM, the entire women's fashion business was an anachronism—controlled by designers who cared not a whit for an increasingly active lifestyle. They were totally out of touch with our consumer.

For Joseph Magnin to survive and continue making money as a fashion leader, it had been my son Donald's opinion that we had to penetrate the major markets. He thought the ultimate answer to keeping JM viable was not more and more smaller stores in Modesto and Santa Rosa. We needed to expand to Chicago, New York, Dallas—cities across the country. And Donald called that kind of move a major crapshoot, because if we were wrong, we could be totally out of luck. If we opened a store, especially with our formula for low-cost leases in a Modesto or a Ventura, and we made a mistake, so what? But if we gambled and opened in Chicago, Houston, Denver or any other major city and made a mistake, our company could have lost some of its credibility which probably would have had a deadening effect on our profits. And at seventy years old, whether I thought Donald was right or not, I couldn't take those chances. I had cut back my active participation in JM to spend more time with my outside interests, and I was looking forward to the time when I could step back, if not down. So when a call came into Walter Newman's office back in 1968 inquiring if Joseph Magnin was for sale, it was the germ of an idea we could no longer ignore.

We had never structured ourselves for an outright sale. I had said to Donald, Ellen, Jerry and Walter that if we got a good offer, I'd like to sell, but I never entertained it seriously until Marshall Weigel for Schwabacher and Company, a lifelong friend of Walter's, called and said, "I've got some people in my office who would like to buy Joseph Magnin. Is it for sale?" Our usual response was that everything is for sale if the price is right. But I said, "No, not especially," because the best way to get the best price whether you're selling a house or a business is not to appear too anxious. The first offer Weigel's buyers came up with was something like $28 per share, which I immediately turned down. They countered again with a higher figure and I turned them down again. Weigel asked what it would take to buy the business and I made up a fantastic figure—"$50 a share," I said grandly, never figuring we'd get it. Our buyers, who by the way were still anonymous, countered with another offer which I turned down, and then I said to Weigel jokingly, "You should learn your English—we want $50 a share," which was 3½ times book value or 28 times earnings. Weigel, on behalf of the client who we learned was a conglomerate named AMFAC, said yes, and we called him back and said that the sale could be on a cash-only basis—no stock. I had seen too many deals fizzle where stock was involved.

AMFAC is an acronym for American Factors, Ltd., a Honolulu-based conglomerate with interests in sugar cane production, construction machinery, appliances, hotels, restaurants and department stores—they owned the Hawaii-based Liberty House stores. They were offering us about $30 million for a company whose real assets—that is, fixtures, merchandise, accounts receivable—were worth only $9.5 million. What they wanted to buy was our reputation and our management team.

The decision to sell was not to be taken lightly. It required unanimity among the family members, and it turned out to be an emotional decision for all of us. For myself, because I had spent most of my life involved with a company started by my parents, and for my children, whose intention it had been to carry on in the Magnin tradition as retailers and fashion pacesetters. Although we were contemplating selling our business to a large conglomerate, a move that seemed to be a coming trend in our business anyhow, AMFAC sweetened the deal by telling us that management was the key to their wanting JM and that all of us would stay on in existing positions. They would bring in the resources to turn us into a national firm. When it came down to making the final decision, however, the family was of two minds, Donald especially.

When Donald went into the board meeting to discuss our options, he said, "Ladies and gentlemen, I am going to wear two hats. I'm going to wear one hat as a director cognizant of this enormous price that's being offered—$33 million for a company worth only about ten—and as a director with a sense of obligation to those 600 stockholders who bought our stock ten years ago. I'm going to vote for the sale." But emotionally and personally Donald said that he was going to vote his own stock against the sale, noting that perhaps he was being selfish yet loved what he was doing. I had made it very clear that if one did not want to sell, we would not sell. However, at the last minute Donald voted his stock in favor of the sale, although to this day he says he wonders if he made the right decision. I think that he suffered more emotional pangs than anyone, but financially there was no question we'd made the right decision.

In the course of our meetings I had occasion to visit with Toni Moran Harley, who'd remained my good friend throughout the years. She had invited me to a party at her home in Ross, a luxurious suburban community in northern Marin County, across the Golden Gate Bridge from San Francisco. I had been mulling over the sale in my mind for weeks and I was disturbed and troubled by the ramifications of selling JM. As I strolled down the driveway at Toni's house with her, I said, "Let's face it, my kids don't want to work like I did. It's nothing against them, but it's the times." Deep in my heart I didn't want to let go of a business that was my life, my love and my religion, but I could never express it that way.

We took our final family vote at Stonestown, which is a typical suburban shopping center store and a place which Ellen thought not to be at all appropriate for such a far-reaching decision. Perhaps she wanted more pomp and circumstance. We went over the terms of the sale—we were to receive two-thirds of the proceeds in cash and another one-third in convertible bonds—a compromise I thought was not good, but we did it anyway. Years before, my father, wanting the business or the cash from same to remain in the family, had structured his will in such a way that we would be living off the income from our stock of which I was made trustee. The principal would then revert to my children upon my death. The money from the sale was divided up according to the structure in Joe's will and the way everything turned out, each of the children was to get a little more than $1 million when the deal was signed—I was to get a little more than they. The rest was put in trust. AMFAC also offered and insisted on five-year contracts at a substantial rate to stay in current positions (they did offer me a little more to stay on as chief executive officer). We believed them. We had such pride in Joseph Magnin that we'd do anything we could to see it succeed in the national marketplace. All of us agreed to sell—even Donald.

But a conglomerate is a different entity from a small, family-owned company. We didn't have Harvard Business School types running around constantly deciding things by committee and were able to move quickly when we had questions to answer. And while AMFAC indicated to us that they were buying our brainpower, they soon made it clear that they wanted to do things their way. At the time of our sale an article appeared in a business weekly which explained it better than I can:

> The main financial reaction to (the sale) is that it again shows the fading interest in the retail world to the family-owned, independent chain. The fact that the JM operation now becomes part of a big conglomerate indicates a trend toward the bureaucratic and public form of business as opposed to the independent and private. Also, many feel that it is the beginning of a drive on the part of JM for the kind of financial backing to move the chain into the national scene . . . Many fashion forces are speculating that the personal touch of JM (the touch that made them famous) is bound now to be watered down and that the store will now have to play the part of the rich dowager.

How sad that what the article spoke was the truth.

Although we had five-year contracts, it wasn't the same as being your own boss, and as Donald said, once you've been your own boss, you can't adjust to someone looking over your shoulder. Donald was in charge of what AMFAC was calling "merchandising operations" and his superior—his first real boss other than me—was constantly double-checking him and demanding: "Do you think you bought too much of that or not enough of this? Don't you think you've stuck your neck out too far?" And Donald's answer was, "You're paying me an awful lot of dough for these decisions. If you want to second-guess me, I don't think you need me." During the time Don worked under the AMFAC rules, he did something he'd never done in his life—he watched the clock.

All of my children loved retailing and, as Donald was to say many years after, "I don't think I could ever again be as intense about anything as when I was working at Joseph Magnin. Aside from pride of ownership and watching the company grow from a staff of 20 to 3,000, I loved working with my family. We had the best of two worlds. Not only were we financially successful, it was fun working. I don't think we ever had a sour moment that lasted . . ."

But when AMFAC announced that it was looking for a new chief executive officer to replace me, it ceased being fun for all of us. The move came within six months after acquisition. We had no idea that AMFAC was looking to replace the family until we found out they were in the market for a new CEO—a person, by rights, I could have had some influence in choosing had I wanted to press my advantage. But AMFAC owned almost ninety-five percent of the stock in the company and they said they felt there was too much family and that the company would do better with someone from the outside. I told them that I did not want to be CEO; I'd had my share of it. However, I made several suggestions of who I thought would be good for the company, including one of my family, and I said that I didn't think that someone from the outside would be beneficial. In retrospect, I think AMFAC would have done better had they listened to my suggestion, but they thought there was too much in-breeding.

There is something magic about the word "president" and I knew that in a company the size of ours someone had to be CEO. Although I could have chosen one of my family to head Joseph Magnin *before* we sold the business, I think I lacked the courage to make the choice. Each one of my children, including Walter Newman, had special abilities. But I didn't want the same thing to happen to my family that happened to my father when Grandma Magnin made John chairman of the board of I. Magnin over him. And whether Grandma was right or not, there was no way of telling. I was too young at the time to know what had really happened, but I could see the results of her decision—the rift it caused between my father and his family. All I wanted to do in 1969 was to keep peace in my family. Of course, when we received the price we did for the business, it did seem to solve the problem of succession for me. But when AMFAC started rearranging the JM corporate structure, although I had some input, it was too late for me to make the choice.

The conglomerate had its own ideas of what to do with the Cyril Magnin family. At the time Henry Walker, head of AMFAC, thought that a change would be healthy and proposed a wholesale switch in positioning for each member of my family. Donald was offered the presidency of Liberty House in Hawaii, a bigger job than what he had at JM as vice-president and merchandise manager. The job carried considerably more salary but he would have had to take his children out of school; Elaine would have had to close her successful needlepoint business and they would have moved to Hawaii. AMFAC had said they had great faith in him. Jerry, who was running our Southern California operation and making quite a name for himself as a visionary, swing-for-the-fences retailer, was asked to manage the Stonestown store and Walter, who for years had been active in civic matters and had just been named to the San Francisco Planning Commission, was told to pull up stakes and manage the Century City store in

Los Angeles. Ellen was asked to remain with AMFAC to be what she always was, assistant to the CEO, who we learned was to be a man named Robert Berry, who AMFAC was bringing in from Neiman-Marcus where he had been the merchandise manager.

Donald said he wasn't going to take any more. He had spent an agonizing period trying to fit into the corporate way of doing things, but after years of being his own boss and accomplishing things through our freewheeling style—our creative anarchy if you will—he was hating his job. Finally Don, Jerry and Walter went to Henry Walker and said, "Let's agree to disagree. If you don't feel we're competent to continue running JM, we'd like to leave." They still had those five-year contracts and by rights could have stuck to them, but they negotiated their way out. The headline in the *Chronicle* read: "Magnin Management Walks Out . . .'It was a breath of spring.'"

The major difference between a conglomerate and ourselves is that AMFAC was an organization and Joseph Magnin was a group of dedicated people. The only thing that mattered to us was that everyone work together. Everyone had responsibilities in their particular area, but they weren't told how they had to accomplish it. They had the freedom to do things and the only thing that counted was the result. The split from AMFAC was a very rough period—after all, we had been a close-knit group, not only as a family, but as business associates, and it appeared that we were finally all going our separate ways. Siamese quintuplets separated after thirty years. There were bruised feelings all the way down the line, but nobody went into shock and fell apart . . . but in the course of disengaging, there was a letdown in drive and loyalty.

At the time there was a series of profiles done in *Women's Wear Daily* about my family and me and their comment about the sale reflected the good front we put on for the public. The article said, "Cyril Magnin has it made . . . With AMFAC stock in his poke, a good contract for his declining years and a well-manicured finger in many civic and cultural pies, he plays the *bon vivant* with characteristic élan . . . he entertains almost nightly and is recognized as an authority on his home town's better restaurants." Fluffy stuff which didn't get anywhere near the truth of what was going on in each of our hearts.

Personally I still had my offices at Harrison and Spear, although officially I was no longer president of the company. I retained the title chairman of the board. I stayed because I thought I could be useful—actually I was asked to stay and said I would to be helpful. It was a goodwill gesture, but I thought I could help straighten some of the corporate fellows out; they were making mistakes that were becoming costly.

While I was still CEO, and before they replaced me, one of the AMFAC people came into my office one day with leases he had negotiated for stores in San Jose and Hayward—expensive leases which he wanted me to approve. I read them over and said I wouldn't approve them, that we didn't make leases where we had to put in all the fixtures and pay a high percentage and a high minimum rent. I told the gentleman that I thought it was bad for the company and he said, "Look, *I'm* telling you what to do." I refused to sign the expensive leases and I guess if I ever made an enemy, I did that minute. He was mad as hell, but I told him, "Your methods are different from mine and we don't agree." I said, "Maybe I'm old-fashioned," but I was so mad myself. I saw that those leases would hurt the company. The mind-set of AMFAC was not geared to what had made JM a success and with the methods they were using with our former stores. They wound up, eight years later, nearly $20 million in the hole before they could find another buyer for Joseph Magnin.

Meanwhile our young leadership—Donald, Jerry and Walter—were considered experienced whiz kids in the retail-

231

ing business and in 1970, shortly after they left JM, they were contacted by Carter Hawley Hale to join them to form a national chain of specialty stores which would replicate Joseph Magnin. They were offered $20 million in investment capital and very substantial salaries plus the time to think about it. Carter Hawley Hale was interested in the specialty store market but had not acquired Neiman-Marcus or Bergdorf Goodman at that point. Donald said he couldn't, that he'd had it. No more big companies. Jerry and Walter could have done it without Donald, but they turned it down also. The offer was a tremendous compliment to the Joseph Magnin organization.

While I had my civic responsibilities and cultural interests to take up my time, my children weren't exactly idle. Donald started Domain Imports (Domain is a contraction of Donald Magnin, Inc.), a very successful and low-profile business. He runs it about the same way old Joseph would have. For years Don reinvested everything in his business, building it carefully. He even typed his own invoices for three years and answered his own phones. Ellen thinks he's very much like Joe—she calls it a "European attitude" about finance because Donald is very careful about money.

Walter Newman went to work for I. Magnin and eventually opened up his own consulting business doing basically what he did for Joseph Magnin for many years—finding retail locations and handling real estate, acquisitions and mergers.

Jerry, meanwhile, is very much like me—down to the way we talk to the way we walk with our shoulders hunched over to the clothes we wear—almost exclusively Ralph Lauren. After years of my dressing him, now *he* dresses *me*.

When Jerry cleaned out his desk at Joseph Magnin in Los Angeles, it was a Saturday. In the Sunday paper he read that an historic old Hollywood restaurant was for sale by order of the court. It turned out to be Chianti, a romantic Italian place built back in 1947 by the famous restauranteur Romeo Salta.

232

Jerry called his pal Larry Mindel in San Francisco and had him fly down—together they went over to take a look at the place with an eye to buying it. When they walked in, there were plastic flowers on the tables and fourteen people in the place the entire night. With a little smart maneuvering, they acquired Chianti and then a few years later they opened another place in Los Angeles modeled on Harry's American Bar in Venice, Italy. They formed Spectrum Foods and opened two restaurants in San Francisco—MacArthur Park, which was one of the original "fern bars," and Ciao, a high-tech Italian restaurant where you can watch the pasta being made.

Jerry also opened a consulting business immediately after he left JM. But on his way out, he was stopped by a menswear buyer he'd hired while at JM by the name of Al Karstensen who asked Jerry if he would back him if he ever decided to go into business for himself. Jerry thought the guy would never leave his job—it was a good one with a good salary and substantial benefits—but Jerry said yes and then promptly forgot about it. Then one day he got a call from Karstensen who said, "I quit my job . . . I'm here." Jerry says that one of the things he learned from me was integrity and that he'd given this man his word and Al had quit his job because of it. They agreed to go into business together. Well, they kicked around a couple of names for a store and finally when it got down to the wire, Karstensen looked at Jerry and said, "You know, we're jerks if we don't use the name Magnin over the door . . . you own it." And so, Jerry Magnin it was and still is. Jerry has since bought Karstensen out.

The former leadership of Joseph Magnin was thriving. Unfortunately Joseph Magnin itself was not doing as well. In 1977 *Business Week* ran an article in its July 4 issue quoting Henry Walker, Chairman of AMFAC, Ltd.: "We're getting out of the women's apparel business because we find we're not very good at it." By then, Joseph Magnin had grown to forty-eight stores and was sporting an after-tax loss of $16 million. The article went on to say that AMFAC would be selling the specialty chain for about $35 million, a loss of some $20 million in goodwill—the excess of cost over equity—carried on its books since the acquisition of the business in 1969 for $33 million. AMFAC had added eighteen stores that boosted sales volume from $50 million to $83 million, but as the article said, "Operations were increasingly turbulent. Earnings were disappointing and [the] merchandising image [had become] blurred as two presidents within a two-year span tried to right its course . . . AMFAC's mistakes with Joseph Magnin, believes Walker, 'stem from a lack of specialty store experience and controls. The chain was over-inventoried and was recently forced to take heavy markdowns which cut into operating margins. For a big company like ourselves, attention to fine detail was hard to find.' "

In 1977 Walter was contacted by AMFAC in his position as a consultant. They asked if he and Marshall Weigel would dispose of ten Mainland Rhodes stores for them, as they were starting to unload their retail operation. Five stores in the Northwest were sold to Marshall Field and five in the Southwest were sold to different outlets. In the course of their success in finding buyers for the Mainland Rhodes shops, Walter and Marshall were asked on a strictly secret basis to find a buyer for Joseph Magnin. AMFAC was, indeed, losing a lot of money—they had lost the top management and with them, the spirit of the family. For when Donald, Walter and Jerry left the company, so did most of our people including Selma Gross, Rita Wohlman and most of our top buyers.

The second Joseph Magnin sale was accomplished through a firm named Gibbons, Green and Rice, a New York investment banking house which specializes in turn-around situations. If companies are having problems, they put a package together to buy a company, bring in management and find investors who are willing to buy it with them. They had been alerted to the Joseph Magnin situation by Ed Gorman, then assistant to the president of J. C. Penney. He told Gibbons, Green and Rice about the underlying value of Joseph Magnin. Gibbons, Green and Rice had worked with a Pittsburgh outfit named Hillman Company and indicated that they wanted to buy JM from AMFAC. Walter and Marshall convinced AMFAC that these people would be the best ones to buy the company. Before that deal was struck, however, AMFAC thought they had a deal with Ross Hall, a holding company in Palo Alto. Ross Hall had agreed to buy Joseph Magnin at a fixed price and they were down to final negotiations when a major disagreement put a spanner in the works and the deal was off. By the time AMFAC sold to Hillman, they incurred a loss of $17,879,000 after taxes as a result of the sale of Joseph Magnin Co.

As for me, I was and still am working out of my office at Harrison and Spear Streets. Part of my job is to keep the Gucci connection alive.

When Robert Berry first came with the company, he had met Dr. Aldo Gucci, the Italian leather magnate, and Barry felt it would be a prestigious thing to have a Gucci boutique in the store. Dr. Gucci thought it was a capital idea. In September, 1971, Gucci opened at the downtown San Francisco store on the fifth floor. For the first time in thirty years I went out on the floor to sell because there was such a crowd that we were shorthanded. I made so many sales that if I'd been on commission, I'd never have been able to afford me. It was during that time that Barry introduced me to Dr. Gucci and we became friendly. After Barry left the company, Dr. Gucci asked if I would watch over his interests. The Gucci connection had been made.

Then JM was sold to Hillman and they brought Ed Gorman from J. C. Penney as the chairman of the executive committee and chief executive officer of the JM stores. By then Dr. Gucci was dealing mostly with me.

Today there are eleven Gucci franchises controlled through Joseph Magnin with free-standing stores in San Francisco, Honolulu, Phoenix, Las Vegas (in Caesar's Palace) and Atlantic City, plus one being built in Lake Tahoe. In Joseph Magnin stores in San Francisco, Honolulu, Las Vegas, Denver and Carmel, there are Gucci departments. The Gucci connection has certainly added a modicum of prestige to Joseph Magnin.

As for me, I'm still working out of my office at Harrison and Spear . . . making contributions wherever I can, especially in the area of Joseph Magnin's relationship with the Gucci organization.

CHAPTER TWELVE ✍

Dinner-Table Diplomat

✍ FOR YEARS MY POLITICAL ASSOCIATES had tried to get me to run for public office and when I refused, they pushed all sorts of appointments at me. Some of them I took, like the Port Commission and the presidency of the Chamber of Commerce, but for the most part I turned everything down, including the numerous offers to run for mayor and even feelers from the Johnson administration to be Ambassador to the Philippines. I had my priorities. Joseph Magnin was to take my creative energies and most of my time. But when we went public in 1960, and even for the eight or nine years before, I was delegating a part of the authority to my children and to the capable management who had grown with Joseph Magnin. It gave me a lot of time to fill.

But I am not the kind of person who can be idle. I like to be on the go almost every minute of the day, and sometimes far into the night. There are just so many restaurants you can patronize, just so many parties you can attend and just so many cultural events available before that kind of social whirl starts to pall. My family and I have never been what I'd consider "café society" (I don't even drink), nor did I ever try to be part of the social elite. So, when I found myself free to indulge a few of my fantasies, my natural impatience to fill time with good works led me to talk to Mayor John Shelley about a dream job—protocol chief of San Francisco.

I had seen protocol in action during our Portola Festival tour back in 1948. Grover Whelan was New York's official greeter and I had seen him alongside the mayor and in a huge motorcade coming down Fifth Avenue with dignitaries, a police escort and sidewalks lined with gawking onlookers. All the ruffles and flourishes of Whelan's office must have impressed me. Besides, I loved the sound of sirens. But his position was a paid one and I knew that San Francisco didn't have money in its budget to support all the niceties of protocol. However, one day, Jack Shelley called me into his office to thank me for my support and everything changed.

Jack Shelley was a big, happy-go-lucky Irishman. He was the gregarious kind of man who would get out of his limousine in front of City Hall to a crowd of children calling him by his first name. He was honest as the day is long and appreciative of those who helped elect him, me included. When he called me into his office back in 1963, he said he wanted me to have first choice of any commission appointment. I was prepared to turn him down as I'd done so many times before and I did it with a little story:

A young Jewish dress salesman had been drafted into the army. He had been a dress salesman all his life, a wholesale salesman who worked on commission. When he went into the army, he was put in charge of the supply department. One day, the lieutenant came along and watched the young private helping several men. The lieutenant noticed that the private got his work done

238

before anyone else. The lieutenant thought, "Gee, this young fellow has great administrative ability, he's a good worker. I'm gonna recommend he get a commission." So, the lieutenant goes to his colonel and says, "Colonel, Private Cohen is a good worker, you should give him a commission. He knows how to handle men; he knows how to get his work finished on time." So, the colonel calls Cohen into his office and says, "Private Cohen, I've got good news for you. The army is gonna give you a commission." But Cohen scratched his head, thought about it for five minutes and said, "Colonel, you're a very nice man and I know you mean good by me, but you know . . . I've been working on commission all my life . . . I'm satisfied with a straight salary."

When I finished telling my story to Mayor Shelley, I said that I didn't want a commission. I wanted to be chief of protocol. And Shelley says, "What's that?" I explained to him that there was only one other city in the United States that had one and that was New York. Shelley thought about it for a moment and mentioned to me that there was no provision for such a position in the city charter—no expense money, either. I told him I knew that but there was nothing stopping him from appointing me his Assistant in Charge of Protocol Matters, and to sweeten it I said I'd pay all my own expenses. As the mayor, Shelley had only a very small entertainment fund for visiting dignitaries and he also didn't like getting up at four in the morning to greet a visiting emissary.

He took his time thinking about it. He was advised by several mutual friends that it would be a good thing for San Francisco's image, and on May 19, 1964, I became the city's official host. Municipal Judge Lenore Underwood said at the time, "My, my, Mr. Mayor, you picked the right guy to be the glad-hand artist of this city." As for me, I told Jack Shelley that I was going out right away to buy a pair of striped pants and a cutaway . . . just like Grover Whelan.

239

Our first official guest to visit the city after my appointment was the sixty-four-year-old king of Burundi, His Majesty Mwami Mwambutsa IV. To prepare for the king's visit, I borrowed a book on protocol from the State Department. I told the press at the time, "I've heard the king is kind of a swinger. Well, I don't mind swinging once in a while . . . our country needs friends." I seem to remember smiling a lot during that visit and fumbling for correct procedure so as not to insult anyone. I got better at it as we went along.

San Francisco is a major stop on most visiting dignitaries' itineraries. For the Asians we are usually the last stopover in the United States before flying home, and for the Europeans and South Americans—ambassadors, prime ministers, royalty and such—we are a city not to be missed if they are in the United States for any period of time. We have the second largest consular corps in the country and it was my intention when I took the job to meet and greet every one of the consuls-general in residence and to make it clear to them that my office was to be their liaison between their consulates and the city. The first thing I did, however, when I took on the job, was to convince Jack Shelley to get rid of the existing key to the city. It looked like a reject from a toy factory. In its place we had a hefty, brass-plated key designed that weighs about a pound and looks and feels impressive. It made getting the key to San Francisco a real occasion.

Protocol ceremonies, by and large, are cut and dry. You can never say what you want or ask questions you'd like to ask. It is mainly a ritual that most civilized countries indulge in. Protocol involves many things on many levels, however, from establishing tight security for national leaders and visiting royalty down to dispatching transportation, adhering to tight schedules, attending to dietary prohibitions and providing entertainment—the theater, opera, ballet, sightseeing, dinners, luncheons, receptions and, in some cases, gala

240

parties with dancing. As we got better at the job, the job grew and eventually outgrew my office which consisted of me, my assistant and my secretary.

Sometimes we got help from the city by way of special mayor's funds. At one point we were helped out by the hotel tax funds, but basically, as promised, I picked up the tab myself until it started to cost upwards of $25,000 a year. Good works breed a fine reputation and as the word spread that we were creating a pleasant and cooperative atmosphere for our visitors, more and more of the famous from other countries decided to pay us a visit—like the King of Norway, the President of France, the Emperor and Empress of Japan. Mayor Joe Alioto, Jack Shelley's successor, remarked that prior to my tenure we did not have nearly as great a number in terms of quantity and quality of important guests. And he felt it was essential for San Francisco to attract such a glorious list of visitors, not only economically, but artistically. We had a primacy in the performing arts because the people of San Francisco rallied around the opera, the ballet and the symphony. They are proud of their city because it has a luster to it, a gleam made even more golden by the presence of so many important people.

As I found out very soon, my office staff and I couldn't carry the job alone. For state occasions we had worked with Bernice Behrens, who was the director of the U.S. Department of State Reception Center. It was a political appointment she held for eight years and when Jimmy Carter took office as President, Mrs. Behrens found herself out of a job. But by then we were handling between 2,500 and 3,000 state visitors per year, including the famous and their entourages. Sometimes they would be on official business or on a well-publicized tour; others preferred to slip in and slip out. Regardless, we had to be prepared to extend the hospitality (and sometimes, the protection) of the city to them. From a protocol standpoint that meant meeting them at the airport, getting them to their hotel or consular residence, providing security and entertaining them.

When Mrs. Behrens's appointment with the State Department was terminated, all protocol functions were transferred to the city of San Francisco, and Mayor George Moscone and I immediately appointed her deputy chief of protocol on a volunteer basis, although my office did pay for some of her services. Funds had been reduced drastically during the initial Proposition 13 cuts—the Jarvis-Gann initiative that turned into a taxpayers' revolt. What little monies we had for entertaining dried up. But the job had gotten out of hand for my pocketbook. We devised a plan to involve key members of the community who had specific interest in international relations. They were asked to join a Host Committee. For this privilege they paid annual dues of $1,000 each, which fills the protocol coffers and provides not only funds for entertaining our distinguished visitors but willing workers to expedite invitations, give luncheons, volunteer their homes for parties, and the like.

Most protocol receptions are filled with appropriate pomp. For the visit of Prince Albert and Princess Paola of Belgium, there was a reception in the City Hall rotunda with a contingent of forty full-dress marine guards and the entire army band from the Presidio. As 1,000 invited guests filed through the high-domed hall, the band played both our national anthems and then struck up, "I Left My Heart in San Francisco." We had learned through their consulate that the Prince and Princess did not want to be entertained by private persons. One of our leading hostesses wanted to give them a luncheon, but on the theory that if they went to one person's house, they'd be expected to honor every request, we had to find an alternative way to entertain them for lunch. We borrowed an eighty-five-foot yacht owned by a man from Seattle who had business connections in Texas and we had

Mama's, one of North Beach's favorite restaurants, cater the luncheon on board. We made arrangements to have the fire boat come out onto the Bay to salute the royal couple. They were greeted by Fire Chief Andy Casper as another yacht floated alongside with TV film crews and various other members of the press aboard.

In the course of the last eighteen years I have met hundreds of the famous, from the late Shah of Iran and his sister, the Princess Ashraff, to the Emperor and Empress of Japan, the King of Sweden, Joseph Cardinal Mindszenty, President Suharto of Indonesia, Ferdinand and Imelda Marcos of the Philippines, various kings, sheiks and princes from the oil-rich Middle East, prime ministers of Israel, New Zealand and Australia and one of the best guests the city ever had to host, Prince Charles of Great Britain. In spite of the fact that his visit was a security officer's nightmare—supporters of the Irish Republican Army insisted in making his stay a noisy protest with threats of violence—the Prince captivated the hearts of everyone in San Francisco.

Before Prince Charles arrived, we received an itinerary book with sixty-two pages of print so small you could go blind trying to read it. It listed arrival times and limousines—who would ride with whom and which security agent would accompany them. The schedule assigned to the Prince was fierce. He would leave the Fairmont Hotel early every morning, would come back to freshen up around dinner time and then would have a full evening ahead of him. On the first day of his visit there was a reception at the consulate, a beautiful brick Tudor mansion in Pacific Heights, hosted by the British Consul-General. The Prince was utterly charming, regal and self-possessed in spite of the tactical squad stationed in front of the residence protecting him from a group of noisy Irish protesters. The party was held in the front rooms of the home and you could hear all the noise outside. The Prince had come through the mob in his limousine and had been rushed into the mansion. There were 200 invited guests and the Prince had been briefed on every one of them, and as the Consul-General took him around the room, Prince Charles shook everyone's hand and talked with them for about two or three minutes. It was a marvelous display of tact and aplomb.

The next morning I had a California Street cable car waiting for him in front of his hotel and we rode down Nob Hill into the financial district where we stopped at the Bank of America and met with A. W. Clausen and the British-born staff. Then we walked across Montgomery Street and met with the staff of the Chartered Bank of London. At exactly 10:05 A.M., we were on board the *Golden Hind,* a replica of Sir Francis Drake's ship. We had a quick glass of sherry and then we drove to the Golden Gate Bridge vista point where we had exactly eighteen minutes to enjoy the view of the city and Marin County. The Prince went on to visit Oakland via BART, met with Lionel Wilson, the Oakland mayor, toured the port, toured the University of California at Berkeley and then arrived back at the Fairmont at 5:20 P.M. in time to go to City Hall to meet our mayor. The next day was equally as filled with visits to the wine country in Napa, then U.C. Davis to see agricultural exhibits and then on to Sacramento to meet Governor Jerry Brown. The Prince flew back to San Francisco to Crissy Field in the Presidio in time for dinner and a performance of *Turandot* at the San Francisco Opera. The opera was not my choice of entertainment for His Majesty. I had wanted to take him, as I'd taken so many, including every member of the consular corps, to see *Beach Blanket Babylon Goes to the Stars,* the witty, inventive and entertaining review produced by Steve Silver. However, "Beach Blanket" was not considered proper enough for a prince. Secretly, I think he wanted to see it himself because during *Turandot* he leaned over to me and said, "Er . . . please tell me. What about this blanket on a beach?"

For the opera Bernice Behrens had suggested selecting

one of the city's prettier debs for the Prince's date, but one of the British advance men said, "Oh no, the gossip columns would have a field day with it. This trip is *strictly* official." With the mayor entertaining in an "official" capacity, we then thought it would be appropriate to have Jennifer Moscone, the mayor's beautiful daughter, in the opera box with the Prince. We wanted to get the center box for the performance and prevailed upon the people who had reserved it for Saturday night to give it up especially for the occasion. It was a request they couldn't refuse. If you're asking a favor like that for the Prince of Wales, you find that most everyone is cooperative.

Not all requests that come through my office turn out to be as pleasant as the Prince's visit. When Prime Minister Fukuda of Japan came to town, we found he was interested in baseball, and after the City Hall reception and press conference we went into his hotel suite to present him a cap and jacket from the San Francisco Giants. Everything was going well when the wife of one of the gentlemen in the room rushed up, put her arms around Fukuda and kissed him. A very bad gaffe, because of all the countries in the world, Japan is one of the most formal. I think that Mrs. Behrens said to the gentleman, "We *do not* kiss Prime Ministers," and he just shrugged, "I can't do anything with my wife . . ."

Because of my protocol job, I work very closely with the FBI, State Department Security and Secret Service. I have developed friendships with a number of agents, including a young chap by the name of Joe Aaron. Often, he and I will have breakfast together and walk to work. Joe is a handsome man—he looks more like film star Burt Reynolds than what you'd imagine an FBI man to look like. We met over an incident having to do with a foreign diplomat in our city whose family had been robbed. I wanted to avert an international incident and asked Aaron who had called me if he could do anything to help our robbery victim. We wanted no adverse publicity for San Francisco and felt that an incident of this kind could have happened anywhere. When the FBI and local police started looking beyond the obvious facts, a few things surfaced.

We found that this particular man, whose family was on holiday, had entertained some ladies of the evening in his hotel suite, had refused to pay them what they asked and had gotten into a real meleé. During the fight, one of the women took his room key and later, her "protector" let himself in and cleaned house.

Through our official association, Joe and I have become friends. Sometimes we walk to work together; however, my regular morning walk-to-work partner is Jim Rudden, my friend from Port Commission days. He and I have been hiking down Nob Hill for the past eighteen years. We don't exactly let grass grow under our feet, as young Aaron found out when he went with us. Once we have come down that very steep hill, we take varying routes through the city. I don't think there's a building that's gone up in the eastern part of San Francisco that we haven't clocked each pane of glass, each extra story or each new business that's gone in. We keep a fairly frenetic pace; we're notorious red-light jumpers . . . and jaywalkers. We don't have the patience to stand and wait. We walk for exercise and don't like to waste time. But we're more careful now. Herb Caen, in his inimitable style, called attention to our penchant for crossing in midstream, remarking in print that I almost got run over by a No. 45 Muni bus while jaywalking across Mission Street.

By and large, the job of official greeter for the city of San Francisco is a rewarding one and it can carry ramifications with it far beyond just my own personal pleasure and ego gratification. My association with Huang Chen, the head of the Chinese legation to the United States and now Minister of Culture for the People's Republic of China, for instance, proved to be beneficial to the entire city.

When President Nixon began an association with the People's Republic of China back in the early seventies, we did not yet grant them recognition. In other words, there was not the usual exchange of ambassadors and consul-generals. However, the Chinese did send members of a legation to Washington. Their first stop was usually San Francisco, and back in 1973 the head of the Chinese liaison was Han Hsu. Part of our welcome for him was a gathering given by crusty Harry Bridges, the former head of the longshoremen's union. The Chinese remembered Bridges for the time he stopped the loading of scrap steel to Japan after the Manchurian invasion. About the same time that Han Hsu arrived, early 1973, we had heard that the Chinese were going to send on tour a marvelous exhibition of archeological finds—a collection of artifacts which had never been out of China; and because of our fine Asian Art Museum and large Chinese population, we made a concerted effort to inform Han Hsu that San Francisco would welcome the exhibition. I'm afraid his answer was an inscrutable smile and a noncommittal nod. The matter was dropped with no resolution either way.

In August, 1973, Yvon d'Argence, curator of the Asian Art Museum, was on vacation in Paris and saw the exhibition. He contacted the U.S. Embassy to see the Chinese cultural attaché in the Chinese Embassy (because the Chinese had no official delegation in the United States) to see if any progress had been made on our request. The Chinese were again polite but noncommittal. In September, 1973, the scheduled American cities on the tour were announced—Washington, D.C., because it is our country's capital, and Kansas City, partially because it is the geographical center of the country and partially because of its fine Asian arts museum. But no San Francisco.

At the request of Mayor Joe Alioto, I traveled to Washington with William Goetz, chairman of the Asian Art Commission and vice-president of the Bank of America to

247

make another plea and was told by John Richardson, Jr., Assistant Secretary of State for Cultural Affairs, that there was no chance of San Francisco getting the exhibit. He confirmed that statement late in May, 1974, by letter, saying that after its stop at the William Rockhill Nelson Gallery in Kansas City in June, 1975, the exhibition would be on its way back to China. Most people would have given up then, but I didn't.

Letters started going back and forth between San Francisco and the Chinese re-emphasizing that our city had the largest Chinese community in the United States. We started having visits from Hsieh Ch'i-nei, the cultural consul, a man of great importance who was well-versed in Western affairs. He was a career diplomat. He came to take a look and still no commitment. It was then that, through my job as protocol chief, we finally got a very lucky break.

In January, 1975, a man named Huang Chen, the chief liaison officer between the People's Republic and the U.S., came to replace Han Hsu. He came through San Francisco on his way to Washington. On the evening of January 22 I hosted a party at the Mark Hopkins—a glittering affair to which diva Beverly Sills, Bing and Kathryn Crosby and a few other well-known people had been invited. We had a marvelous dinner of mulligatawny soup, tournedos Rossini, asparagus Hollandaise, fresh strawberries Romanoff and fine wines to accompany. And in the spirit of friendship, Mayor Joe Alioto got up after dinner to make a few remarks. Now, let me say that Joe Alioto is probably the best extemporaneous speaker to ever emerge in San Francisco politics. He got up to make a toast as we presented Huang Chen with the key to the city. Mayor Alioto said, "We suggest to the Ambassador that inanimate objects might get tired on their long journey back to China and we suggest that a place be found where they could 'rest' and get over their jet lag." Everyone applauded and sang out with "San Francisco, San Francisco." Through one of his interpreters, Huang Chen called San Francisco "the golden city." There was a feeling of good fellowship, but still, no commitment . . . yet.

Now, I have always called Huang Chen "Mr. Ambassador," although at the time there was no Chinese of that rank in the country—we did not fully recognize Huang's country until the Carter administration. Huang was a diminutive man—my size really—who dressed in well-tailored olive drab uniforms with Mao-styled collars and jaunty peaked caps. During the course of our time together I found out he was a wine buff—he had spent time as a diplomat in France and had developed quite an educated palate. Through architect Tommy Hsieh, a tour of the wine country was arranged, including a tour of the Napa Valley in a custom-fitted Gray Line bus with a fully stocked bar and leather swivel seats. We not only toured the Sterling and Mondavi wineries, we had a barbecue at Franciscan and a complete wine-tasting at Inglenook vineyards. The table was so covered with different sized glasses it looked like a sea of crystal. After Huang Chen tasted a particularly fine and rare wine, a 1955 Cabernet Sauvignon at Inglenook, he smiled and said, "I feel I am back in France."

I thought that Huang Chen and I had quite a bit in common—even though we did not share the same language or the same political ideologies. We shared a certain *joie de vivre* and interest in some of the same things. As we established a friendship that needed few words in common, I felt free enough to approach him about the Chinese exhibition. I told him that I thought both San Francisco and China needed each other—that we were the gateway from the East to the rest of the U.S., that we had a large and active Chinese community and that we were the ideal city for the exhibition. Then he said to me: "Why should we send the exhibition here? San Francisco has only about 650,000 people—not nearly enough to warrant stopping." Then I made a very rash comment. I told him that, indeed, the city itself had only 650,000, but that we were in the center of a potential audience of nearly 40 million people. Huang Chen nodded and with a twinkle in his eye turned what had been only noncommitment from previous diplomats into a definite "maybe." At the end of his stay he invited me to Washington where he said he would return all the courtesies I had shown him.

Meanwhile, to back up my claims of 40 million potential visitors, I did a little homework. I had a map of the western United States laid out on my desk and I marked all the major cities from Denver westward, added up the populations, and what do you know? The figures totaled nearly 38 million people. I had been very close to my estimate. I then spoke with Joe Alioto, who was president of the United States Conference of Mayors, and asked him to write letters to the mayors of each of the cities I'd marked on the map for their support in promoting the Chinese exhibition. They, in turn, wrote official letters to Mayor Alioto, promising their enthusiastic support. When I journeyed to Washington to see Huang Chen, I came armed with my map, a bunch of thumbtacks to mark the cities, little slips of paper with the populations of each city written on them and an adding machine tape with a tally of the population total on it—plus the letters from all the mayors pledging their support. It was a very convincing presentation. I said, "Look at this—you've got all these people to play for," and then I took a chance and told him that I thought San Francisco could draw more people than Washington or Kansas City. It was a calculated risk that we would, mainly because of our large Chinese population and our reputation as a tourist center. He said, "It looks good and I'm going to recommend that you get it."

The next day, when I returned to his office, he told me that Kansas City had the exhibit for four months and that they would either have to take two months away from some other city or give it to us for only two months. We knew the exhibition was going to only eight cities in the world—Vienna, Stockholm, Paris, London, Washington, D.C., Kansas City, Toronto and now, us. Whereas the other host cities had a year to prepare for the display, we had less than ninety days. We got official notification in April and on June 28, 1975, we were to open the exhibition at the Asian Art Museum in Golden Gate Park for two months, closing on August 28.

We broke a world record for attendance for that particular tour, which was officially called "The Exhibition of Archeological Finds of the People's Republic of China." And that was for only sixty days, not the four months each other city had been allotted. I had estimated that 600,000 people would see it and was off by one-third. Before the last artifact was packed and on its way to Bejing, exactly 835,891 visitors had filtered through to see it—a logistical problem that was handled with grace and efficiency and eighteen-hour days.

The exhibition itself consisted of 385 pieces, including a 2,000-year-old burial shroud of Tou Wan, consort of Liu Sheng, Prince Ching of Chungshan of the Han Dynasty, unearthed in Mancheng, Hopei, in 1968. It was 2,160 platelettes of opalescent jade sewn together with golden thread. There was also the celestial flying horse, a bronze figurine discovered in Wu-Wei, Kansu Province, in 1969. These were rare and beautiful pieces that required a fine display space. It took fifty carpenters, cabinet makers, painters and curators working day and night to put up nineteen walls, eighty display cases and silk and velvet-covered pedestals covering 23,210 square feet of space. That was the easy part.

The exhibit was to occupy the entire first floor of the Asian Art Museum except for the Magnin Jade Room, a collection of jade miniatures housed in a facility donated by myself to honor my wife and my parents. The entire exhibition, some of which was funded through the National Endowment for the Arts, was to be free. We had to account for crowd control, publicity, education, security and hospitality for the Chinese curators. The technical aspects of building proper cases and handling the packing and unpacking was enormous. While I had the complete cooperation of Yvon d'Argence and the museum staff, who worked day and night, as chairman—and a "hands-on" chairman at that—I felt obligated to do the best I could from beginning to end. Even when I was out of town at Cape Canaveral watching a space lift-off which linked the U.S. up with the Russians, I phoned San Francisco daily to make sure things were proceeding all right.

We planned everything down to the last detail, especially what to do with the mobs of people who were waiting for their turn to go through the exhibit. We invited members of the Western and Merola Opera groups and just about every fine street entertainer in San Francisco to play at scheduled times in the plaza in front of the museum. The crowds were so well-behaved that a woman who misplaced her purse found it later where she'd dropped it—complete with the $3,000 worth of travelers' checks she had inside.

In October I received an official letter from Huang Chen, who had been present for the opening of the exhibit. He was at the end of his term as chief liaison officer to the United States and he said:

> It is my great pleasure to have established friendship with you. The memory of the many pleasant meetings between us is still fresh in my mind. I wish to take this opportunity to express once again our thanks for your warm hospitality accorded us in all these years, for your vigorous support and assistance to the Exhibition of the Archeological Finds of the People's Republic of China and for your unremitting efforts in promoting the understanding and friendship between our two peoples.

How are your daughter Ellen and her husband Walter and your grandson Bobby? They are friends of mine and I wish them all well. Bob is a bright and able young man. Young people are our hope. With the friendly feelings cherished by the young generation towards the Chinese people, the traditional friendship between our two peoples will surely continue to develop from generation to generation.

We may not have the opportunity to meet again before I leave the United States, but I hope that we shall see each other again in China in the future.

Yours sincerely,
[signed in Chinese character writing]
HUANG CHEN

On a less official note Huang Chen, who used to call me "Cyl," once told me that he wanted me to do him a favor. He wanted my family and me to come to China as guests of the Chinese government. He invited me and three others. I told him that he wasn't asking me to do *him* a favor; he was doing *me* a favor. I told him that the greatest desire in my life was to visit China, and in October, 1975, I found myself, Ellen, Walter and my sister-in-law, Adele, on the way to China, where I was to discover we would be treated like visiting royalty. Prior to our invitation the only people able to visit China were diplomats. Very few Americans had been invited in. We found that they were giving us the very best. I don't think the President of the United States could have gotten better treatment.

Bowie Kuhn had invited me to the World Series, but on the first afternoon, as the first pitch was being thrown, we were on our way to China. We flew Pan Am to Hong Kong, and took a train from Hong Kong to Canton, which was having a huge fair. As we cleared immigration, we were asked if we were coming to the fair. We said no, and this Chinese fellow who spoke English said that we weren't allowed to

253

come there, we needed special permission. I started to tell him that we were guests of the government when a man walked up and asked, "Are you Mr. Magnin?" I found out later that he knew who we were because he had pictures of all of us. From that moment on we had no problems. We had guides and three separate cars. We were given first-class accommodations, albeit a bit strange.

In Bejing (Peking back then) I had a beautiful suite. Half of it was a living room and the other half, the bedroom, which was decorated in the Chinese style with a gorgeous carved bed and chairs and filigree fretwork around the door. But the living room was ultra-modern. Adele said it looked as if everything had been bought from a Sears Roebuck catalogue—all very plain and functional. And right behind the couch was a brand-new white refrigerator. Our guide explained that the Chinese were beginning to manufacture refrigerators; they had never had them before, and they wanted me to see it. So they brought it in and put it right in the middle of the living room. It didn't have a thing in it, but the lights worked.

We were wined and dined and were treated to several large dinners, including the traditional Peking Duck feast. The Chinese food in the United States doesn't compare with the beauty and flavor of the food they served us in China. Everything we ate was a picture of proportion and color— each plateful a work of art. There was no waiter to speak of. The people whose guests you are sit at opposite sides of the round tables and they serve you. We were told that food is a very high priority to the Chinese and because of potential shortages, there isn't any food allotted to feed dogs and cats as pets. The Chinese, we were told, had killed off the animals. Adele and Ellen weren't at all sure what they were eating half the time, and as a joke they would look across the huge circular table at each other and whisper, "Dog? Cat?"

Being in the fashion industry, we were all very conscious

of what the Chinese wore. As we visited Kwangchow (Canton), Bejing (Peking), Changchou, Nanking, Soochow, Shanghai, Hangchow and four other cities, we noticed that most of the men and women wore the same kind of outfit— the Mao jacket and pants. In the summer months the women switch to dresses because of the extreme heat in the southern cities. When we were entertained, the women wore beautiful pantsuits. The children, we discovered, were the colorful ones. Since the men and women work, the children attend day-care centers. The little girls wore ribbons in their hair, and both boys and girls wore pant outfits of bright red, blue, green and pink. Adele wanted to buy costumes, turn-of-the-century robes worn by concubines who entertained the emperor and empress. Some of our Chinese hosts told Adele they thought it was bourgeois of her to do so, but she explained that she wanted to buy the old silk robes to show fashion students at home. The Chinese weren't happy, however, until she bought a Mao jacket.

During our visit Henry Kissinger and George Bush, who was then the liaison officer to China, were in China. It was the only time I've ever met Mr. Bush. But by and large our tour was social, not political. Adele did conduct a bit of business. She was interested in buying cottons at the Canton Fair. We would go up to a booth and would ask how much the material was, and they'd ask how much we were going to buy. The price depended on the quantity. We would bargain to get the best price. Adele settled on a dollar a yard and bought 4,000 yards of pure cotton which she wanted to turn into blouses. It arrived back in the United States six months later, too late for her line. As she told me, "It was packed so beautifully, I hated to unpack it. The cotton came in perfect condition; there wasn't a flaw in it."

We saw so many marvelous things in China like the underground city, museums, the theater, schools, even a soccer match between the Chinese and New Zealand. The

Chinese are dedicated fans. They root every minute. We made a trip to the Great Wall. Ellen was carrying a Polaroid camera and when she took an instant picture that developed right in front of her subjects, she was almost trampled by the curious. All of us got a mild flu, but Adele was felled by a bad case and had to be hospitalized in Hong Kong before we flew home in mid-November to a party, a Chinese theme, of course, given for us by famous attorney Melvin Belli and his wife, Lia.

Of course, I credit my protocol post for giving me the opportunity to serve both San Francisco and our country. But the post has allowed me to be of the kind of service I was in helping to get the Chinese exhibition. I was used again in the same capacity for the King Tut exhibition. It had been offered to the de Young Museum, but museum officials turned it down on the first go-round, thinking that we couldn't accommodate the crowds. Those of us in the art community knew from the way we had handled the Chinese exhibition that we could indeed accommodate King Tut, even though another major exhibition, the Dresden Museum exhibit, had been booked prior to Tut and required a lot of time and effort. I took Walter Newman and Ian White of the de Young to Egypt and visited with President Sadat and the Minister of Culture, trying to negotiate our change of heart. Unwittingly, the de Young had purchased a piece of Egyptian sculpture, not knowing that it had been stolen from Egypt. When the Minister of Culture pointed that out to us, I told our museum to send the piece back immediately while we were still in Cairo. And as we waited anxiously for it, wouldn't you know, the piece got on the wrong plane and was lost for a few hours. The Egyptians, understandably, got very upset, but the artifact finally arrived, safe and sound. Everyone was greatly relieved and happy; so happy, in fact, were the Egyptians that we had confirmation that King Tut would indeed stop in San Francisco after all. We wanted President Sadat's marvelous

wife, Jahane, to come for the opening and she promised that
if at all possible, she would. But the whole situation in the
Middle East was too critical. It was around the time of the
historical Camp David meetings between Begin of Israel,
Sadat of Egypt and President Carter, and it was impossible for
her to make the trip West. I think that had it not been for our
success with the Chinese exhibition, our presentation of King
Tut would not have been so smooth or so gratifying. Again,
with Tut, we broke all attendance records, playing to
1,369,000 people.

And now San Francisco is getting its third prestigious art
exhibit in seven years in the spring of 1982, "The Search for
Alexander." Securing this exhibit for the de Young was
accomplished through a bit of personal sleight-of-hand between George Christopher, myself, Walter Newman and the
Greek government.

The Greek parliament approved a resolution when the
Alexander artifacts were discovered in what was thought to
be the tomb of Philip of Macedon. George Christopher was
in Greece at the time and he visited the magnificent white
marble tomb in Vergina with the brother of the Greek Prime
Minister. When he came back, I asked him what our chances
were to get the exhibition for San Francisco, but five cities
had been tentatively announced—New York, Boston, Washington, D.C., Chicago and Houston. I said to George when
he got back, "We're not on the list, we've got to do
something." Around ten or eleven at night, George and
several others came to my apartment and we waited until past
midnight to make a direct call to Constantine Karamanlis, the
Prime Minister in Greece, whom I'd met when he was head of
the Greek government in exile during the years of the junta. I
told George that the shortest distance between two points
was a straight line and put in the call which was answered by
one of the Prime Minister's aides who said, "What the devil
are you calling me at this time of day—it's 7:30 A.M.?" I put

George on the phone and he said, "There is no way I can explain that as a man of Greek descent and a former mayor, that San Francisco isn't getting this exhibition."

No contracts had been signed yet and the five cities were only penciled in. George had talked with the Minister of Culture, a man named Nianias, and he had been hesitant about changing the plans. It placed George in a terrible position—he told Nianias, "I can't fail." I gave George a fistful of information about the two other major exhibits we'd brought in, including the final attendance figures on both the Chinese and Tut exhibits. They proved conclusively that San Francisco is a major drawing card. It was proof enough for the Greeks who decided that we were to get the exhibition, not Houston.

In the past seventeen years I have received a lot of honors and decorations from various governments. I have served four mayors in this position and have met countless diplomats, heads of state, princes, kings and queens. When I give talks to young people, I always like to make a point of telling them never to limit themselves. I use myself as an example. I created the job of protocol chief for myself—I wanted it and I went after it and through hard work and conscientious effort, I have been able to keep it.

CHAPTER THIRTEEN ❧

Me and San Francisco—
A Perfect Match

❧ I HAVE OFTEN WONDERED if I could have turned out the way I am in any other city. My daughter seems to think that I would have developed into Cyril Magnin had I emerged from under a rock. But there *is* something special about the city I was born in that allows the uniqueness of each of its citizens full flower.

San Francisco is a city that has produced trends that have captured the curiosity and favor of the entire world. It was a mecca for adventurers from those first rough-and-ready gold rush days. It was always considered daring, especially during that brief period at the turn of the century when the Barbary Coast flourished with bawdy vitality. And while San Francisco, only about 130 years old, has taken on wealthy dowager status, some of the Barbary Coast deviltry comes out in her. During the late forties and early fifties, she became a hotbed of intellectualism, spawning days of Beatnik glory around Lawrence Ferlinghetti, Lenny Bruce, Jack Kerouac, Allen

Ginsberg and the numerous poets and artists who hung out in places like the City Lights Bookstore, the Co-Existence Bagel Shop, the hungry i and the numerous jazz joints that populated North Beach. Our city played host to the flower children during the "Summer of Love," a fact most San Franciscans would like to ignore; but until those dreamy-eyed, gaily dressed kids were replaced by the commercial drug dealers, we enjoyed the fruits of their labors—the colorfully painted buildings in the Haight, the energy of their music, a reputation as the center of the Love Generation. Actually, as Joe Alioto has said, the hippies had great taste. They picked a beautiful area—between Golden Gate and Buena Vista Parks—in which to set up shop.

San Francisco has had its share of oddities, too. Topless-bottomless dancing was a steady tourist attraction during the sixties and an atmosphere of sexual promiscuity pervaded Broadway and parts of North Beach. But the essential goodness of the city has kept it from becoming another Sodom and Gomorrah. The spirit of its people helped it rally after the horror of Jonestown and the tragic shootings of Mayor George Moscone and Supervisor Harvey Milk. It was the people with their modest donations who helped build the Louise M. Davies concert facility; it is the people who support the opera, the symphony, the ballet and the museums. And it is the people of San Francisco who have enough pride in their city to make it a welcome place for the many tourists who flock to see our wondrous sights.

San Francisco has been triply blessed. We have a spectacular blend of mountains and sea. Built on seven hills, San Francisco has vistas unparalleled in the United States. Our weather is temperate and can produce those glorious sun-washed days that make our beautiful city sparkle and shimmer like a casket full of jewels. And there is a pervasive attitude of "do your own thing," a *laissez-faire,* that allows people, especially people like me, to grow and develop.

There are very few limits placed on a creative person in San Francisco. Usually if someone moves to The City from elsewhere in the country, he or she is allowed the time to make his own niche. San Francisco can be almost impassive to a newcomer—the city does not require of its new residents a full disclosure of past life. Instead, it prefers that if you say you can do something or are something, that you deliver what you've promised.

Fresh starts and new opportunities abound in what is still, basically, a village—a place where Maestro Kurt Adler of the San Francisco Opera takes his own shirts to the laundry; a place where Mrs. Gordon Getty and her friends play basketball in a neighborhood park. Or a place where citizens rally to save the cable cars, those wonderful anachronistic rattling relics from a less frenetic age. In other words, people make a city. You can have the most spectacular buildings in the world and if the people aren't nice, what good are they? The people of San Francisco are vivacious and are special. For instance, I used to eat in a little Italian restaurant many years ago where you could get an entire dinner for fifty cents and lunch for thirty-five. I said to Nick, the fellow who ran the restaurant, "Why don't you fix this place up? You'd get more people." He called me De Mag and he said, "You know, De Mag, I have all the business I can take care of now—and it's what you put on the plates that counts. You can have the most beautiful restaurant in the world and if the food isn't good, people donta come." I think that is typical of San Francisco—a generosity of spirit in the people. We're proud of this city and also very protective; I don't think there's any other city that has a more loyal population than San Francisco.

Of course, the city has changed over the years with the influx of peoples of all races, creeds and colors. Yet, it is still a city of neighborhoods. It is a city to be walked and enjoyed for the delights around each corner. The pungent espressos and steaming cups of cappuccino in North Beach cafés; the delicate *dim sum* brunches at restaurants throughout a China-town crowded with traffic and children and shoppers; the spicy foods and the lilt of Latino music and language in the Mission or the sophistication and glamour of drinks at the Top of the Mark, dinner at L'Etoile or luncheon at Le Central. There is something for everyone in San Francisco—and everything for me.

I have been a city dweller most of my life except for that brief period when my family and I lived in Hillsborough. When my second wife, Lillian, and I broke up, I moved back into the city, choosing for a while to live in the Fairmont Hotel. But for the past seventeen years I have lived right in the hub of things, atop Nob Hill in the famous Mark Hopkins Hotel. My apartment is a mini-penthouse on a corner of the building with a magnificent view of the Bay, the financial district, the Bay Bridge, Telegraph Hill and Oakland and Berkeley and beyond.

The hotel is very much a convenience for me. I am not versed in the arts of homemaking—I can barely boil water. At one time I contemplated taking a penthouse in a beautiful condominium on Nob Hill, but as my daughter Ellen pointed out, "Who would take care of you?" Well, at the Mark, everyone does. I have maid service, clean towels and clean linens every day. I can have room service just like any other guest or I can take my meals in the hotel's Vienna Coffee House or the Nob Hill Restaurant. For several years I have adhered to the famous Pritikin diet and the hotel has been gracious enough to attend to my special food needs—I am known in the city as the man who takes his own bread to a banquet. The special Pritikin bread, that is. The hotel's front desk helps me in many ways by screening my calls (although I must say, I am still very accessible). Even though the calls go through the hotel switchboard, I am bound to tell them, "Put it through," ninety-nine percent of the time. I guess I am very curious as to who is calling.

I am one of three permanent residents who live in the Mark. Unlike most hotel guests, however, I have a four-footed roommate, one of two pets that have lived in the Mark. My cairn Tippycanoe is very well-known. He gets fat from his many friends who slip him a dog biscuit when he so conveniently sits up. He, like his master, is constantly on a diet. Tippy's predecessor, Robbie MacPherson, also lived with me at the Mark. He was a gift from Ellie Ford. Master Robbie was a marvelous animal and I grieved terribly when he died. Ellie went right out and bought Tippy for me, but I wouldn't have anything to do with him. I would visit Eleanor and she'd urge me to take Tippy home with me, but I was still loyal to the memory of Robbie. One afternoon, however, when Tippy was probably about a year old, he followed me out to my car and, unbeknownst to me, hopped in the back seat and rode home with me. He's been with me ever since.

Dogs can be very territorial. Years ago, when former General Manager Pierre Bultinck moved in with his poodle, Grocky, his pooch of course thought that *he* was the hotel mascot. It was a case of jealousy at first sight. To prove his point Grocky came up to my suite one day and walked in when the door was left open by the maid. He left a small deposit on the floor, claiming Robbie's territory for himself. We had some quiet negotiations and my dog ruled the roost— at least on our floor.

I have discovered that no matter how cute and well-behaved they are (and I think that Tippy has become quite civilized coming to work with me every day, wearing his Gucci collar and matching raincoat), dogs are not loved by everyone. On one occasion we were entertaining the Prime Minister of Ireland and his wife. Now I usually take Tippy with me as a matter of course when I greet visiting dignitaries. On this occasion Tippy was riding in my car with Mrs. Behrens and the wife of the Irish Prime Minister. Bernice turned around to the lady and said, "Don't you just love dogs

. . . and isn't Tippy cute?" The woman looked up at Bernice and scowled, "No . . . I hate dogs." We had to find other transportation for Tippycanoe.

There are times when living in a hotel has definite disadvantages, such as the night that a fire in a second-floor bathroom filled the lobby with thick clouds of smoke. It was about eleven o'clock and I strolled very calmly out of the hotel wearing a gray pin-striped suit. I was just about ready to undress and go to bed when I heard the fire engines and decided to come downstairs to investigate. Like most small boys, I've never lost my fascination for fire engines or sirens. But had the fire broken out fifteen minutes later, I would not have been so sartorially attired.

When I moved into the Mark, the suite I occupy was in need of personalization. It was a lovely three-room suite with a glassed-in porch, but other than that I felt that it not only had to reflect my lifestyle, it had to be a place where I could entertain and then, when I needed it, a place to relax and recuperate. I set Eleanor Ford, an extremely talented interior designer, to the task of decorating the place for me. She felt that one of the ways we could go with the apartment could be with classically good eighteenth-century furniture, **Coromandel** screens and expensive and busy Persian carpets. Ellie showed me samples of what I could expect and I didn't like anything. We were in a quandary as to where to go from there, and then I saw a tapestry by a man named Mark Adams and decided that I had to own it. The tapestry dictated the entire apartment.

The Mark Adams is called *The Great Wing.* It is a huge piece that covers an entire wall; it was woven in Aubusson, France, but by a San Francisco designer. It is a gigantic wing in flight on a persimmon background. The colors are gorgeous and lush—from a hearty burgundy to deep navy and royal blues, to chartreuse and orange and red, to fuchsia; it is spectacular and it is such a strong piece that either you like it or you don't. I happened to love it.

264

I first saw it at the Legion of Honor when President Pompidou of France was in San Francisco. He was a guest of the French colony in our city and as protocol chief, I accompanied him along with the Secret Service. He had stood up and was giving a long speech in French, a language of which I know perhaps four words. Everyone was applauding, and to be courteous I applauded also. But I thought that it looked like we were going to be there for a long time, so I wandered off to tour the galleries. I knew there was a Mark Adams exhibition in the museum and I wanted to see it. As I walked into one of the galleries, I saw this marvelous tapestry. I had just taken the apartment and could envision the piece hanging in it. I knew it was exactly what I wanted to live with day after day.

I called Mark Adams right away from the Legion of Honor and told him who I was and that I wanted to buy the tapestry. He said, "You're kidding." I'm afraid he didn't believe me. After all, it was a call out of the blue at nine o'clock at night. I told him to call the Mark Hopkins to verify that I lived there. I also mentioned that although I couldn't show him my credentials over the phone, somebody could vouch for me. He knew who I was and said he didn't think I'd be buying a tapestry off the wall, especially at that hour of the night. I told him I wanted it . . . if the price was right. I never let a seller know how anxious I am for anything. It's a cardinal rule of buying. But truthfully, I wanted the tapestry so badly I think I would have paid any outlandish price to get it. I was familiar with Adams's stained-glass work and his smaller tapestries and I recognized his superb design ability. When you're in the fashion business all your life, you learn to recognize inventiveness and creativity in design. Besides, the colors made me happy and I thought, "I don't know how anybody could look at this marvelous thing and not like it."

However, the tapestry was so vibrant and so strong it needed a neutral space to go around it and not conflict with it. We had to do some restructuring of the wall on which it was to hang because the piece was so long it draped on the floor. The ceiling above was torn out and lifted and four optical projectors were put in with display lights to show off the color range to best advantage.

Ellie Ford did a masterful job of coming up with a livable design for my apartment. The place was so distinctive that the apartment was chosen to be featured in the February, 1974, issue of *Architectural Digest*; then later, out of thousands of homes, castles, mansions, gardens and apartments, my apartment was one of thirty-six chosen to go into the *Architectural Digest* coffee table book. What Eleanor assembled was a place of texture and shine, but in neutral colors so as not to "fight" with the Adams. She turned my apartment into a purely classical backdrop for art.

Eleanor scrapped a fake fireplace and pink velvet walls in favor of oyster leather and Tennessee pink marble. Actually the floors are beige-ish tiles which match the dimensions of the tiles on the floor in the Legion of Honor. Ellie chose them for their practicality—Robbie MacPherson was prone to accidents and would have ruined a good carpet. The walls are covered in neutral nubby linen which Ellie also used for roman shades and lamp shades. The couch is a banquette-style sectional which covers two whole walls and is upholstered in soft off-white leather. It had to be made in several sections because the entire thing couldn't fit into one of the elevators. The carpet (which we try to keep Tippy off with a special screen across the doorway) is also a light buff, specially woven to match the pattern of the marble floor tiles. Ellie knew I entertained a lot so she had small, convenient round pedestal tables placed strategically at intervals in front of the couch for nonspot surface just in case a drink spilled. And behind the sectional she put in ledges for plants and art.

My combination library-dining room is sunny and filled with white oak furniture and bookshelves lined with plaques, pre-Columbian pieces and antiquarian books, another hobby started with the help of Ellie Ford. The apartment also has a small kitchen, where I brew coffee and little else, and a tiny bar. While the living room is very formal and extremely functional—I have had as many as 150 guests there at a time—my bedroom is my sanctuary. The walls are butterscotch and the bedspread is a plaid in butterscotch, red, green and black—very much in keeping with the kinds of dogs I've loved over the years, Scottish and cairn terriers. The bed is a comfortable resting place for Tippy, who usually ignores his doggie bed and props himself up on the pillows when I'm out for the evening.

Because the apartment is such a perfect place in which to display art, we chose what we put into it carefully. Ellie suggested primitive art—some pre-Columbian but mostly African pieces. I could envision the very modern pieces I owned with the tapestry, including the chrome Pristini sculpture Donald had picked out for me, but Ellie's suggestion of African art was brilliant. It blended perfectly with what I had. But I didn't know a thing about African art and I never get involved with things on a financial level until I've had time to study them. To acquaint myself with the art of collecting primitive statuary, Ellie and I visited the Primitive Art Gallery which is run by former jockey Billy Pearson, who had won a lot of money on the "$64,000 Question."

Eleanor loaded up the pieces she thought were appropriate in a station wagon and we brought them up in a freight elevator and put them all over the apartment. I came in and selected what I liked and then Ellie wandered out of the living room and left Billy and me to talk price. She said the negotiations between Pearson and me got too tough for her. When I'd selected what I wanted, I called someone from the museum who came by to tell me what it was all worth and then Pearson and I struck our final deal.

My idea for buying art ultimately reflects my one criterion: would a museum want this piece? I like to buy art, but I always buy with an eye to giving it all away. I once bought an expensive Arp and two years later, when Arp died, the painting appreciated at a rapid rate. I really loved the piece, but the Modern Art Museum in San Francisco kept after me and finally I donated it to them. I think that secretly I've always regretted that decision because it was a favorite painting.

I was, myself, an amateur painter—a Sunday painter, if you will. I did only a few canvases, one of which hangs in my daughter Ellen's foyer. It was an abstract in brilliant pinks, oranges and reds. I gave up the hobby because it was so time-consuming—I like swifter pursuits and I can't sit for the length of time it takes to complete a canvas. I'm too impatient. But Ellen seems to think that I had great promise as a painter.

My interest in art had led me to be active on several museum boards, including the Asian Art Museum. I got involved in a very intimate way when Avery Brundage, former president of the International Olympic Committee and a curmudgeon of the first order, lent his priceless jade collection to the Asian Art wing of the M. H. de Young Museum under the proviso that it not only be displayed properly, but that it be maintained in a style to which it could be advantageous to both Brundage and the city. We at the museum were thrilled to get the collection—Brundage had been romanced by several major museums throughout the country—but, unfortunately, monies were not sufficiently appropriated to keep the promises we had made Mr. Brundage. Word got back to Mayor Alioto via Gwin Follis who was in Brundage's city, Chicago, that Mr. Brundage was on the warpath and was threatening to remove his collection from San Francisco. The jades comprised the most valuable collection of Asian art outside of the Far East and it would have been a loss of prestige if the jades were removed.

At the request of Mayor Alioto, I got on a plane that night

and flew to Chicago to meet Gwin Follis. Together we would go up to see Brundage and try to heal the situation. At the time Brundage owned the La Salle Hotel and had offices on the top floor. Follis and I called on Brundage the next morning and he was in a rage. We didn't keep our promises. The jade was lying in the dirt and he was taking back his collection. He yelled that we had promised him a special place for his jade and he hollered, "It's lying in the basement!"—which it was. I told him to cool down, that we were going to try to see that he got what he wanted. That's why I had flown all the way from San Francisco to see him.

The first part of Brundage's extensive collection had been committed in 1959. There had been a California connection for Brundage through Santa Barbara, not San Francisco, but the Society for Asian Art lured him to San Francisco. I believe George Christopher was mayor at the time. Brundage had been solicited by every major museum in the United States but decided to park his collection in San Francisco. But there was a big problem due in part to lack of space and partly because he continued to buy large amounts of art. And in the next ten years there was almost a second collection. The entire collection consisted of about 10,000 pieces covering 4,000 years and representing various periods and styles. There had been several stipulations to the initial gift. Although there was never any mention of money, the city agreed to display the jades in an independent section of the museum and promised to provide enough money for public programs. The museum was to have a governing body and the collection was to be administered by a competent staff. The city made all these commitments and year after year cut budgets and laid people off. It was doubtful, also, that the museum could be open seven days a week as originally planned.

I knew, however, that the city didn't have the funds to help anymore. Weeks before Joe Alioto took office in 1969, he'd visited with Brundage and pledged to him that he'd appoint a blue-ribbon committee of citizens to take care of the collection and to raise funds for its maintenance. Another $50,000 was pumped into the M. H. de Young Museum budget . . . but a year later, not much had been done and Brundage was not happy. When Follis and I went to Chicago, I had just sold my business to AMFAC and had enough money to help out. I donated $100,000 right away to keep the Brundage Collection in San Francisco and then I pledged more money and aid to build a Jade Room in honor of my parents and my late wife. The offer cooled him off.

He gave me his list of complaints and we adjudicated most of them. I flew back to San Francisco and with the help of Skidmore, Owings and Merrill's Chuck Bassett, we made plans to build a jewel-like circular room in a wing of the de Young which was called the Asian Art Museum. Skidmore volunteered the architectural work for nothing and we worked with a man named Jim Hill who designed the Magnin Jade Room.

There were particular problems inherent in designing a room in which to display a rotating selection of 1,200 small pieces (a fraction of what was available in the entire Brundage collection). The unusual aspect of the collection was that there were a large number of animal figurines and pendants. We had to design light-filled spaces to show off the translucency of the jades. We also had to hang the pieces on fishing line so they wouldn't get broken during an earthquake. In effect, what Jim Hill came up with were jewel boxes in which the pieces were swimming in light. The original room was a cavernous space with no character. Hill designed circles within circles that when lit glow like a fine jewelry emporium after dark.

As the room was being finished, I was standing there talking to Skidmore's Charles Pfister about improving the lighting when in walked Mr. Brundage. He looked at me and didn't say a word. He had told me at our meeting in no uncertain terms that unless he approved what we were doing, we still had a chance to lose the jades. I was sweating blood, afraid that in some way we'd displeased him with our rather expensive gesture. He spent about an hour just walking around, examining every curve and every case. Then he came over and put his arms around me and said, "You're the only one in this goddamned city who kept his promise. It's beautiful." It was like taking the Himalayan Mountains off your back. He was as tough as nails and had a reputation for being a real hardnose. I mean, how do you deal with someone like that? Really, you don't. We had passed muster. He was pacified. The room cost better than $250,000, and it's really the only place in town that has my name on it.

Over the years there have been quite a few cultural events that have had my name attached to them—usually they are of a fairly sensual nature like good food, beautiful women and marvelous music. I combined both beautiful women and gorgeous music when I met Beverly Sills and became not only what she and her husband call her "West Coast Family," but her patron as well.

In September, 1969, I flew to Manila in the Philippines with my daughter Ellen to attend the farewell concert of Miss Beverly Sills, the former "Bubbles" Silverman of Brooklyn, at the Meralco Theater. It was the formal opening of the Philippine Cultural Center and my family and I had been invited to take part in the festivities. Beverly had been invited by a man named Lopez, who owned the electric light company and a newspaper in Manila. He invited famous artists to sing free concerts, and the year the cultural center was opening, Mrs. Imelda Marcos had invited Ellen and me to attend. We all arrived simultaneously, were wined and dined and wound up having a marvelous time together. As new friends are apt to do on parting, Beverly, Ellen and I promised each other we'd meet again, especially since Beverly was coming to San Francisco to sing. I said, "Be sure to call us," and that's how our long friendship began.

The first time that I saw Beverly perform in San Francisco was when she played the title role in *Manon.* We became even better friends. She took the suite across the floor from me in the Mark so we could have breakfast together—me, Beverly and, of course, Tippy. When her husband, Peter Greenough, was in town, it was as if I had another daughter and son-in-law. Beverly and I went everywhere together—especially Trader Vic's, which is a favorite after-performance restaurant. Ellen and Walter also became very close to the Greenoughs and when Ellen was in New York on business, Walter would take Bev, an inveterate moviegoer, to the films.

One evening when we were together, I turned to Beverly and said, "I'd like to give you a present," and she asked what kind of present. I told her I wanted to buy "my best friend" an opera.

I have been going to the opera for years. My family has had an opera box since the days when Mary Ann would sit in one and Grandpa Isaac would rub elbows with the standees. Opera is one of my consuming passions and I felt that it would be a fitting memorial to my father if I donated an opera in his name. So in 1971 I got my feet wet as more than just an opening night ticket-holder. I gave the San Francisco Opera money for a production of a one-act opera, *Il Tabbaro,* or *The Cloak,* starring Leontyne Price. But for Beverly I wanted a special opera—something which would show off her glorious coloratura voice. I gave $150,000 for scenery and costumes for one of the grandest of the *bel canto* operas, Donizetti's *Lucia di Lammermoor.* It was a historical *Lucia* which opened to rave reviews and starred Beverly and Luciano Pavarotti, one of the most inspiring tenors of all times. Carl Toms designed the sets, Tito Capobianco directed the production and Jesus Lopez Cobos conducted. Beverly sent me a model of a bicycle built for two and one of her many lovely notes—

she is a marvelous correspondent and will jot down a hurried and warm epistle in pencil to keep in touch. She said, "To my darling friend, let this little tandem be a symbol of our joint venture tonight—our first 'Lucia' together. Lots of love, hugs and kisses, Beverly."

Through the years, when Beverly has breezed into town, it has always been an occasion. I try to make her visit as pleasant as possible. When she was rehearsing *La Traviata*, I welcomed her with a bouquet of flowers in the shape of a "Walkyrie" helmet—a memento of her debut into the chorus of *Die Walküre* in 1953 when she played what she calls "one of the screaming ladies" of that opera and her helmet fell off her head. Then there was the time we walked into Bill Frey's super hamburger joint out on Clement Street in search of the Beverly Sillsburger (with Swiss cheese). Beverly ate it with great enthusiasm although, as she said at the time, "It makes me feel just a bit cannibalistic."

I didn't limit my support—my stage-door Johnny act, if you will—just to her performances in San Francisco. There are times when I've flown to New York to see her perform, especially in April of 1975 when she made her debut at the Metropolitan Opera in *The Siege of Corinth*. She was forty-five years old when she first sang at the Met after years of performing right across the courtyard at Lincoln Center at the New York City Opera. I was also invited to see her last performance in 1980 when she stepped down as the reigning diva to become the director of the New York City Opera. It was a laughter- and tear-filled evening. She sang Rosalinda in the ball scene from *Die Fledermaus,* and as usual, her voice was glorious—she was filled with high spirits and the impish sense of fun which has endeared her to everyone she knows. I admire her gumption and her courage and I also admire her practicality. It isn't every first-rank star who can quit at the peak of a career to go onto another venture. She is a woman of very strong ego, but at heart she's still "Bubbles" Silverman from Brooklyn who broke into show business as a youngster on the "Major Bowes' Amateur Hour."

I gave "Bubbles" one other present—another opera. This time it was in 1976. She made a gorgeous *Thaïs*." We were sitting in the Villa Taverna one afternoon having lunch when she proposed I do *Thaïs* for her. It was to be a co-production between the San Francisco Opera and the Met; when Anthony Bliss, director of the Met, flew out for the opening performance (and we had to scramble to find a box seat for him), he thought it was marvelous and agreed to book it into the Met for twelve performances the following spring.

The production was designed, again, by Carl Toms. Maestro Adler was in London when the model of the set was completed. He was staying at the Carlton Towers during the days when terrorists were setting off bombs all over the city. The hotel security was understandably tight when Toms walked in with this weirdly outsized package—the model for the *Thaïs* set. The detectives stopped him right away and almost tore the package into shreds trying to find a bomb. The production was a fancy one and the model was quite ornate, but it certainly wasn't lethal.

The *Thaïs* debut in San Francisco was a true gala evening but it was just part of an entire month of occasions starring Beverly Sills . . . and a new baritone—me.

To benefit the Merola Opera Fund, we gave an evening at the Stanford Court Hotel called "This is Your Life—Beverly Sills," a *very* comic opera written by Paul Blake, a director at the American Conservatory Theater. It starred some famous names like Maestro Adler, Calvin Simmons, then assistant conductor of the Los Angeles Philharmonic (and now permanent conductor of the Oakland Symphony), and Jussi Bjorlinsky a.k.a. Cyril "Golden Pipes" Magnin, singing his theme song, "I Can't Give You Anything But Cash, Baby." Calvin Simmons played Maestro Adler to perfection, Viennese accent intact, with lines like, "Beverly Schtills was nossing until I discofert her and has she vonce phoned me to vish me a happy birthday? I am a very humble person and I don't keep score . . . of course, Beverly, you know you will never sing for me again. I only put you in *Salome* because my horoscope said, 'This veek there's goink to be a lot of b.s. in your life.'" It brought down the house.

Before *Thaïs* opened I didn't miss one of the rehearsals. I was the opera's "angel," someone who spent nearly $250,000, and I guess it was a privilege of the house that I got to see the opera from beginning stages to the finished product. Beverly, gracious as ever, presented the city of San Francisco a gift in return. She gave a free concert in Golden Gate Park for more than 30,000 people. It was not your average concert. As the press put it at the time, it was an operatic "love-in," a love affair between an adoring public and a true American super-star. Afterwards I took Beverly, her husband, Peter, and their seventeen-year-old daughter, Muffy, to see one of my favorite "operas," *Beach Blanket Babylon Goes Bananas*, where another talented soprano, Nancy Bleiweiss, sang an aria from *La Traviata*—with her eyes crossed. You could hear Beverly's infectious laughter all over Club Fugazi.

As I have said, the Greenoughs consider the Magnins their West Coast family. Ellen, Walter, Beverly and Peter— sometimes me and all of my family as well—spend Christ-mases together either in San Francisco or in Hawaii. We are in constant communication and share an affection for the same things—small, affectionate dogs, quiet breakfasts together, the morning paper and, of course, the opera.

I used to be as passionate about food as I am about the opera and pretty women. But I was always a little overweight. Although I've never been sickly, I was advised to go easy on my food and visited the Pritikin Longevity Institute in Southern California. I was placed on the Pritikin diet and for the past three years have stuck to it almost exclusively (although I've been known to cheat once in a while with a nibble of cookie or a piece of something that looked appetizing). While my entire outlook about consuming food changed, I did find myself involved with fine cuisine on a different level.

For years fine American restaurants have been staffed by European chefs. But it has become increasingly difficult for Escoffier-trained, Cordon Bleu chefs to get green cards—the government figures, why let a European take a job that can be filled by an American. Unfortunately there weren't too many places where American youngsters could get Cordon Bleu training. That's where Danielle Carlisle and the California Culinary Academy came in.

Back in 1977 when Danielle wanted to open a school for chefs, she came to my office in search of support—not for money, but for advice. She couldn't get anyone to support her idea and she wanted to meet me because she knew that I was very active in the training and education of young people through my work with the Fashion Institute and the American Conservatory Theater. She thought that I would recognize the merit of a European culinary academy. She called my office and was confronted by Meg Starr who told this unknown person that I was already on too many boards and that she didn't think I'd lend my name to such a risky venture. Although she'd been turned away, Danielle was persistent. She says that she decided on the spot that she wanted me for an advisor—that she had her mind fixed on me. But it was six months before we met.

Meanwhile she made a tour of banks, was turned down right and left, and where a less ambitious person would say, "forget it," Danielle persevered. Somehow the California Culinary Academy got off the ground and six months later it seemed to be taking off. Then Danielle, who knows nothing about cooking, by the way, ran out of working capital. She had just two weeks to make a $20,000 payroll—she had to pay her teaching chefs and her restaurant staff. She went to a major bank in desperation; she said they put her through a grueling, nearly humiliating set of conferences and still turned her down. And then, one lunchtime, I walked into the Academy's restaurant with a publicist named Donna Ewald who had been doing some work for the C.C.A. and finally met Danielle.

I recognized instantly the merit of what she was doing. I decided that I could risk my name and some money, if need be, to help support this effort. I was told that a major bank wouldn't give her the time of day so I called the bank's president and even I was turned down. I offered to sign the note for Danielle but she refused to take any kind of money from me, even when the bank called her back and said that she'd been covered. She felt that if she didn't get the loan on her own merit, they could just rip up the check. We put our heads together and decided that since she had been turned down at a number of banks, that the way to go was through the Small Business Administration. Marks Kavanaugh was the Western Regional Director of the SBA, and I enlisted his aid. I told him, "Please help this young lady," and we arranged for a loan through the California-Canadian Bank for the SBA to take ninety percent of the loan and the bank to take the other ten percent. I like to get loans where I don't have to take the risk and I told Cal-Canadian that they had a good deal here, being guaranteed by the SBA. Still, the statements from Danielle's venture weren't very good; she was losing money and Cal-Canadian balked. Finally I got Marks to talk with them. He thought it was a good idea to loan the C.C.A. some money—after all, the SBA was recruiting minority business-people, and women, at the time, were considered minorities. But the president of the bank said no, and then I reminded him that his vice-president had indeed said yes, and what kind of bank were they to go back on their agreement?

We not only borrowed $20,000 for Danielle to meet her payroll, we got an additional $180,000 so she wouldn't be

277

undercapitalized. And in an advisory capacity—because she still wouldn't take any money from me—we found her another accountant, got her books into line and helped get the restaurant on a paying basis. We took out another loan for $200,000 to buy more equipment, bought out her original backer and soon the C.C.A. started to make money. Danielle was very pleased, so pleased, in fact, that she wanted to make me an active partner—she wanted to give me twenty-five percent of the business. I told her I wouldn't take it. But we did swing a deal. For my expertise as an advisor and member of her board, Danielle offered to serve my meals gratis. The C.C.A. bakes my special bread; they always have a table for me when I bring visitors in—and I'm there with various visitors and dignitaries about twice a week. One evening we opened the kitchen to tenor Luciano Pavarotti who is a fabulous pasta cook. I wanted to bring him to the Academy because of his love of cooking and because the kitchen there has the finest of everything in it. It was a gala evening. We both wore the high white toque of the master chef (although, as I've said, I can't even boil water successfully) and Pavarotti put on a feed fit for a Renaissance prince.

I speak at C.C.A. graduations and find myself a welcome visitor in the Academy's kitchens and dining room. Those young people are so talented and they always have a kind word for me. They learn everything about running a first-class restaurant from buying fine produce to pricing out a menu to turning out a fancy buffet to making dessert. In searching for something clever to put on my Christmas card in 1980, I made arrangements with the C.C.A. to have them make a gingerbread doghouse for Tippy, and when it was finished, the students and staff of the Academy joined Tippy and me in a wonderful picture. We had trouble keeping a chef's hat on my dog. I think he was more interested in gobbling up one of the delicious cakes in front of him, but after about ten "watch-the birdies," we got a marvelous shot.

Danielle has become one of my dearest friends. She is a tall, slender woman with titian hair and a spectacular pair of legs. She is an astute businesswoman—a trained chemist, actually, from Pittsburgh, Pennsylvania. She would have made an excellent addition to the talented Joseph Magnin staff were she old enough to have been around during our heyday in the fifties and sixties. We often double-date and there are times when Danielle will play hostess for me at some kind of protocol function or party.

Ultimately I find it ironic that a woman who can't cook and a man who's not allowed to eat rich food have put together a business as successful as the California Culinary Academy, but as I've said, San Francisco is a magical place. Anything can happen . . . and usually does.

CHAPTER FOURTEEN ✍

The Fun Begins for Reel

✍ I HAVE NOT INDULGED MYSELF seriously in pondering the "what ifs" of my life. Were I to have done so, I probably would have wasted a lot of time becoming who I am. I worked hard all my life doing the things I believed were right for my family and myself; but in some quieter moments, those times when a person's thoughts belong only to himself, I thought that if I *could* live my life once again, it certainly wouldn't have been as a blond, to paraphrase that old Clairol ad, but perhaps, I would have lived it as an actor.

The Magnin progeny did not fare so well in that profession, or at least, my unfortunate Uncle Victor didn't. As he died an ignominious death, a penniless and sick actor-musician in New York, my grandmother never spoke of him again. But from my earliest memories I loved the magic of acting, of pretending I was someone else. Barking for my Uncle Manny in front of the wheel of fortune and the cooch dancers in Neptune Park or becoming a process server for

Leon Samuels or even getting fancied-up in formal attire for a protocol function—it all has been a lovely game, a way to use my imagination. They have all been ways for what is still a shy little boy to get out of himself. A way to have fun.

When there came that period in my life, after working so hard for Joseph Magnin, that I started to relinquish some of my authority, not only did I fill the time with civic and philanthropic work, I was able to indulge some of my wilder fantasies. I would get dressed up in costume at the drop of an eyebrow pencil. Once I dressed as Harpo Marx for a benefit for *Beach Blanket Babylon Goes to the Stars*, and once I was turned out in full royal regalia as the Caliph in *Turandot* as part of the Opera Faire. Everyone who attended the fair could be made up to look like their favorite opera character for a small donation. As I sat in front of the light-wreathed make-up mirrors in the make-up room in the bowels of the Opera House, I saw my complexion go from ruddy pink to a deep, exotic tan. I was given a Fu Manchu mustache and an elegant pointed beard. I dressed in a great jeweled turban with feathers and a heavy, spangled robe of brocaded silk which replaced my customary Polo suit. I turned from Merchant Prince to Prince of China in a twinkling—it was marvelous. Perhaps I was born with greasepaint in my veins and I never got a chance to find out until just recently.

As president of the Chamber of Commerce, I came in contact with all sorts of people who had plans and schemes for the betterment of their own coffers and, sometimes, for the betterment of San Francisco. But perhaps none was so interesting or close to my heart than what was to become our fifteen-year, ongoing association with the American Conservatory Theater.

In July, 1966, a vibrant and prestigious young acting troupe was booked at Stanford University in Palo Alto—the American Conservatory Theater, a repertory company which had its roots in the fertile ground surrounding the theater department at Carnegie Tech in Pittsburgh, Pennsylvania. The company found itself with plenty of competition between the fine Carnegie-based theater and the Pittsburgh Playhouse and it had taken to the road with a series of eight plays in revolving repertory. It was one of those marvelous coincidences that brought ACT to the Bay Area at the exact moment when San Francisco's only resident theater company, the Actors Workshop, was folding to a $75,000 loss.

The directorship of ACT had gotten wind of the demise of the Actors Workshop and sent a man named Bill Baer to see me and COC headman, Bill Dauer. Baer came flying into my office, anxiety written all over his face. He pointed out the obvious—that San Francisco didn't have a rep company, but now it had a vacant theater with no company to fill it. He felt it was our civic duty to fill that vacuum and hopefully, to fill it with ACT. The man's intensity and perseverance were attractive to me—I have always appreciated people of passionate conviction and besides, he piqued my interest with his challenge. The least we could do was to take a look.

With the help of Mortimer Fleishhacker and Mel Swig, the chamber organized a busload of prominent San Franciscans to travel down to Stanford for a performance of *Charley's Aunt*, starring Rene Auberjonois. We loaded ourselves—fifteen of us in all—into a custom coach complete with drinks and hors d'ouevres for the hour's drive to Palo Alto. We arrived at Stanford in time to be duly impressed by what we thought was a wonderful production full of gifted performances. We were extremely pleased with what we saw.

Sometimes what you don't know can't hurt you. And what our *ad hoc* committee of San Francisco's leading culture vultures didn't know was the backstage tumult that preceded our arrival. As I've said, the company was playing eight works in repertory. They rehearsed one play in the daytime and performed another at night. They had already opened six plays before we got there, but for *Charley's Aunt* they hadn't had two basic rehearsals—there had not been a technical rehearsal or a dress. To add to the confusion, half the cast had been rehearsed in Connecticut and half in Stanford—the two halves had never met and they were to play an antic farce which involved flawless comic timing and scads of props with no rehearsal in front of fifteen backers who were either going to extend to them the offer of a permanent home or turn thumbs down to a sloppy group of players purporting to be the American Conservatory Theater.

Says Bill Ball, resident founder-director of the company, "I'd never seen a play in worse condition, but I borrowed a trick from a friend of mine. I felt that the players were not going to get anywhere if they saw *me* panicking." So Ball tried to maintain a happy façade. He was prickly with excitement, stage fright and flop sweat all at once and when he went backstage, his players' faces were ashen. They were struggling to remember their lines; they hadn't had proper rehearsal time and they were feeling their usual stage fright compounded by the fact that *we* were out front with the money. In spite of everything Bill Ball seemed to think that ACT and San Francisco were fated to be together because the performance the backers saw was nothing short of terrific—Rene Auberjonois was superb; the company was skillful, energetic and full of high spirits. They impressed us so much with their ability that we almost had no choice but to start negotiating to make a home for ACT in San Francisco.

In the course of our negotiations we went to see ACT several more times. Morty Fleishhacker especially liked the Pirandello play, *Six Characters in Search of an Author*, and invited the company to his home for a party. The Fleishhackers had a swimming pool, and during the course of the evening one of the company decided to take a skinny dip, doffed his clothes and dived in. Instead of being horrified, Janet Fleishhacker was so amused that her guests were free enough to act themselves, the incident was forgotten with a good laugh and a comfortable, familial link was established.

The company performed in Palo Alto for four weeks and than headed to Chicago where its reception was equally enthusiastic. So far we hadn't made a commitment to ACT and when they were ready to leave Chicago, they found out that they were wanted in the Windy City as well as in San Francisco. Soon there was negotiating in two directions—who would get ACT? A plan was struck that ACT spend half a year in San Francisco and the other part of the year in Chicago. But according to Equity rules, one of the cities had to be the home city and the other had to be considered a road city. Again, by Equity rules, an actor is to be paid more on the road, which would have made the presence of ACT in the road city more expensive. At the last minute Chicago's civic leadership was not able to raise enough money to guarantee a first season for ACT. And through some very heavy negotiations, San Francisco, backed by Mel, Morty, me and the COC, invited ACT to become our theater company.

It is no small chore taking on a repertory company. We promised to raise $200,000—the amount needed to support ACT's first season in San Francisco. Morty, Mel and I primed the pump with $35,000 of our own and then went on every radio and television show that would have us to pitch for city-wide support. By September we had raised nearly $50,000 in pledges and advanced ticket sales and by opening night, January 21, 1967, we had raised $202,000. It was an ambitious undertaking, that first year. In January ACT was to mount the first of 16 productions in 22 weeks employing 47 actors playing 187 characters. As one writer in the *Examiner's* California Living section said, "It was a dazzling display of energy."

Opening night was a glittering affair. ACT presented Moliere's comic romp, *Tartuffe*, and opened it to rave reviews of all the critics in attendance, including Cecil Smith of the *Los Angeles Times* who said, "The applause roared on and on. The actors on stage, having done all their curtain call tricks, finally just stood, many with damp eyes. ACT founder-director William Ball wept and Cyril Magnin, one of the prime civic movers in the movement to establish ACT permanently here, did a victory dance in the aisle, grabbed a nearby woman gave her a resounding kiss." All I can say about that night was that the play was marvelous, we were all jubilant at our success and the woman I kissed must have been cute.

At fifty, Bill Ball is a ball of energy. He can be as flamboyant as his position dictates. He once affected a gaucho hat, toreador pants and a campy West Point cadet jacket. Since, he's traded his costumes for more comfortable turtleneck sweaters and casual slacks. But his intensity and drive have not changed. He is an arresting-looking man with baby pink skin, a balding head, piercing brown eyes and eyebrows that move when he talks. His hands speak with an eloquence all their own. He's the sort of person who couldn't talk were he to be sitting on his hands. Bill has a short fuse and can be very temperamental at times, but he has the respect and adoration of his actors and the admiration of the business community with whom he's dealt these past fifteen years.

I try to keep our fund-raising efforts as far away from the creative energies of the players as possible. Bill Ball has been a good liaison between the money end and the performing end and has been most generous in working with us to keep the company solvent and happy. It's difficult to raise money for something as ephemeral as the spoken word. You can't put a brass plaque on an actor as you could on a building or a street lamp. And every now and then we'd look at the books to find they were written in screaming red ink. It was time to get out the old fund-raising muscle. I tend to speak in hyperbole at times like that and would go running off to see the mayor who had discretionary funds tucked away for emergencies—the hotel tax fund or a donation from a civic organization earmarked for certain things. Mayor Joe Alioto says he could always count on my visit concerning ACT at least once a year. He had a certain fund donated by the San

Francisco 49ers for youth-oriented projects. One day I rushed in and said, "This is it; we're locking our doors," and then Joe pulled $50,000 out of the 49er fund for our youthful company justifying the funds because the acting company sponsored youth activities, such as their apprentice program and school. Somehow or other we always made our deadlines.

Repertory theater is hard to finance and expensive to produce. You have to support a huge staff of actors and technical people. It's not like performing the same play over and over where you don't need a large staff or a collection of rotating sets. But with repertory it's an opportunity for the public to see the classics performed and then, perhaps, some new works by both new and established playwrights.

We have found through experience that when we've experimented, we've had poor seasons at the box office, but when we've stuck to the classics like Shakespeare, Shaw, Moliere, etc., we've done quite well. However, there are always exceptions to the rule, especially when Tennessee Williams comes to town with a play for the company. In 1976 we presented the world premiere of Williams's play, *This Is (An Entertainment)*. About it, the elusive Williams said, "It's a comedy but different than anything I've ever done." He had high praise for ACT, calling it "the best acting company in America." I was at a party when I heard that and I turned to my hostess with tears in my eyes and said, "That's what I've been telling everyone for years. Now . . . maybe somebody will believe me."

The play was to open on January 20, and on January 17, I received a typewritten note from Williams which read:

Dear Mr. Magnin,

It is very unusual for the happiest experience of a man's professional life to be held in reserve for such a long time that it appears to be close to the end like the kiss that was reserved for the end of old-fashioned movies. But that is just what has been my very unusual luck in finally

287

participating in the creation of a new play, *This Is,* with America's greatest repertory company—San Francisco and America's A.C.T. With its amazing corps of actors, directors, technicians, designers—you name it and they have it and there's none better! To quote from *Menagerie*—it's for me "The long delayed, but always expected something that we live for" . . . I'm sure that I'm expressing their sentiments, as well as mine, when I say that this company is also very fortunate in having such a devoted and appreciative patron as you.

Very sincerely yours,
TENNESSEE WILLIAMS

After years of searching for fun ways to raise money for ACT, one of our board members, Lita Vietor, came up with a novel way to serve the whole community at the same time we were raising money. We enlisted the help of San Francisco's celebrities and society folk, Hollywood stars and major interior designers in what we call "An Elegant Celebration of Christmas." The designers and the glittering folk were to come up with Christmas tables or Christmas rooms which would be on display from the end of November through the middle of December. The Elegant Celebration was to be in a wholesale furniture design center, a place where the general public was not allowed to come unless they had a designer with a resale license in tow. There were a few doubters that first year—who would want to spend six bucks to see a bunch of Christmas decorations? But it was a huge success and we have repeated it as a new San Francisco tradition every year. Our list of glitterati has grown to include Kathryn Crosby, Elizabeth Taylor, the Joseph Cottens, the Jimmy Stewarts, Lee Radziwill, Carmella and Boz Scaggs, plus members of the San Francisco smart set and . . . me. One year my table for two was covered with a Kilim Persian rug and decorated with a towering vase of pheasant feathers, Portuguese pewter dishes and obelisks, thistle-patterned wine glasses from Scotland and mock sheep for benches. It was designed by John Withers who was redoing the JM store in Century City. Another year I had a tropical oasis designed with a sandbox for Tippy and a gaily striped tent.

While ACT dug in and became an integral part of the cultural fabric of the city, there was a young man named Steve Silver who found himself working for ACT in an unusual way. Steve had met Bill Ball who found out Steve's knack for theatrical presentation. Bill enlisted his help to put on entertainments for the company—in other words, instead of working his way up from the prop room, Steve was hired to throw parties.

Like myself, Steve Silver is a native San Franciscan who went to Lowell High School. At San Jose State he was an art major—Steve is a talented painter. He used to sell tickets at the hungry i and then he started a very inventive business called "Rent-A-Freak" where he would provide strange people for special occasions—such as when he sent a 250-pound gorilla in pink tights on roller skates into one party or the time a girl served strawberries through a funeral wreath. He also had a ballerina who would "die" at a party and then be carted off by six cotton clouds.

Steve met Bill Ball at a fund-raiser for ACT where bits and pieces of that year's repertory were being performed for the benefit of the cameras of KQED. Steve was fascinated with the production values, the costumes and all the pageantry and made inquiries as to whether he could be part of it, too. When he went to see Ben Moore, the company's business manager, Moore saw slides of Steve's work and said, "Don't call us, we'll call you." Steve was in the hospital recuperating from gall bladder surgery when a call came from ACT with the request to plan a party in the next two days. Steve remarked with customary understatement, "I'm having an intravenous feeding at the moment, let me get back to you." Thus began his association with ACT, throwing parties and, yes, working in the prop room. His wonderful *Beach Blanket* reviews started evolving from the little bits of fantasy and business he'd put together for ACT.

Although Steve had been working for ACT, we'd never talked at length, or at least, not until one evening when we were in the same restaurant, Capp's on the corner of Powell and Green Streets right down the way from Steve's Club Fugazi. Before I was on the Pritikin diet, I loved to eat at Capp's. There were times when you could get an entire dinner for $3 to $4, and on certain nights they would have lamb or beef stew and oxtail soup—my favorites. One night, sitting next to me was Steve Silver with one of our people from ACT. He turned to me and said hello and I said hello back. I had been introduced to him while he was doing props for the company and I knew he'd since left, but I had no idea what he'd gotten himself involved in. I asked him what he was doing and he said, "I've got a show next door . . . do come and see it. I'll have two tickets at the box office for you . . . no arguments. You're my guest."

It was *Beach Blanket Babylon Goes Bananas*—a melange of campy theatrics, solid singing and dancing, and outlandish props like dancing Christmas tress, a walking-talking Mr. Peanut and, of course, the hats of Brobdignagian proportions that surpass anything Carmen Miranda wore. One of the hats is so elaborate it cost $7,000, weighs forty pounds and has the Transamerica pyramid growing out of the top of it along with the rest of the San Francisco skyline. Anyhow, the moment I saw *Beach Blanket* I recognized that this was terrific stuff and that I'd be back quite often. As chief of protocol I brought consuls-general, foreign dignitaries, prime ministers, princes —anyone who had a spark of excitement in them, I knew would love it. I have seen both *Beach Blanket* reviews more than 200 times.

I became a regular and Steve always sat me at the same table which he called the "Cyril Magnin" table. It became a landmark in the Club Fugazi and when Steve is giving directions for setting up the hall, he'll often say, "put so-and-so to the right of Cyril's table." After my 100th visit to *Beach Blanket*, Steve gave me my own chair which he hauls out if he knows I'm coming; and for my 200th visit, I got my own personal table with my name on it. If I go much longer, I'll probably have enough furniture to outfit my own nightclub.

Sometimes it's as entertaining in the audiences of one of Steve's shows than on stage itself. And I've been both places. One evening Charles Lowe, Carol Channing's husband, called Steve and said, "Listen, we're coming to the show; we don't want to make a big deal about anything, but we would like to arrive a few minutes before showtime. Would you usher us to our seats up front?" Steve said he'd be more than happy to help, but when Channing arrived, in a limousine, she emerged head to tail in white mink with a big white purse, big white boots and her cotton-candy white hair. Steve said it was like a pigeon flying through a black room and as she walked in, the whole audience applauded her. She took her boots off and settled in to watch the show.

In Steve's review Snow White leaves San Francisco in search of her prince. She goes to Los Angeles to find fame, fortune and her prince charming. We thought it appropriate to take a real prince charming to see *Beach Blanket*, and several years ago, when things still seemed "normal" in Iran, the Shah's son, Prince Reza, came to the performance with me. The only person in Steve's organization who knew what we'd intended was Steve. The Secret Service was all over the theater, checking out the bathrooms and all for bombs, but none of the players knew about their special guest. I walked in with the Prince and sat at the Cyril Magnin table, and soon there is Snow White on stage singing, "Some Day My Prince Will Come." Prince Reza leaned over to me and whispered, "Did they write this specially for me?" He didn't believe they hadn't until the show was half over.

When it was decided by someone in the British consulate

that we not bring Prince Charles to see *Beach Blanket*, I saw to it that Steve and several of his staff people and performers would be invited to the official reception to meet the Prince. When I brought Prince Charles over to meet Steve and his company, the Prince said in his very elegant and clipped British accent, "Oh, I do believe . . . aren't you the gentleman with the *Beach Blanket* thing . . . tell me about this beach with this blanket." In this case, it was Steve who was charmed by a Prince.

There are a number of San Franciscans who have remained Steve's biggest fans, although I'd wager a five or a ten that no one has seen the show as many times as I have. But every Christmas and New Year's Eves, the "faithful" get into the act. There will be a regular performance of the show and then, during the finale, Steve will have written a special little skit, starring his friends. One year Steve dressed all the waitresses in his club as Snow White and when the curtain opened, there was one of our city's leading artists, Catherine Cebrian, being peeled out of a banana by seven gorillas. The pageantry built until at the last moment, another curtain opened to reveal a silver-haired John Travolta in profile. Me. I took disco lessons for two weeks before to learn the *Saturday Night Fever* dance steps to go along with the three-piece white suit. Another year I was Disco Tut and usually on Christmas I'll get myself up as Santa Claus. I don't know if I've ever had the chance to thank Steve for allowing me to live out my dearest fantasies, but I know that it was Steve who I have to thank for my movie debut, and perhaps the beginning of a whole new career.

Back in 1977 Steve's old friend from San Jose State days, Hollywood director Colin Higgins, was in San Francisco preparing to film *Foul Play* which was to star Chevy Chase and Goldie Hawn. Higgins was looking for spectacular locations, including a grand hall to represent the entrance of the Opera House (I guess he felt that the actual Opera House's foyer wasn't grand enough). He seemed to be having some problem with the city officials about securing the City Hall rotunda, so Steve called me to see if I could do something about it. I took Steve and Colin over to City Hall to show them the place and a few days later Colin called Steve and said, "Listen, I think that Cyril Magnin would be the greatest Pope in my movie. How do you think he'd react if we cast him?" Steve said, "He'd love it," and Colin said that he wanted to call me immediately. Steve warned him to be very sure that I was who he wanted and he told Colin, "I feel very protective of Cyril and I wouldn't want him to be hurt or disappointed in any way if you change your mind."

When Colin Higgins called me and explained to me that he wanted to cast me in his movie—the film was about a plot to assassinate a visiting Pope—I thought he was kidding. He was very convincing, but before I agreed to do the part, I told him I wanted to see the script and to have a copy of it. I didn't want to offend any of my Catholic friends, so I had a copy sent to Father Anthony of St. Mary's Church and to Archbishop Joseph McGucken and they both said they saw nothing objectionable in the script. When I told Higgins I'd do the part, I plunked down my dues for the Screen Actor's Guild—about $550, which I got back many times over—and started to work. I flew to Los Angeles where I was fitted for my papal robes and did a couple days' filming before we came back up to San Francisco to do my big scene at the Opera House. Colin Higgins had thought the Opera House itself to be marvelous with all of its gilt trim and plush red upholstery. He said, "It lends an old-world look to the surroundings." But he said also that the real entrance to the Opera House wasn't as great as the interior and he wanted something grander—like the majestic staircase in City Hall, which is how we came to film there.

In the film the Pope comes to the Opera House to watch a performance of *The Mikado*, not knowing that his life is in danger. I didn't have any lines, but the camera was on me quite a bit during the scene. As I watched what was on stage, I unconsciously got into the music and started tapping my foot, something I always do. I saw the camera panning down to catch me, so I stopped the scene for a moment. I thought I was doing something wrong and Higgins said, "No, no, go on. Keep tapping; that's fine." As I watched more of the movie being filmed, I realized that actors often flub their lines or business and that there have to be re-takes. There were almost no re-takes in my scenes and I became known as a one-take person.

For the Opera House scenes the audience was filled with people from the Bay Area, actually, some of San Francisco's own wealthy set decked out in their own furs and jewelry. In addition Paramount agreed to donate $6,000 to the Children's Hospital Branches, Inc., which was raising funds for a new medical center, if it would deliver 425 male and female "extras." When there was such a tremendous response, Paramount was so pleased they donated an extra $15,000. It was an amusing sight to see all of these socially prominent people, curious about movie-making, dressed up in their finest, eating box lunches and taking time away from work to be in the movie.

I wasn't the only San Franciscan who was offered a part in the film. Bill Ball wanted to be in the movie and volunteered to do anything—play a janitor, even. He told me he wanted to be there while I was being the Pope. At first he was cast as a priest in the Pope's entourage, then he was elevated to monsignor, and by the time we filmed, he was a full cardinal. We ended up in the same scenes together.

The scene filmed in the rotunda was one of great pomp and elegance. It was the Pope's entrance to the Opera House, and for it I was to wear the long white robes of office with the vibrant red cape and walk down a six-foot-wide red carpet and up the stairs—a marble staircase with this huge carpet pulled all the way up some eighty feet to the top and a magnificently carved pair of eighteen-foot-tall oak doors. On every other step there were the colorfully garbed Swiss Guards with plumed silver helmets and drawn swords. It was a very impressive sight and for a moment I forgot that it was all make-believe. That is, until I tripped on my robe. As I was climbing up those carpeted stairs trying to be regal and Pope-like, I stopped and hollered, "Dammit! Cut! Not acceptable. Not even for a Jewish Pope!" Then I muttered under my breath, "I've been selling dresses for fifty years and this is the first time I ever had to wear one."

The world premiere of *Foul Play* was several days after my seventy-ninth birthday in the summer of 1978. There was a screening of the movie at the Palace of Fine Arts and then a huge party in the Hyatt Regency ballroom where a neon-trimmed discotéque had been constructed. The film company was making a promotional TV show, a special, and there were loads of entertainers, including "The Fonz," Henry Winkler, and the Spinners, flown up for the occasion. It was a marvelous night with flashing lights, a catered buffet and dancing. Of course, afterwards, we were all very anxious about the reviews. We were not disappointed.

Reviews for *Foul Play* were marvelous. The *Chronicle*'s John Wasserman wrote, "Oh yes, our own Cyril Magnin [was] the visiting Pope Pius XIII . . . Cyril, it hardly needs to be pointed out to those familiar with his cherubic countenance, looks more like a Pope than most of your actual popes. Pope-watchers will see a basic John XXIII type." Stanley Eichelbaum of the *Examiner* said, "The pope is played by San Francisco's own goodwill ambassador, Cyril Magnin, who's quite convincing without uttering a line." (Well, I did have a few words to say—"bravo, bravo"—for which I was coached by Beverly Sills.)

When the film opened in San Francisco, it played at the Regency Theater and on the marquee was, *Foul Play*, starring Goldie Hawn, Chevy Chase and . . . Cyril Magnin.

I have Steve Silver to thank for so many things—mostly it

gives me great joy to be around someone so inventive and full of talent and life. But for my eightieth birthday, Steve went all out and produced something so special I don't think I could ever repay him.

In the Club Fugazi there was an unused basement area with a small stage. Unbeknownst to me, Steve turned the place into a nightclub called Cyril's. He took a copy of my signature and that became the logo for the new club. On the walls he had painted all sorts of figures—mostly the loyal fans who had supported *Beach Blanket* all through the years. There was Catherine Cebrian who took part in his New Year's Eve entertainments and San Francisco's hardest-working charity fund-raiser, Charlotte "Tex" Mailliard, and then there was Beverly Sills and yours truly. I was not to discover any of this until the evening of a surprise party Steve threw for my birthday.

Steve sent out invitations in red and white with the *Beach Blanket* logo, which was usually a silhouette of a girl standing on a pedestal, kind of like the Oscar statue, with a huge hat on her head. Instead of the girl, Steve had placed me on that pedestal which was a three-tiered birthday cake dripping with icing. A big number 80 wreathed in stars and flooded with spotlights was on the top of the page and the print read, "Beach Blanket Babylon Goes to Cyril! (It's A Surprise)." The date was for Thursday, July 5, one day before my birthday, and it was for curtain-call cocktails and a stage-door supper. All of my family and friends had been invited—there were mobs of people, about 300 in all.

Now, the Fugazi is an old Italian opera house and Steve felt it appropriate that there be an Italian theme to the evening. The food was Italian, catered by my son's restaurant, Ciao. I was to be made an "honorary" Italian. Lita Vietor, one of our hard-working society women, had driven down to Tijuana from her vacation home in La Jolla and had bought a garlic lei to bring back, and Charlotte Mailliard came dressed as an eighteenth-century waitress. She served drinks all night and washed dishes.

When I walked in, everything was a total surprise. Steve placed the lei of garlic around my neck and put a loaf of french bread under each of my arms. There was an Italian band and loads of commotion—and, there were those paintings on the wall, not to mention an entire club named for me. I had always thought that perhaps, someday, in San Francisco, they'd name a street or a park after me, but never a nightclub. (And I'd always said that if they ever named a street after me, I hoped it wouldn't be one with horses on it.)

During the evening a huge birthday cake in the shape of the Mark Hopkins was wheeled in, and by the waning hours of the party the french bread under my arms was beginning to look a little shoddy. I had been so moved during the evening that I was crying and had used the ends of the loaves of good old San Francisco sourdough to wipe my eyes. The next day I was invited to the Top of the Mark, ostensibly for a KCBS radio show. Instead, there was another surprise party for me with my favorite bistro pianists, Peter Mintun from L'Etoile and Bob Moonan from the Mark bar, sitting there playing my favorites.

Whenever I'm asked about my admiration for Steve Silver and young people in general, I have to say that I like young people, not because they are young, but because we seem to think alike. In my age bracket, perhaps people age sixty-five and older, most people *don't* think the way I do. I've often said that I'm going to die young, not chronologically, perhaps, but certainly young in my thinking. I dislike anything that has the connotation of old age, unless it's something fine, rare and wonderful, like the Tut exhibit.

I have spent my entire life surrounded by young people. My business was a smashing success when we started catering to the young and those who thought young, and in retrospect I think that my life reflects those precepts over and over again. I would like my life to be an example for our country's young people at a time when, perhaps, we should be reminded of some solid, American values.

I feel that young people should dedicate themselves to their objectives, keeping in mind always their family, friends and their community. They must work diligently and hard to achieve what they want—as the man said, there is no free lunch. They should also try to keep in mind their treatment of others as well and remember that ambition does not give them the right to step on someone else to get what they want. They should be thankful that they live in the United States, a country founded on freedom and initiative—a country which opened its doors and hearts not only to the Magnins, the Davises and the Silvermans, my ancestors, but to the thousands who flood our shores daily.

And finally, for the young, I would hope that like me, they would always stay youthful in their thoughts and ideas, never closing their minds to anything new. It is the new, the innovative and the future which has excited me and still does.

EPILOGUE

AND OF CYRIL MAGNIN, perhaps no one has refined the scope of his life down to eloquent terms better than his friend, Bill Moyers, who said, "I've seen few men who work as steadfastly as Cyril does at the process of life itself. And he does work at life. I wouldn't say that it's a fetish with him and I wouldn't say it's an obsession with him—it's like much of Cyril's other commitments. There's a tenacity to it. And he is tenacious about his friendships, his business, his loyalties—tenacious about his family. Tenacious about his protocol work and anything else he takes on. Therefore, it's natural that he works hard to hold on to life."

INDEX

301